The Alchemy of Slavery

AMERICA IN THE NINETEENTH CENTURY

Series editors:
Brian DeLay, Steven Hahn, Amy Dru Stanley

America in the Nineteenth Century proposes a rigorous rethinking of this most formative period in U.S. history. Books in the series will be wide-ranging and eclectic, with an interest in politics at all levels, culture and capitalism, race and slavery, law, gender, and the environment, and regional and transnational history. The series aims to expand the scope of nineteenth-century historiography by bringing classic questions into dialogue with innovative perspectives, approaches, and methodologies.

The ALCHEMY *of* SLAVERY

Human Bondage and Emancipation in the Illinois Country, 1730–1865

M. Scott Heerman

PENN

UNIVERSITY OF PENNSYLVANIA PRESS

PHILADELPHIA

Published by
University of Pennsylvania Press
Philadelphia, Pennsylvania 19104-4112
www.upenn.edu/pennpress

Printed in the United States of America
on acid-free paper
1 3 5 7 9 10 8 6 4 2

Library of Congress Cataloging-in-Publication Data

Names: Heerman, M. Scott, author.
Title: The alchemy of slavery : human bondage and emancipation in the Illinois Country, 1730–1865 / M. Scott Heerman.
Other titles: America in the nineteenth century.
Description: 1st edition. | Philadelphia : University of Pennsylvania Press, [2018] | Series: America in the nineteenth century | Includes bibliographical references and index.
Identifiers: LCCN 2018007657 | ISBN 9780812250466 (hardcover : alk. paper) Subjects: LCSH: Slavery—Illinois—History—18th century. | Slavery—Illinois—History—19th century.
Classification: LCC E445.I2 H44 2018 | DDC 306.3/620977309033—dc23
LC record available at https://lccn.loc.gov/2018007657

CONTENTS

Introduction. Slavery and Freedom on the American Continent 1

Chapter 1. Making the French Negroes 17

Chapter 2. Another Law and Empire 38

Chapter 3. Remaking the French Negroes 58

Chapter 4. Contesting Bondage in the Slave North 82

Chapter 5. Paths to Independence 109

Chapter 6. Freedom Practices, Freedom Politics 135

Conclusion. North of Slavery, South of Freedom 160

Notes 169

Bibliography 205

Index 229

Acknowledgments 235

INTRODUCTION

Slavery and Freedom on the American Continent

It could be a difficult crossing. The Mississippi River spanned more than a mile between the French village at Kaskaskia, in present-day Illinois, and St. Genevieve, now part of Missouri. For much of the 1750s, the Reverend Father Alexandre Xavier de Guyenne, curé of Kaskaskia, frequently traveled between Catholic parishes on opposite banks of the Mississippi. Four parishes operated on the east bank of the river, and a new one had just opened on the west bank. But the parish in St. Genevieve had no priest, and so the Jesuit superior of the Kaskaskia mission tended to its members, instructing residents in the pillars of the faith, as well as "visiting the sick and in relieving the poor."[1] As he went to and fro, he trusted his fate to a "slave, who alone guided the canoe."[2] The crossing was no simple undertaking. The current would challenge even seasoned rowers, and the wind gusts brought "danger of perishing, if in the middle of the river" the canoe "had been overtaken by a violent storm."[3] Despite the challenges, a sense of mission brought Father Guyenne back and forth across the Mississippi. But what motivated the unnamed slave to keep returning time and again between the banks of the river and not trying to head off to freedom?

Answering this question would require teasing out some of the details of the enslaved rower's life, which proves to be a difficult task. Pinning down the identity of this single slave, as well as surmising his or her motivations, is so challenging because a range of enslaved experiences existed in Illinois. Slavery was at once a form of coerced labor and a method of indigenous politics, and these different ways of organizing enslavement operated simultaneously. During the 1750s, the Jesuit fathers in Illinois owned over thirty slaves, some of them of African descent, some of them indigenous slaves, and it is impossible to know which or how many of them ferried Father Guyenne back and forth across the Mississippi. When Jesuits or other slaveholders spoke of slaves, they could have meant people of African descent brought to the region to labor on the fields, people of Indian descent adopted into French society through a politics of captive exchange, or an enslaved person born in Illinois who shared both Indian and African ancestry. Enslaved people coerced to serve the Jesuit fathers could have had an array of different racial origins and be held in slightly different statuses, and that fact uncovers the reality that slavery never operated in any one framework or served any one function.

Taking stock of the slaves that the Jesuits owned and speculating about the identity of this enslaved rower shed light on the different processes of enslavement that trapped people in bondage in this colony. For instance, the rower could have been Louis, an enslaved man of African descent who appears to have observed at least some elements of the Catholic faith; he married in the church and together with his enslaved wife Therese had his daughter baptized. If Louis had been the unnamed navigator, perhaps a duty to the faith, the joy of seeing his wife and daughter, and a community he called his own could have kept him returning. However, enslaved Indian women also lived in the Jesuit parish in Kaskaskia and could have been guides to the missionaries in the Mississippi Valley. These enslaved people had not been brought to the region to clear and work the land. Instead, indigenous bondage operated as a form of Indian diplomacy and undergirded alliance systems in the region.[4] Perhaps, then, if Guyenne's slave was a woman of indigenous descent, she returned time and again because her adoption into a new society, coerced though it was, gave her some tie of kinship that she would not want to sever.

Whoever it was that brought Guyenne to and fro, it is clear that over time, slaves of diverse origins came to live side by side in the tiny Illinois outpost. Most of the Jesuit slaves probably worked in the colony's lucrative agricultural economy that could "produce all things needed to support life, and even to make it agreeable."[5] Enslaved Indians who had been carried into the region through a system of captivity, exchange, and adoption joined enslaved Africans in these tasks. Rather than indigenous and African slavery existing as separate institutions, masters drew on different kinds of enslavement and held slaves of diverse origins on the same estate. In the process, they forged different kinds of enslavement into one localized form of slavery that trapped diverse people in bondage. Indian- and African-descended slaves at times intermarried, bore children, and shared birth and death rites, and the two different forms of bondage worked alongside one another as masters turned many slaveries into one. By the turn of the nineteenth century, this community of enslaved people would become the "French Negroes," an invented legal category for a diverse group of people enslaved in Illinois. But they would not be the only types of slaves in the Prairie State.

* * *

Sometime around 1818, William Wilson moved from the Missouri Territory into the Illinois Country, and he brought with him two enslaved young "negro" women, Judith and Lindah. By terms of the 1787 Northwest Territory Ordinance, the U.S. government had made "slavery and involuntary servitude" illegal in Illinois.[6] In summer 1818, just as Wilson made it to the state, politicians and other local notables met to craft a new state constitution, which would ban slavery's future introduction into Illinois. Yet slavery's illegality did not mean Wilson had to free Judith and Lindah. Instead, he converted them into indentured servants, which entitled him to hold them to terms of labor for ninety-nine years without pay. He also had the right to hold any children they might have as servants until adulthood. Once he registered their contracts with the local county clerk, Illinois law permitted Wilson to buy and sell his servants as chattel.[7] Their status as servants did very little to spare them from bound labor's brutality. Wilson had nearly unfettered power over them: he could beat and whip them or violate them sexually. Across the state, servants like Judith and Lindah were clapped into chains, sold as property at auction, and brutalized in a variety of ways.[8]

The adaptations to slaving practices were on full display when masters like Wilson turned slaves into lifelong servants. While politicians met to create a new state charter that purportedly banned slavery, masters signed slaves into lifelong indentureships to keep human bondage alive by other means. This legal dodge operated under the fiction that the two enslaved women consented to their servitude and signed onto new terms, making their unfreedom nominally voluntary. Even though the two women were enslaved at the time they signed these contracts, the law treated them as voluntary servants. Wilson could then put them to work either in the state's agrarian districts or in its salt mines, where hundreds of servants and slaves did the brutal work of harvesting, processing, refining, and shipping salt. In time, the Illinois Supreme Court would uphold indentures like Judith and Lindah's as legal and not interpret them as a violation of the ban on slavery or involuntary servitude. Just as indigenous and African-descended people both fell victim to different slaving practices, Judith and Lindah's experiences point to another framework, contract bondage, that shaped the life of enslaved people in southern Illinois. As one of Illinois's leaders later observed, the servitude system "is but another name for slavery."[9]

Masters found ways to manipulate the law of slavery, but slaves like Judith and Lindah rarely accepted their status. Time and again, slaves with servitude contracts found ways to contest their subordination: some bound workers managed to accrue small amounts of money and purchase their freedom, others ran north to escape slavery, and still others sued in court for freedom claiming that their master violated specific conditions of their contracts. Judith and Lindah may have lived out their lives in servitude or risked running away and escaping into freedom. Whatever the fate of these two particular slaves, men and women trapped in forms of contract bondage contested their unfreedom, and those disputes provided the bedrock of a wider political struggle over slavery and freedom. At first, this attack on slavery rarely relied on help from abolition organizations and, unlike in other states that had gradual emancipation statutes on the books, Illinois's laws concerning slavery and servitude made escape all the more daunting. Still, as the nineteenth century pressed on, conflicts over the "French Negroes" and lifelong servants would help to transform the state's politics.

* * *

In 1848, three men kidnapped Wade, an African American man from Cairo, Illinois, and trafficked him to Missouri.[10] Southern Illinois was notorious for its racism, and it might have been easy to assume that few people would have cared about his captivity. Yet Wade had lived in the state his whole life. According to one account, he "is what is usually in this State denominated a 'French Negro,'" whose mother had been kept in bondage under a legal loophole. In 1818, lawmakers barred the future introduction of slavery but did not make that prohibition retroactive to include people like Wade's mother.[11] As a result, Wade inherited his mother's status and had lived as a slave for much of his life. He most likely had family and friends that worked to liberate him. Whatever the inspiration to act, local officials secured kidnapping indictments for Wade's three captors in the Alexander County

Circuit Court. Yet because the three men had gone to Cape Girardeau, Missouri, with their hostage, local officials needed the Illinois governor in their quest to free Wade. Illinois's governor at the time, Augustus C. French, was a Democrat who never embraced abolition, and he was no ally in the slave's cause. Perhaps surprisingly given his politics, Governor French wrote Missouri Governor Austin King to request "that said individuals shall be arrested."[12] The Illinois governor got involved in the extradition request because he felt that "kidnapping has been carried to a disgraceful extent in this state."[13] Through kidnappings like this one, Governor French declared, the enemies of emancipation could "reduce free men to Slavery."[14] The Missouri governor denied the request, and although there was a protracted political struggle between the two governors, Wade's captors never stood trial in Illinois.

The kidnapping came at a fortuitous time in Illinois's history of slavery and emancipation. Only a few years earlier, *Jarrot v. Jarrot*, a marquee ruling from the state supreme court, had promised people like Wade their freedom. "French Negroes" had been kept in slavery under a reading of state law that only forbade the future introduction of slavery but did not require all slaves to be freed. In the eighteenth century, the "French Negroes" referred largely to the people of African descent whom French masters enslaved, as opposed to the indigenous slaves or enslaved African captives from the Anglophone world who also lived in the region. Yet by the nineteenth century, the term "French Negroes" had ceased to refer to a social group within the enslaved population and had come to have a specific legal definition. By the time of Wade's kidnapping, it referred generally to all enslaved people who had lived in the Illinois Country during its colonial history, regardless of their racial origin or country of birth. The first state constitution in 1818 exempted these people from emancipation, and people like Wade became "French Negroes," regardless that he was born in Illinois long after the French empire ceased to claim it. But that local arrangement regarding "French Negroes" grew tenuous over time. Joseph Jarrot, one such "French Negro," sued his master, and in 1845 the Illinois Supreme Court issued a new directive. In *Jarrot v. Jarrot*, it found that children born of "French Negroes" were unquestionably free. The court went further to make Illinois free soil; it ruled all forms of slavery illegal and promised "to break the fetters of the slave and declare the captive free."[15] Lyman Trumbull served as attorney for Joseph Jarrot. While in time Trumbull would go on to push forward the Republican Party's platform for national emancipation and chair the Senate committee that drafted the constitutional amendment to abolish slavery, at this earlier date, he engaged in a local freedom politics in Illinois involving lawsuits in local courthouses and the daily work of asserting black freedom.

Yet just as Trumbull would confront after the Civil War, the promise of total emancipation had to contend with local communities who defined slavery and freedom in their own terms. In southern Illinois, "French Negroes" like Wade had long been considered slaves. Notwithstanding important antislavery victories, like the one in 1845, proslavery groups constantly opened new fronts in the attempts to preserve slavery. Facing the prospect of emancipation, masters reinvented how slavery would function, and black kidnapping kept forms of bondage alive. Just as masters adapted to incorporate indigenous bondage and lifelong servitude into their slaving practices, black kidnapping was another way in which masters exerted power over African Americans to enslave them. In the eighteenth century, enslaved people of African descent, like Wade's ancestors, traveled upriver from New Orleans to Illinois as part of a French design to create a plantation economy. By the eve of the Civil War, the flow had reversed, and African Americans in a variety of conditions of unfreedom, including some like Wade, traveled downriver as captives, falling victim to slavery's latest reinvention.

* * *

Each of the three scenes above arrives as a postcard from a different time and place, and each offers a different picture of how slavery functioned in Illinois. Yet they have some things in common. In each case, masters had to adapt and innovate their slaving practices to reckon with the larger political and legal realities in Illinois. Frenchmen had to accommodate systems of indigenous bondage, southern migrants into Illinois reinvented slavery under the guise of servitude, and masters responded to landmark antislavery rulings by kidnapping African Americans into bondage. Viewed in succession, they encourage readers to set aside a very common idea: that slavery was an institution. The "institution of slavery" stands out as a ubiquitous phrase in our histories. Yet, slavery in Illinois lacked institutional trappings because no common purpose shaped the various types of slavery that marked the region. Masters enslaved people to serve a host of different social and economic functions, and no one framework for defining slavery ever prevailed for long.[16]

Together, these three snapshots from the archive reveal that slavery in Illinois existed as an adaptable set of practices. Louis, Judith, Lindah, Joseph Jarrot, and Wade each experienced a different side of human bondage that marked Illinois over a century and a half. All of them were slaves, and yet the set of slaving practices that defined their lives in bondage differed drastically. Over this long stretch of time, slavery was not a fixed status but a dynamic power relationship that enveloped a diverse cast of people, subject to endless contestation and reinvention. As a consequence, slaves occupied a variety of different statuses, and the power over them took new forms and responded to new threats. Slavery was at various times a system of indigenous diplomacy, the bedrock of a colonial economy designed to enrich distant merchants, a means to support racial hierarchy and white supremacy, and a form of coerced, degraded labor.

What follows is a tale of alchemy that traces the ins and outs of slavery's nearly perpetual reinvention. It is a story that shows how slaveholders turned one form of bondage into another. Masters changed Indian captives into slaves, a polyglot cast of Indian- and African-descended slaves into "French Negroes," black slaves into lifelong servants, and free African Americans back into kidnapped captives, and they used this array of shape-shifting slaving strategies to adapt to changing political and economic realities. For more than a century, masters turned to many slaveries and slaving practices to make a single, localized slave system. The final act of transformation in this tale is in some ways the most enduring: enslaved people changed themselves into freed men and women. At each moment in this history, enslaved people had powers and allies of their own that they could summon to make their own alchemy, helping to turn Illinois from a society dedicated to slavery into one committed to its abolition.

The Alchemy of Slavery foregrounds the interactions of enslaved people who had different routes into bondage—be they Indian captives in the eighteenth century or kidnapped freedmen in the nineteenth century—to show that slavery existed as a fiendishly adaptable power relationship. Slavery across the Atlantic world varied immensely, and human bondage in West Africa, the Caribbean, native North America, the Chesapeake, the Deep South, New France, and New Spain all had different defining traits.[17] Rather than studying different regions to see how different forms of slavery took shape, *The Alchemy of Slavery* tells an entangled history of human bondage in one region that foregrounds how different iterations of enslavement mutually played out simultaneously.[18] Instead of analyzing indigenous and Atlantic slaveries, lifelong servitude, and black captivity as separate institutions of slavery and then tracing their connections, *The Alchemy of Slavery* reveals a kaleidoscope of different coercive practices that together comprised the work of enslaving people, allowing masters to render a diverse cast of Indians, Africans, servants, and captives into enslaved people.

In light of this changing landscape of enslaving people, *The Alchemy of Slavery* offers a continental perspective on human bondage and emancipation in mainland North America. Rather than tracing slavery's expansion from the Atlantic world into the heart of North America, *The Alchemy of Slavery* turns that analysis inside out. It looks at the long history of human bondage in the interior of North America and traces its connections out to the larger and changing empires that controlled the region. It argues that the adaptations to human bondage in French and native North America shaped the landscape of slavery and freedom in the United States. Illinois's political leaders, like Lyman Trumbull, had to contend with France's colonial legacy as they confronted a population of enslaved "French Negroes" in the nominally free state. On the eve of the U.S. Civil War, political leaders, including Abraham Lincoln, Stephen Douglas, and Richard Yates, worked to liberate the descendants of enslaved people brought to the region generations before. Freeing these slaves necessitated more than passing laws and winning court battles; it required a robust set of local freedom practices to keep African Americans out of bondage. Across a century and a half, masters, slaves, servants, and free residents, including some of the nation's most important leaders, clashed over the boundaries of slavery and freedom, which led human bondage to take so many different forms. In Illinois, slavery never became an institution and abolition barely became a movement.

* * *

Taking stock of slavery's adaptability, *The Alchemy of Slavery* escapes the institutional framework that often frames the inquiry into human bondage. For decades, historians of North America and the Atlantic world have relied on Orlando Patterson's trailblazing work and adopted a conception of slavery that all too often transcended time and space and treated slavery as a status that served a single purpose.[19] *The Alchemy of Slavery* joins a growing scholarship that goes beyond Patterson's framework, in an attempt to explain the dynamic, changing variety of conditions that enslaved people experienced.[20] If scholars now recognize that slavery had many different forms, *The Alchemy of Slavery* shows that those different types of bondage coexisted alongside one another in the same community. Masters adapted to the reality that slavery never had any one single purpose, and out of many slaveries, they made a single, localized slave system over time. It shows that the power to hold people as slaves was never fixed and stable, but it changed and adapted across different epochs. Foregrounding how masters, chameleon-like, enslaved people in many different ways invites a rethinking of the enslaved experience, the struggle for freedom, and the power of the law to define both bondage and emancipation in North America and the United States.

The Alchemy of Slavery tells the history of human bondage in the heart of North America and connects that story to the wider forces of the Atlantic world.[21] To that end, it takes what one scholar calls a "surf and turf" approach that can explain how changes in the Mississippi Valley took place because of Atlantic processes that played out over great distances.[22] It explores how slave labor took root in colonial societies without plantation economies, far from the Atlantic basin. Some of the hallmarks of Atlantic economies also defined the Mississippi Valley: the use of slave labor to produce a commodity that could command an international market, the free and forced migration of people across imperial boundaries, and the making of new people and new cultures far from colonial metropoles. Traders, travelers, merchants, and laborers across the Atlantic world connected previously remote locales, and that connectivity extended to include large swaths of the Illinois prairie. *The Alchemy of Slavery* joins a growing list of works that show how processes commonly thought of as Atlantic and confined to the oceanic basin transferred deep into the heart of North America.[23]

Looking at slavery beyond the Atlantic basin sheds light on an entangled history of indigenous and European colonial slaveries.[24] Scholars of indigenous bondage have identified structural differences between the two forms of slavery, stressing that one was a kin-based system of captivity and alliance formation that colonizers appropriated to coerce labor out of Indians, and the other was a racially coded, legally defined system primarily run on the plantation complexes of the New World to profit the master class.[25] In light of these structural differences, scholars have often taken to writing of *slaveries* to note the diversity that prevailed in different times and places.[26]

However, in Illinois, masters forged a single, localized system of slavery that drew on diverse origins. While key distinctions between types of slavery did exist in certain times and places, *The Alchemy of Slavery* grapples with the reality that indigenous and European colonial slavery were never entirely separated, did not always operate in different geographies or chronologies, and were not always remote from each other.[27] Masters enslaved people of diverse origins for a variety of different reasons, and those adaptations to slaving practices gave rise to an economy where Indian- and African-descended slaves lived and labored alongside one another.[28]

By foregrounding how slaves of diverse origins, like those owned by the Jesuits, found themselves bound together in a larger set of slaving practices, *The Alchemy of Slavery* sees beyond the institutional frameworks that orient much of the scholarship to date, and it highlights similarities between the kinds of power that plundered enslaved Indian and African bodies. Rather than looking at the transitions and tension between two institutions of slavery, *The Alchemy of Slavery* integrates the experiences of enslaved Indians into a larger story of U.S. slavery and freedom. Scholars of slavery have lately produced excellent work on the movement into a "second slavery" in the nineteenth century that saw slavery adapt into capital-intensive, technologically innovative, modern, and productive labor relations that generated enormous wealth in the cotton economy in the U.S. South, the sugar economy in Cuba and Puerto Rico, and the coffee economy in Brazil.[29] *The Alchemy of Slavery* tells an earlier tale of reinvention. It traces how indigenous bondage interacted and overlapped with forms of slavery that targeted African-descended people and how adaptations to enslavement in the eighteenth century shaped the contours of slavery and freedom in the nineteenth-century United States.

Recognizing that slavery, Atlantic or indigenous, operated as a dynamic, adaptable power relationship requires a reimagination of the kinds of freedom politics needed to emancipate people. To date, a rich vein of scholarship has re-created the struggle against slavery before the Civil War by focusing on the U.S. North, mostly along the eastern seaboard, and the protracted battles over abolition that played out there for decades.[30] These historians have documented how abolition organizations sprang up in the wake of the U.S. War for Independence and pushed to make their societies free from slavery. Across New England and the mid-Atlantic, abolition societies pressured legislatures and eventually won the passage of gradual emancipation acts.[31] These acts freed all children born after a certain date, so-called *post-nati* emancipation. With these laws as tools, members of abolition societies shifted their focus. They tried to enforce the laws and guard African Americans from kidnapping and reenslavement, and some abolitionists argued for black citizenship in the Early Republic. African American communities in northern cities were no bystanders in these developments, and they played a crucial role in dealing slavery a deathblow.[32] Yet this analysis argues that the peculiar institution could be abolished by winning court rulings or passing laws and then working toward their rigorous enforcement.

Looking at slavery as a series of adaptations requires looking for different struggles for freedom, ones that had local roots, ones that required a diverse array of freedom practices, and ones that did not need abolition laws or antislavery institutions to succeed. In Illinois, the central drive for emancipation came out of enslaved people's resistance to their subordination and the help from residents of a series of all-black towns in rural southern Illinois. Residents of these towns succeeded in building lives apart from slavery, despite the fact that for many years in Illinois, no abolition law or society existed. These black villages acted as incubators of emancipation in the rural landscape.

This new conception of a local freedom politics necessitates a revision of the relationship between slavery, freedom, and the law that decouples the power to enslave people from the legal authority afforded masters. *The Alchemy of Slavery* does not rely on the law for its definitions of slave and free spaces. Over a century and a half, residents in Illinois wielded a local knowledge that often could trump laws passed by legislatures, congresses, parliaments, and kings. French settlers ran their slave economy according to local arrangements and not in ways envisioned by the *Code Noir*, the legal proclamation meant to govern slavery in the French empire.[33] When the British claimed the region, no civil jurisdiction or law of slavery extended to cover Illinois. Yet the region's bound workers remained enslaved, despite the absence of a law defining slavery. Similarly, settlers in antebellum Illinois, like William Wilson, kept hold of their slaves through local power arrangements, and they spawned a society with slaves not envisioned by the U.S. Congress or Illinois State Constitution, both of which forbade slavery. Over this long stretch of time, masters held people as slaves without specific sanction from the law, and slave status was less a legal fact to be applied and more a set of power relationships that at times operated independently of the law.[34]

The system of slavery that existed in Illinois required masters to adapt to changing legal regimes. As the French, British, and Americans attempted to create a law of slavery, settlers on the ground navigated those changing landscapes to make a slave economy that suited their own designs. In Illinois, the law had social and cultural dimensions that extended far beyond the courtrooms.[35] Over a century and a half, the courts and laws played a contested role in slavery's perpetual reinvention: they did not only act as a tool of the master class or as a vehicle for emancipation. At times, masters used the law to sanction bondage and reinvent slavery in new guises, while at other times, slaves like Joseph Jarrot turned to the courts and undertook the challenging work of finding freedom. Laws and legal institutions mattered enormously in the great battle over emancipation, if only because they gave both masters and enslaved people the tools to advance their own interests. But the law did not determine the course any one community would take.

* * *

Although the law alone did not sanction slavery's existence, and slavery never took on institutional form, human bondage still had a definition. Taking stock of the variety of slaveries that marked Illinois, it is clear that human bondage was distinct from other forms of unfreedom, such as apprenticeship or forms of debt peonage.[36] *The Alchemy of Slavery* looks at the various iterations that slavery took in the Illinois Country but largely excludes other kinds of coercion and unfreedom. Slavery was more than captivity, and it also cannot be reduced to a system of commodity production. First, slavery in Illinois was a long-term, usually lifelong, and frequently an inheritable and generational status. This set it apart from other forms of servility, which tended to be shorter and more episodic. Second, slaves were transactable. Most notoriously, this took the form of the "chattel principle" that allowed masters to sell human beings as mere property. Indigenous systems of bondage did not have a similar concept to chattel, but slaves in Indian communities could be moved, transferred, adopted, or displaced within political and social networks at their superiors' will. So it was with lifelong servants, who were traded and trafficked by masters to make a society and economy that suited their designs. Third, slavery in Illinois empowered a few to define who belonged to free society and who stood outside its boundaries. By defining outsiders, slavery let masters establish themselves as insiders, and in that way, enslaving people gave them a measure of power over society. Slavery's function allowed a class of freemen in Illinois to accrue profit and power through their long-term mastery over a salable, foreign people, no matter if that took the form of trading in indigenous captives, signing slaves as lifelong black servants, holding African Americans as inheritable bondsmen, or kidnapping black freed men and women.

Slavery exhibited this dynamism in part because Illinois had different and changing political boundaries that helped to inform what function bondage would have. Over a long period, Illinois went from Indian Country to European colony, from borderland of the U.S. South to bulwark of the free North. In each period of reconception, slavery changed to meet new situations. In order to follow the long story of human bondage in Illinois, *The Alchemy of Slavery* for the most part focuses on the land between the Mississippi and Wabash Rivers, as well as between the Ohio River and the Great Lakes. Before the nineteenth century, the Illinois Country had more expansive boundaries, and understanding how slavery functioned requires looking west of the Mississippi, south of the Ohio, and east of Lake Michigan. After 1787, the Mississippi and Ohio Rivers became nominal dividing lines between slavery and freedom, and *The Alchemy of Slavery* follows the history of slavery's adaptations in that newly minted free soil space, leaving the story of what became Kentucky, Missouri, and Indiana to others.[37]

Even as Illinois's boundaries became increasingly fixed over time, migrations played a critical role in the region's reinvention. In the eighteenth century, Indian slavery relied on travel that sent Illinois Indians on captive raids, carrying their hostages back into the Illinois Country. Before long, European migrations brought French men and women into the region. These newcomers imported enslaved people of African descent to work in staple agriculture. With rival groups moving into the region, different forms of bondage came into contact, and Illinois was at once Indian Country and part of a European empire. By the nineteenth century, U.S. migration again transformed slavery's place in the Illinois Country. White southerners from Virginia and Kentucky poured in, and many of them brought their slaves in tow. Before 1830, settlers coming from the Upper South populated Illinois and arrested attempts to end slavery. Instead, local white communities looked for ways to keep human bondage alive, and they largely succeeded. Yet after 1830, a new wave of migration reworked those local arrangements that kept slavery in southern Illinois. Free African Americans came out of Tennessee and Kentucky and settled in all-black towns in the state's southern districts. These enclaves of black freedom took root in the same communities where slavery survived. As free African Americans worked to liberate enslaved people, they found new allies among the white immigrants who poured into Illinois. By the 1840s and 1850s, settlers from New England, the mid-Atlantic, and Western Europe had come to call Illinois home, and they again remade the state's politics of slavery. They joined the small abolition societies, pressed for new antislavery laws, and helped to make Illinois a free state by supporting a local freedom struggle in southern Illinois. Across this long arc, the movement of people in and out of Illinois made, remade, and eventually unmade slavery's place in the state.

As Illinois's borders and population changed, masters reconstituted their power to enslave others, but they never achieved total dominance. They did not have a monopoly on state authority, and they likewise could not control religious institutions or civic society. Notwithstanding the limits to their influence, masters living in this marginal slave economy still managed to coerce labor from generations of enslaved people and to work their slaves in a wide array of industries. Slaveholders wielded political power in local courts and state legislatures, and before 1830, inhabitants routinely elected slaveholders to statewide office. Those officeholders passed draconian Black Codes that degraded black citizenship. By the 1850s, the state legislature had banned black immigration into the state. As a diverse cast of free and enslaved adversaries beat back slaveholders' power, masters turned to systems of black kidnapping to keep slavery alive in new guises.

The Alchemy of Slavery relies on a diverse assemblage of archival sources spanning the late seventeenth to the mid-nineteenth centuries. The opening chapters draw most heavily on diplomatic correspondence and other records from the French and British colonial archive. These official records tell a story of imperial expansion, explaining why the empires invested so heavily in making a slave economy in the region. However, the travel descriptions, Jesuit accounts, notarial documents, baptism entries, and occasional business record books that survive from this period reveal how slaveholders adapted to the circumstances they discovered in Illinois. By the turn of the nineteenth century, when the newly minted United States claimed the region, the balance of the source base had changed. Owing to the county and state governments that the United States created, officials in Washington, D.C. spent less time administering the region, giving rise to a rich set of local legal records that comprise the archival base for most of the rest of the period under study. Most of these legal records reside in county courthouses in southern Illinois, where they sit crammed under staircases, shoved into crawl spaces, often suffering every imaginable form of neglect. Another key change came in the second decade of the nineteenth century, when newspaper editors set up the first printing presses in the region. By the 1820s, the state had a handful of newspapers that usually printed weekly. In time, the volume of print culture exploded, and by the mid-nineteenth century, daily newspapers abounded in the state. Over this long stretch, correspondence between colonial officials in three empires, baptismal records, notarial records, travel descriptions, bills of sale, merchant's accounts, "negro registries," books of emancipation, criminal indictments for kidnapping, probate inventories, freedom suits for slaves demanding emancipation, newspapers, and speeches and debates from the state's leaders all tell a new tale of slavery and freedom in the United States.

Each set of sources offers its own window on the contours of slavery and freedom in Illinois, and each has its own set of limitations. The colonial archives reveal how slavery in this one region belonged to a wider history of New World colonialism, and they reveal that different imperial contexts inspired slaveholders to reinvent the slave economy time and again. Yet if these records help unearth the alchemy of enslaving, they also project an imperial control over the region that local settlers rarely had. The thin remnants of the local archive from eighteenth-century Illinois only point to the general outlines of the ways that slaveholders adapted to the local slaving practices of the region's powerful indigenous inhabitants. Almost none of these sources speak directly to enslaved people's thoughts, identities, or motivations, making their voices and experiences all the more obscure. As the volume of local sources exploded in the nineteenth century, the fine grain of the power struggles over slavery and freedom comes into fuller view. Yet, these records only provide a fiction of a complete and true record of the lives of masters and enslaved people. Local legal case files rarely make mention of the major changes—from industrialism, new political alignments, changing ideas of racial hierarchy, and sweeping demographic influxes—that shaped enslaved people's lives. Throughout the long span of this project, global forces and local adaptations played off of one another and propelled the movement from slavery to freedom, even if the archives rarely tell the full story in their own right.

Drawing on such a wide array of sources, Illinois's case shows how slavery and freedom were perpetually renegotiated and redefined according to local politics, economics, and social norms. Throughout this long history, grand forces of nations and empires never determined the outcome of struggles over slavery. Instead, local knowledge and local arrangements commonly held sway. The history of slaveries in this one location unearths new dimensions of the work of enslaving that for so long drove much of U.S. history. Illinois was not a world that slaveholders made, but neither was it free soil. The transition from slavery to freedom is a familiar one in U.S. history, but in Illinois, that movement ran its own course and had its own logic. Understanding that movement requires grappling with the reality that slaveholders drew from many different kinds of slavery, stretching back centuries, in order to make a single, localized slave economy. Over a long span, slavery, then, was not a fixed status but a changing and contested power relationship that masters forged over indigenous captives, African bondspeople, African American servants, and many others. This story of seemingly perpetual reinvention begins at the turn of the eighteenth century, with the making of the "French Negroes."

CHAPTER 1

Making the French Negroes

Late in 1748, a convoy of bateaux descended the Mississippi River from Kaskaskia in the Illinois Country to New Orleans. The convoys had become a regular fixture of life on the Mississippi, semiannually bringing grain, corn, naval stores, furs, and foodstuffs from the Upper Mississippi Valley into the Crescent City. But this particular convoy also brought Marie Jeanne, an enslaved woman of African descent, south to New Orleans to stand trial for infanticide. The case had begun some months before, on July 7, 1748, when Jerome Matis, a *habitant* in Illinois, discovered "the arm and parts of the skull of a child" near his home and "upon searching . . . found a grave and several other pieces of the body in the pig sty and the barn." After finding the child's corpse, Matis accused Marie of "having given birth to a child in a stable, burying the same in a manure heap, there to be devoured by hogs."[1] Other witnesses confirmed that "a child's skull was found among the animals" and that "debris of a child" was "in the barn."[2] With gruesome detail of blood and dismembered body parts, a cast of French settlers were certain that Marie had birthed, then killed, an infant girl.

Marie disputed these charges, maintaining that she miscarried the pregnancy but that she knew very little else about what transpired. Marie declared that she had given "birth to a soft mass of flesh, but not to a child."[3] In her telling, on July 4, already several months pregnant, she was minding the cattle in Matis's stable when she "fainted from pain."[4] She surmised that "whatever happened must have been during a long period of unconsciousness from which she awoke in a barn to find herself soaked with water."[5] When she collapsed, "Lisette, an Indian slave girl," had doused Marie in an attempt to revive her. Lisette, however, could not shed much light on the course of events, as she spoke no French, and her statements were confused.[6] What's more, Lisette may have been gone for most of Marie's ordeal. Right before the fainting spell, Marie "scolded her to make her work" and sent her from the barn to gather some corn.[7] Without a witness to corroborate her version of events, Marie could not refute the charges.

At trial, the Superior Council of New Orleans ordered doctors in New Orleans to examine fragments of a skull that supposedly belonged to Marie's slain child. The Master Surgeons of New Orleans and the Surgeons Major of Louisiana conducted an "examination of the bone of the skull of a child . . . coming from Illinois." Their conclusion was that "the bone submitted is not that of a new-born child, but that of a child several months old." If the skull fragment had belonged to a stillborn child, "the membranes should adhere [differently] which leads them to believe that the bone is older than they say."[8] Marie seemed to know her fate; as she explained to an interrogator, she sat in New Orleans "so that they could take her life."[9]

The mid-eighteenth century has long been seen as a watershed moment in the history of racial slavery, the period when proto-scientific forms of racial thinking came to support and justify African slavery as an institution.[10] The court that relied on examining a skull to determine the nature of black motherhood and infancy in some ways anticipated a later period of scientific racism, where cranial analysis would be the basis of proslavery ideology. This development had important consequences also on North America's native populations. As racial categories matured in the mid-eighteenth century, French officials came to think of native North Americans in racialized terms. For centuries, agents in the French empire imagined that natives could be "Frenchified" through intermarriage and Christian conversion.[11] Yet by the 1750s, many French officials had come to believe that America's Indian population belonged to a foreign race. These changes to racial thinking led many French officials to believe that Indians, as a race, were too free to be enslaved and Africans, as a group, were to servile to be free.[12] This discovery of race thinking was a key moment that shaped both the forces of colonialism and slavery. An emerging scholarly narrative argues that by the mid-eighteenth century, Indians and Africans had drastically different experiences with enslavement, and Indians were increasingly exempted from bondage while many Africans fell deeper into it. In this approach, no matter the similarities between indigenous and Atlantic slaveries, the two groups of people had divergent experiences with enslavement as the nineteenth century approached.

Marie's case offers a different portrait of slave life in early North America, one that does not cast indigenous and African slaves as trapped in separate institutions of bondage. This in turn provokes a reconception of the ways that indigenous and Atlantic slaveries interacted with one another. Rather than seeing two forms of slavery grow apart over time, the ties between Marie and Lisette suggest a different trajectory for this region. Masters like Jerome Matis, as well as many others, owned slaves of diverse origins who remained in constant contact. Indian- and African-descended slaves shared long-lasting, even intimate bonds as they worked, lived, and suffered alongside one another. They found ways to overcome language barriers and communicate with one another. Marie and Lisette's relationship, obscure though it is, highlights the larger reality that Indians and Africans found themselves bound together by acts of enslavement that did not fall along racial barriers. Instead, masters brought slaves of diverse origins into French colonial society, at once appropriating forms of indigenous bondage and using Indian slaves to serve their own colonial desires. Different enslaving practices existed alongside one another, and masters innovated to make a slave system that drew on indigenous and Atlantic sources of bound labor. By drawing on diverse tactics to enslave people, French settlers helped to make many slaveries into one.

This diverse landscape of slaveries operated in Illinois because many of the processes that defined the Atlantic world also transformed the Upper Mississippi Valley. Slavery played a crucial role in the Illinois economy. Frenchmen looked to Illinois as a provisioning ground for their empire, and slaves did the work of growing grain as a staple commodity that could command an international market. Over the course of the eighteenth century, Frenchmen imported enslaved workers to clear and farm land, and as the acreage under cultivation expanded, slaves worked in the alluvial fields to help construct a budding export economy. Enslaved men and women also labored in mills and other artisanal roles to process and refine grain into flour; they staffed the convoys that sustained the Mississippi shipping economy. In time, a handful of French settlers owned tracts of developed land and dozens of slaves to till it. French officials and *habitants* aspired to make a plantation economy, staffed with enslaved Indians and Africans, that could send surplus grain to lower Louisiana and the Caribbean. Although Illinois sat a thousand miles from the ocean, its history resembled other European colonies of the Atlantic world.[13]

Yet slavery was not a colonial imposition on Illinois. Frenchmen, in fact, found themselves having to adapt to indigenous forms of bondage that predated their arrival. Indian slavery had existed for centuries, and the powerful Illinois Indians carried on an active trade in Indian captives.[14] Through raiding and warfare, the Illinois Indians amassed power over the diverse indigenous peoples in the region, controlling trade and migration networks that stretched south and west. Slave trading played a role in their ascent because indigenous bondage was not simply a labor system—it also served important political functions.[15] By controlling captives of diverse nations, the Illinois Indians became important brokers in a long-distance trade in slaves. For Frenchmen to exploit Illinois for its fertility, they had to forge a lasting alliance with the Illinois Indians. This required them to participate in indigenous systems of human bondage and modify their colonial ideas about plantation slavery. Farmers and would-be planters could amass wealth because they adapted their slaving strategies to meet local circumstance. Despite the important differences between indigenous and European slave systems, masters relied on both forms of human bondage as part of a larger colonial objective to make Illinois a provisioning ground for the French empire.

Slavery in Illinois operated through the negotiations that French settlers, Illinois Indians, and indigenous and African slaves made.[16] Rather than the French constructing a colonial slave economy based on dominating enslaved Africans and displacing Native Americans, the French joined existing systems of Indian slave trading in their efforts to form native alliances. In native Illinois, the exchange of enslaved women had long operated as a fundamental way to structure connections between rival communities, and the French found themselves drawn into this local politics. Simultaneously, French masters drew on their own Atlantic conceptions of slavery and trafficked people of African descent to Illinois to help construct their desired staple economy. By the 1730s, Indian slavery and European colonial slavery had coexisted in the Upper Mississippi Valley.[17] Indian- and African-descended slaves lived in the same homes, married into the same families, and labored in the same fields.

* * *

Figure 1. A map of Louisiana, featuring the Illinois Country at the junction of what is presently called the Ohio and Mississippi Rivers. Le Page Du Pratz, 1775. *Carte de la Louisiane colonial française avec le cours du Fleuve St. Louis, les rivières adjacents, les nations des naturels, les etablissems. Français et les mines* [Paris, 1758]. Retrieved from the Library of Congress, https://www.loc.gov/item/74692885/. (Accessed June 14, 2017.)

From the earliest moments of French settlement in Illinois, settlers had to accommodate the more numerous and powerful Illinois Indians. At the turn of the eighteenth century, Frenchmen, mostly from Quebec, came to Illinois and began to make alliances with the Illinois Indians. French *coureurs de bois* came in pursuit of the region's lucrative fur trade. Although French colonial officials had banned traders from traveling to and trapping in the Far West, a handful of voyageurs nevertheless trapped beaver pelts, buffalo robes, and deerskins. Joining these early traders, Jesuit missionaries established outposts in Illinois. Fur traders intermarried with Indian women, which in turn afforded them access to indigenous trade networks. Jesuit missionaries sanctioned these bonds, hoping to "Frenchify" the nations of native North America, and these cross-cultural liaisons sustained French settlement and helped Frenchmen build a colonial society.[18] In an illustrative 1702 case, Maria Rouensa, the daughter of a powerful leader of the Illinois Nation, renounced her family ties and married a Frenchman, Michel Accault, in a Catholic ceremony.[19] Rouensa would live for more than two decades in Kaskaskia, a Franco-Indian village. She remarried after her husband's death and had her children baptized in the Catholic Church.[20] Other Indian women followed Rouensa's path and took French husbands.[21] These cross-cultural marriages began to make a colonial society in the Upper Mississippi Valley.[22] By the first third of the eighteenth century, a handful of French Canadian families resided in the Illinois Country, with many of the French migrants married to Indian women, in part because so few French women lived in the region.[23] These marriages won sanction from French priests and colonial officials as part of a larger attempt to "Frenchify" native North America, by turning Indian brides into French subjects.

French colonial officials saw Illinois as a key strategic outpost: it sat halfway between Quebec and New Orleans, and its place on North America's waterways could help link the two arms of the France's North American empire. By 1719, French officials had further warmed to the outpost's potential when *habitants* discovered that Illinois's alluvial land would sustain staple agriculture. After a few booming grain harvests, the French settlers appeared to have found a commodity that they could sell in New Orleans and other colonial markets. In a few short years, slaveholders and enslaved Africans trickled north out of the Lower Mississippi and began to erect an export economy.[24] It seems likely that the earliest enslaved Africans in the region had been brought to New Orleans from West Africa and then sold further north.[25] Almost immediately, this northern migration had an impact, with a growing number of *habitants* devoted to grain agriculture. In 1723, one Louisiana official remarked of Illinois that "French wheat grows very well there and of a fine quality of which they gather a fairly large quantity. . . . Several habitants also have horse tread mills of their own with which they grind their French wheat."[26] The following year, Pierre Dugré de Boisbriant, the New Orleans–based governor of Louisiana, commented, "Everyone here [the Illinois] is devoted to agriculture."[27]

In short order, Illinois ceased to serve exclusively as a fur trade outpost, and the rise of export agriculture gave it a new role in the French empire.

The shift to staple agriculture attracted new farmers, facilitated a reorganization of French towns, and occurred just as French officials reorganized their North American empire. By the mid-1720s, French settlers had imported roughly 200 enslaved workers to sustain the grain economy, while the free population grew to 500.[28] Enslaved men and women made up roughly 25 percent of the population, and in these early years, men made up the majority of the enslaved population of African descent. By 1725, French *habitants* had reorganized their villages. While during the opening decades of the eighteenth century, mixed French and Indian villages dotted Illinois's landscape, by the mid-1720s, Frenchmen had resettled their two largest towns—Kaskaskia and Cahokia—away from the Indian grounds they had called home.[29] The new towns were formed in the "long lot" style, with farms radiating out from the nucleated village, in order to expand French access to arable land. Before the 1720s, these villages had hosted mixed French and Indian populations. The new settlements excluded the local Peoria and Kaskaskia Indians and focused the colony's efforts on export agriculture. This turn toward an export economy happened as the French state reorganized its overseas holdings. In 1724, France transferred Illinois out of Quebec's jurisdiction and made it a district of Louisiana.

French officials simultaneously expanded the *Code Noir*, a set of laws that governed slavery in the Caribbean, to apply to North America, including Illinois.[30] Originally passed in 1685 to regulate slavery in the Caribbean, the *Code* set out an empire-wide slave law. It made provisions for the birth, marriage, death, purchase, sale, and punishment of slaves. It defined slaves as salable and inheritable property, codified enslaved status through the mother's line and not the father's, and proscribed a set of punishments for various crimes. It also made provision for the baptism of enslaved people and their instruction in the Catholic faith, and it gave slaves the right to seek redress from an excessively violent master or one that deprived enslaved people of basic necessities such as food and clothing. Yet, as was common in other empires that had similar slave codes, it was selectively applied on the ground, including in Illinois. Looking at the trial records for several enslaved people, one scholar has concluded that Illinois *habitants* knew about and invoked the *Code Noir* regularly, but they frequently deviated from its provisions. Notably, one enslaved person was spared death when a chief of the Kaskaskia Indians intervened, indicating that the law of slavery had to be fit to the local circumstances in Illinois.[31] Still, by the 1720s, a legal framework had come into being that shaped some of the terms of slavery and freedom, even as those legal norms accommodated local circumstances.

Illinois's staple crop and its labor demands shaped life in bondage on farms and emerging plantations. Wheat demanded grueling labor only during planting in spring and harvest in the late summer, and slaves likely worked in gangs during these labor-intensive seasons.[32] During its growing season, however, wheat cultivation did not involve the careful tending and weeding required by tobacco, indigo, or cotton, and in the slack seasons, slaves did other work. French settlers relied on enslaved labor to clear land by felling timber, removing dense grasses, and preparing soil for planting. With steady effort, Illinois's economy underwent a steady expansion as the acres of developed land increased. Given the demand for grain in distant markets, the high yields these lands produced, and the large number of slaves relative to the free population, Illinois in the eighteenth century met some key conditions for becoming a plantation economy.[33]

Slaves also played important roles in milling grain to prepare it for export. Several techniques for milling grain existed, and slave labor was useful in all of them. The crudest method separated the grain from the chaff by flailing it on top of straw before sending it through a millstone. Standing in a circle, workers would walk slowly and beat the piles of grain on the ground in front of them. Another common technique was to trot horses on the grain, but the horses needed careful guidance, which made for an inefficient method. Planters more commonly used a gristmill run by water or horsepower to separate the grain from the chaff before funneling it to the millstone. Elaborate machines that needed careful calibration, gristmills also relied on several crude and laborious tasks. For instance, millstones generated heat, which would cook the flour and make it less desirable. Once the flour emerged from the stones, slaves would have to rake the flour until it cooled. This created a bottleneck in production, as a mill could produce a thousand pounds of flour per day and would thus need several rakers working around the clock to prepare the flour for barrels.[34]

Once packaged, slaveholders needed to transport flour to New Orleans for sale. With thousands of pounds of grain to ship, the convoys could grow to scores of bateaux that would descend the Mississippi at once. Rowing and navigating the Mississippi's waters demanded much from the crew and always remained dangerous, and the journeys down river and the return to Illinois could take months. Moving so many ships en masse required a large labor pool, the convoys always risked attack, and masters used slaves to meet the needs of these arduous journeys.[35] Consequently, enslaved labor was not mere surplus between planting and harvest: slaves did all the work of connecting the commodity with the buyers, a vital function that sustained the emerging plantation economy.

Frenchmen and women erected a staple economy that relied on enslaved workers to harvest, mill, and ship grain, but settlers also adapted to local circumstances and appropriated existing systems of indigenous bondage. Indigenous slavery played important political roles, and it was not simply a form of labor. The Illinois Indians, in particular, used it to organize power and forge diplomatic ties between diverse people in the Upper Mississippi Valley.[36] Illinois Indians would conduct raids on nearby regions and take women and children captive. Those captives would be traded among foreign nations, and in time they would become slaves when they were adopted into new societies. Women and children exchanged in this manner became "agents and objects of diplomacy" in part because they forged kin ties between groups.[37] This kin-based system of captivity, which was brutal, often leaving its victims physically maimed and scarred, sustained indigenous forms of bondage and erected a local politics of alliance.[38]

Frenchmen needed to accommodate the larger political reality concerning slavery. They could not simply sustain an export economy without also reckoning with the reality that Indians outnumbered them as colonial newcomers. As a consequence, Frenchmen participated in systems of captive exchange, knowingly or not, to maintain local alliances. During the early eighteenth century, nearly 10,000 Illinois Indians resided in the region, compared with fewer than 1,500 people of European and African descent.[39] As a result, Frenchmen adopted enslaved Indian women into their societies in order to sustain Native American alliances and brought Indian-descended captives into their growing slave economy. Before long, the Indian slave trade left a mark on French society. Census data in French Illinois indicate that women comprised the majority of Indian slaves.[40] Many enslaved women in time took baptism rites in the Catholic Church, and the people who partook in those rituals appeared to have come from the trans-Mississippi West.[41] The effect of this captive trade was not merely local: over time, French colonial officials modified the laws of New France to permit Indian slavery. While holding Indians in bondage remained illegal for much of the seventeenth century, by the early eighteenth century, French laws permitted Indian captive exchange and enslavement as part of an accommodation to the political reality in French North America.[42]

Once they entered the French community, Native American women trafficked as slaves experienced bondage in ways that differed from enslaved people of African descent. Women made up the majority of Indian slaves in French Illinois, in large part because Indian raiders tended to target women and children. It appears that Indian women more commonly served in household economies, although some labored in staple agriculture.[43] The sexual exploitation endemic to slavery fell disproportionately on Indian women in Illinois's society. This was especially true when masters sired children with enslaved Indian women. For instance, in 1726, an "Indian woman belonging to Louis Turpin" gave birth to a daughter who had an unidentified French father.[44] Cases like this were not unique. More than mere sources of coerced labor or targets of sexual violence, captive Indian women also joined in the making of a local colonial society. Over several decades, intimate relationships between Frenchmen-enslaved Indian women were recognized, and mixed-race children received baptismal sacraments.[45] As Indian women came to terms with their masters' power over them, some found ways to escape bondage. Intimate ties with their owners and mixed-raced children recognized by the church offered some Indian women access to manumission. It is impossible to say how many Indian women came into their freedom, but in several instances, freed women appear in church records with French husbands.[46] Not knowing for certain how these women understood their sexuality or eventual emancipation, it is still clear that enslaved Indian women changed the nature of French colonial society through the work of mothering children and helping to birth a new culture that mixed French and native peoples.

However, incorporating Indian *slaves* into colonial society did not mean French masters incorporated indigenous *slavery*. Ultimately, French masters participated in forms of captive exchange as part of a colonial strategy to forge a lucrative trade and export economy. Indian slaves, then, went to work on the grain fields and in the households of French farmers. Enslaved Indians may have entered French colonial Illinois through systems of kin-based exchange to sustain a politics of alliance, but many of them soon found themselves trapped in forms of coerced and degraded labor, sold as mere chattel between slaveholders.[47] Masters manipulated these slaving practices and in time managed to make a slave economy that could enrich themselves and the wider empire while also accommodating the powerful Illinois Indians that controlled much of the region.

Atlantic and indigenous bondage in Illinois did not operate as parallel institutions, but adaptable slaving practices gave rise to entangled relationships between slaves of diverse origins. While black and Indian slaves had divergent experiences with bondage, with most Indian slaves being women and most African slaves being men, they nevertheless forged some common bonds. After all, both had been seized from their native lands, trafficked into a distant colonial society, and coerced to labor in a growing agricultural economy. Slaveholders owned both enslaved Native Americans and people of African descent, and they undoubtedly worked alongside each other. For instance, in 1732, one slaveholder owned six bondmen of African origin and five Indian slaves. In another case, a master had two indigenous and two African-descended slaves.[48] In a third instance, a *habitant* owned at least two Indian slaves and acted as a godfather to a black slave.[49] On smaller farms such as these, the two types of slaves tended to work side by side. Similarly, in other parts of the colonial economy, differences between slaves likely broke down. In June 1736, several captive Chickasaw Indians arrived on the Mississippi convoy and were likely sold into the agrarian economy.[50] As enslaved people of African descent worked this convoy, they undoubtedly had sustained contact with the fresh shipment of enslaved Chickasaw Indians. And as enslaved Indians traveled on convoys staffed with black slaves as rowers, it seems likely they began to bridge divides. In all these ways, sustained contact between Indian- and African-descended slaves, on farms, on convoys, and in church life, would have tended to provide at least some common experiences among slaves.

As different enslaved populations interacted with French masters and comingled in the slave quarter, two separate groups of enslaved people began to make a shared life together. Throughout the eighteenth century, the parish life revealed how slaves of diverse origins became part of colonial society. Through much of the first half of the century, baptisms and burials of Indian- and African-descended slaves regularly marked church life.[51] The Jesuit Priests seem to have taken seriously their charge to Christianize the region's slaves. In addition to providing "almost daily instruction" to free French children, they oversaw "instruction of the negroes and the savages, slaves of the French, to prepare them for baptism and for the reception of the other sacraments." This included "on Sundays and feast-days, two instructions in the catechism . . . one for the French children and the other for the black slaves and the savages."[52]

The church provided one venue for slaves of diverse backgrounds to build a common life. On rare occasions, Indian- and African-descended slaves intermarried, formed stable families, and had their children baptized in the Catholic Church. For instance, in 1743, a "pagan Negro Slave" and a "Pawnee Indian Woman" who belonged to the same slaveholder had their two children baptized.[53] When slaves of Indian and African descent married, they crossed from very different landscapes of slavery onto a common ground. This immediate family, as well as other polyglot households, shows that Indian and African slaves could be incorporated into a single, adaptable, and localized system of bondage. The handful of instances when slaves of different races intermarried and had children suggests that elsewhere in the colony—on convoys, in the fields, and in cramped living quarters—slaves, whatever their origin, would have shared a common place as slaves in French colonial society. Rather than Indian- and African-descended slaves having divergent histories in this colonial society, slaves of diverse backgrounds came together as enslaved workers. Although Indian slavery had once been illegal, and slaves of African descent had been targeted for bondage due to their supposed racial inferiority, slaveholders assembled their coerced labor force by drawing on and appropriating different slaving practices. French colonial bondage thrived in part because masters could reinvent the process of making people slaves and could turn differing frameworks of slavery into one local system.

The local innovations to how human bondage functioned helped build a slave economy that made Illinois a place that could furnish the French empire with grain, furs, and naval stores. By the 1730s, colonial officials in New Orleans had noticed the region's growing output. Writing in 1731, the former governor of Louisiana, Pierre Dugué de Boisbriand, was relieved to hear that *habitants* in Illinois had ample seed to increase planting. Anticipating a surge in exports, the governor urged these *habitants* to fell timber and provide the southern end of the colony with lumber because lower Louisiana "lacked boats for commerce."[54] He stressed that more settlers and troops were necessary to increase production but underlined that land and military protection alone "is not sufficient," and the *habitants* needed to have access to "negroes' labor."[55] He "recommended that the inhabitants supply flour" to the Lower Mississippi River Valley, going on to say that "it is in the interest of the inhabitants to cultivate it . . . and support commerce" on the Mississippi.[56]

The steady expansion of Illinois's export economy convinced French administrators of the region's importance. They urged Frenchmen to develop the export economy further. Boisbriand remarked, "The post was established . . . because of the bounty of the land." He continued, "The corn comes as if it is from France, they have constructed mills and the provisions of all kinds are in abundance, they have discovered mines of copper, lead, silver and it is in great quantity as well as quality, which are near the way you pass to get to Canada."[57] He looked to Illinois's "most agreeable . . . fecund terrain" and knew it could create lucrative commodities "if they would work it with surety."[58] Colonial officers recognized that relying on Illinois for grain required giving "inhabitants in this post the liberty of the land" and "use of their negroes."[59] With enslaved Africans to labor on plantations and work in convoys, Boisbriant was certain that "the upper colony can provide enough flour for the base of the colony."[60] Writing in 1731, Boisbriant reported to the French minister of the marine in Versailles, Jean-Frédéric Phelypeaux, Comte de Maurepas, "This quarter must be regarded as the most important in the colony." The governor continued, "This colony merits the attention of your Greatness, the river is a great port for France."[61] By the 1730s, with enslaved laborers working the harvest, grain periodically arriving in New Orleans, and a growing colonial population, French Illinois had in some ways begun to find its footing in the larger empire, even if that progress was fragile, contingent, and subject to reversal.

It was during the Fox Wars of the 1730s that French officials learned just how important it was to sustain Indian alliances and how fragile Illinois's security was. Members of the Fox Nation—upset that Frenchmen held their kin as slaves—began conducting raids and skirmishes against the French.[62] The conflict cut off Illinois's trade routes to the Lower Mississippi Valley, and the tenuous nature of Illinois's export economy became manifest. In January 1732, Boisbriant lamented that "the pirogue of the Convoy of Illinois" came under attack and that "a Frenchmen and a slave were killed by a party of five or six savages."[63] In October of the same year, he reported to his superiors in France that "war sustained with the savages" disrupted trade and that farmers "were not able to make a route within this country." The convoy "languished, particularly because they could not find an outlet for their foods which consists of flour, pork, and other goods."[64] Regrettably, he continued, "they were not able to descend the Illinois and above all ascend without a larger company [of soldiers] in the convoy." In light of these disruptions, he remarked that "their meats and their flour which is the principle resource . . . [for] the inhabitants at the base of the colony" cannot be trafficked and consequently the convoy "must find a new route to Illinois."[65]

The Fox Wars quickly concluded, but they did not trigger a total abandonment of Indian slavery in the Illinois Country. Peace came after a devastating 1731 French attack on Fox warriors. The war did not bring an end to the enslaving of natives, but as part of the peace terms, trade in Fox Indians subsided. The wars in turn inspired a series of efforts to curtail Indian slavery's wider political impact. The longtime colonial governor in New Orleans, Jean-Baptiste Le Moyne, Sieur de Bienville, instructed the Jesuit Priests in Illinois "to prevent unfair treatment of Indian slaves in the missions." He wanted to curtail any danger that came from the trade in Indian slaves because Indians' place on Frenchmen's farms led to "wars that they foment among the savages."[66] Yet the reforms that took shape after 1732 had their limits. Even as the trade in captive Fox Indians subsided, exchanging Indian women continued as part of the native alliance systems that were the lifeblood of the French empire.[67] New Indian slaves continued to arrive in Illinois: in the wake of the 1736 war between the French and Chickasaw Indians, who resided near modern-day Memphis, Frenchmen seized Chickasaw captives and deported them to Illinois. As late as 1752, nearly 150 Indian slaves lived in French Illinois, constituting roughly a quarter of the entire enslaved population.[68] The Fox Wars taught Frenchmen that their export economy depended on local collaborations, which would shield them from attack. Participation in captive trade with the many nations of the Mississippi Valley was an important component of those indigenous alliances.

It became a governing principle among French officials that Illinois's export economy could only survive with local Indian alliances to support it. For one thing, the large convoys—often dozens of boats with thousands of pounds of flour—made for easy targets. Jean-Baptiste Le Moyne de Bienville recognized this fact and repeatedly strategized about it. Writing about the need to sustain "the current state of tranquility [that] renders possible the Navigation of this river throughout the Illinois," Bienville urged his superiors in the ministry at Versailles to encourage traders to establish ties "in each of the different Nations of this Continent."[69] Over and over again, Bienville stressed the importance of the convoy needing to travel in "perfect tranquility" and that sustaining peace with the "Illinois Indians and the Chickasaws" was key.[70] Bienville boasted about the traders' ability "to overcome the difficulties with the Savage Nations of the Continent" and "accelerate all the advantages" of the Illinois Country.[71] Boisbriant, now a former governor of Louisiana, observed the "tranquil" state of affairs in Illinois, noting the Indian nations had stopped harassing "the people and negroes that ascend the river."[72] France should expect benefits to the whole empire from "the flour . . . that will descend every month to Louisiana and Canada."[73] With Indian alliances intact, the distant Illinois Country could maintain a growing export economy and serve as a provisioning ground for Louisiana and the wider French empire.

Even under these improved circumstances, Illinois merchants made only tenuous progress toward integrating their export economy with the wider French empire. A crop failure in the 1730s led to a disappointing export. Writing in the spring, a colonial official in New Orleans lamented that a convoy from Illinois arrived "charged with flour, pork, bear oil, [and] pelts" but only "in small amounts because they say that the winter was long and rough."[74] A few months later, this disappointment was still on his mind, as he wrote that Illinois suffered from the "misery of last year from the loss of almost all of the crops."[75] He nevertheless concluded that "this little help does give some relief at the bottom of the colony which was wanting for any kind of food."[76] Whatever the region's shortcomings, Jean-Baptiste Le Moyne de Bienville declared that Illinois was "equally necessary for Canada as for Louisiana. It provides to this colony and province all the flour that is necessary and to Canada the means to stage their infinite commerce."[77] Illinois's exports made "the Post of Illinois respectable for its force, useful for its fertility and advantageous for its happy situation . . . for New France and its commerce."[78]

The local slave system helped propel Illinois's export economy and make the enslaved population one key component to the colony's place in the empire. By the late 1730s, Illinois masters reversed their setbacks, and staple export agriculture helped define Illinois's place in the French empire. As midcentury approached, Pierre de Rigaurd, the Marquis de Vaudreuil, the incoming governor of French Louisiana, had concluded that a larger garrison "would enlarge their Agriculture and provide to the lower parts of the Colony a larger quantity of flour" because "it will impose on the savage nations of this continent."[79] He insisted the dispatch of troops was necessary because Illinois was "the chief country of this colony . . . and a principal post" in North America. He argued that "a good crop will require considerable troops in this country to promote an advantageous commerce with New Orleans."[80] Enlarging the garrison would give "the inhabitants of Illinois the ability to multiply their crops. . . . This will allow them to considerably increase the flour" sold in New Orleans, a key imperial objective.[81] While Vaudreuil may have simply wanted more resources from France, he nevertheless accurately assessed Illinois's economy and the reality of trade on the Mississippi.

The Illinois export economy grew steadily, and New Orleans reaped the benefits. Between the 1730s and the 1750s, the percentage of slaves in Illinois rose, the total acreage under cultivation expanded, and the value of land appreciated. In 1732, enslaved workers constituted roughly one-third of the population, and in 1752, they approached 50 percent. In 1752, over 1,300 people lived there: 785 white *habitants*, 446 enslaved Africans, and 149 enslaved Indians. As the population grew, the acreage and value of land under cultivation increased nearly tenfold. In 1732, planters had cleared a little more than a thousand acres of land, valued at 827 livres—or a couple hundred British pounds. Twenty years later, that number jumped to a few thousand cleared acres valued at 7,250 livres.[82] Although not a vast sum—it equaled roughly 1,500 British pounds—the trend showed that important changes had begun.

By the 1750s, slave-grown wheat monoculture had pervaded the region, and Illinois looked like a typical staple economy. Within the context of the wider French Atlantic, colonial Illinois always remained a tiny outpost, and lower Louisiana, to say nothing of the Caribbean, dwarfed the upper region. What's more, the land was mostly not organized into plantation complexes, where fields, mills, and the other machinery of processing grain into flour sat within a single plot. Still, the changes to the colony over time pushed it toward that goal, and Illinois hosted a few wealthy farmers and a large enslaved population. Given the thousands of pounds of grain that Illinois exported annually, the crop required a near-total mobilization of Illinois's relatively small working population.[83] With their cultivated acreage steadily expanding, *habitants* quickly found that their economic fortunes depended on slave labor. A wide cast of settlers owned slaves, with 46 percent of free white men owning at least one enslaved worker. Yet by 1752, a few slave masters had ascended to the top of Illinois's society and consolidated their control over slave labor: a mere 4 percent of slaveholders owned 49 percent of the slaves in Illinois.

Several planters acquired dozens of slaves and a growing acreage of land. Antoine Bienvenu, with fifty-nine slaves and two estates totaling nearly 600 acres, ranked top on that small list of aspiring grandees. As late as the 1750s, he owned four enslaved Indians who worked alongside the black slaves on his estate. Bienvenu had been born in New Orleans, and upon relocating to the Illinois Country, he set to work building his operation. He routinely shipped grain on the convoys, and his large holdings of land and slaves testified to the profit he could reap.[84] Bienvenu did not chart this course toward a slave economy alone. Several other prominent planters owned over a dozen slaves and large tracts of land. The would-be plantation masters also owned scores of draft animals and slaughtering animals, including dozens of head of cattle. One such estate claimed thirty-seven slaves and land approaching fifty acres and produced grain for the king's warehouse. Another planter, Antoine Buchet, owned twenty-eight slaves, valuable developed lands, and scores of cattle and horses. A few others had almost twenty slaves and similarly sized land holdings. This small cast of landowners attempted to monopolize labor, owned the boats on the annual convoys to New Orleans, and held the longest tracts of cleared land, which made them indispensable to Illinois's export economy.

Staple agriculture was not confined to the ranks of the few, however. Just below these larger farmers, a few slaveholders owned midsized estates and several slaves. In 1752, seven farmers, a tiny fraction of the French population, owned between ten and fifteen slaves and their land was valued, on average, at over 100 livres. Another sixteen *habitants*, again a small sliver, enslaved between five and ten workers and owned land valued, on average, at just over 80 livres. A few Frenchmen in this last category owned fewer than ten slaves but expansive tracts of developed land and dozens of draft animals. These midsized farmers no doubt sought to increase their labor pools. Yet it seems that wealthier *habitants* monopolized land, labor, and shipping routes to cut off any significant growth of their rivals' estates.

By using adaptable forms of bondage, masters managed to create an export economy and sustain peaceful ties with neighboring Indian nations. By the 1750s, Illinois had become a reliable source of grain, and the region was increasingly well integrated into France's North American empire. Reporting back to the minister of the marine in France, Governor Bienville summarized the state of affairs in Louisiana, concluding "the gardens thrive . . . producing abundance for all."[85] He asserted that "the flour milled . . . from Illinois makes bread . . . very nicely."[86] His assessment concurred with another official's conclusion that, "despite the remoteness of this quarter," it was of great importance because of "all the relief in flour" shipped to "the base of the river."[87] Bienville hoped to make the "movement to Illinois every year in January. The trip will be easier and shorter in regard to the season of winter where the maladies and the threat of wars are less likely."[88] Summarizing several of his contemporaries' opinions, Bienville concluded that "the greatest advantage for this colony was the Agriculture its lands produce."[89] He noted the region's importance, "given where it is situated on the continent relative to Mexico, it can be an entrepôt of commodities and useful for Rich Commerce with New Spain which is forbidden by the sea."[90] Writing at midcentury, Bienville reported to the royal minister in France that "the commerce between the [Caribbean] Islands with this colony changes every day" but that Illinois recently provided "twelve boats filled with wine, flour, etc. and we send back boats with wood."[91]

By the 1750s, grain traffic had accelerated, and masters sent provisions to several outposts in French North America. A 1748 convoy went "to the different posts [that] were in a bad state."[92] Similarly, the 1751 spring convoy sent grain to various posts along the Mississippi River.[93] The commandant of Illinois reported that "7,000 weight of flour remains" in the warehouses of Illinois.[94] The colonial governor of French Louisiana noted that planters were attempting to "augment by a large amount their crops that they will provide to the base of the colony."[95] He added that "inhabitants . . . make lucrative, advantageous commerce with France and the Americas and very favorably with the colony [of Louisiana]."[96] Illinois's commandant reassured administrators in New Orleans that he would "encourage the *habitants* to double their grain crops."[97] The following year, he was satisfied with "the great quantity of flour [that] has passed here."[98] Illinois's production had increased to the degree that the *habitants* "have provided a great deal of flour and it has just descended [the Mississippi] stopping at every post on the route." This was a "great service" to the "interior of the colony," and goods from Illinois would "provide considerable goods for voyages to France."[99] Almost every year, the governor of Louisiana "confirmed the expectation . . . of an abundant harvest in that country . . . some individuals reported 100 thousand weight in flour" would annually descend to the Lower Mississippi River Valley.[100]

Illinois's abundance enabled it to become a breadbasket for posts along the Mississippi, towns across New France, and settlements on the Gulf Coast.[101] Each winter, French colonial officials and ordinary residents in New Orleans assembled provisions to last until spring. They had come to rely on the convoy of provision goods from the Illinois Country. Writing in 1756, Jean Jacques Macarty, the French military commandant for Illinois, boasted that "Illinois [is] very well suited to agriculture of wheat and other grains." He added that in addition to the "black, light, fertile" soil of the Mississippi basin, its "pastures are excellent and the European cattle reproduce abundantly." In fact, he said, so good was the soil that in 1753, this outpost "provided New Orleans with more than 8,000 weight of flour during a single winter." In addition to trade down river, another 4,000 weight of flour was sent to Quebec. As one French traveler reported at midcentury, "the post of the Illinois . . . seems placed where it can always, despite all the navies of the world, export grain and meat."[102]

When warfare—in the form of the Seven Years' War between France, Britain, and Spain—broke out, the region proved its worth. In 1754, just as the slave economy was booming, global events reached this distant region of North America. During the war, the French empire mobilized all its resources to defend against British attacks, and though Illinois saw no hostilities, colonial officials called upon the region to aid the war effort. They were not disappointed. In 1756, Fort Duquesne, near modern-day Pittsburgh, came under attack. The fort's commander begged the commandant in Illinois for provisions, but Illinois's commandant wrote to New Orleans reporting that he found it difficult to arm a convoy.[103] New Orleans officials dispatched eighteen soldiers and some bateaux. In June, a shipment carrying staples from Illinois amounting to 120,000 weight of flour and 40,000 weight of "cured meats" arrived at Fort Duquesne.[104] Illinois became a constant source of "pork, beef, horses, wild game" as well as grain.[105]

Because of the effect of the hostilities on French trade routes, the war had a crippling impact on the region's economy. British soldiers harassed grain shipments, and the reliable convoys that had begun to integrate Illinois into the French empire grew more erratic. With many Indian nations fighting the British, the raids that had once been a reliable source of Indian slaves tapered off because Indian leaders focused on defeating British forces, not raiding to seize new captives. Moreover, Illinois masters could no longer buy slaves in New Orleans, and labor became scarce. At the war's conclusion, statesmen in Europe would transfer Illinois to British authority, which would have important consequences for the local slave economy. But before that transpired, wartime disruptions ground Illinois's continued expansion into a plantation economy to a halt.

* * *

Yet even before these global events upended Illinois's economic growth, the region's success as an export economy remained precarious, and it required collaboration with Indian powerbrokers. The risk of raids on the Illinois convoys always remained. Indian diplomacy and staple agriculture were equally important to Illinois's success, and accepting Indian captives to sustain alliances, while also using slaves to labor in the grain fields, remained fundamental to Illinois's role in the French empire. Indigenous and Atlantic slavery served both important political functions among indigenous nations and important economic roles among French farmers. The French empire in North America had in Illinois a reliable provisioning colony whose residents also maintained peaceful relations with Peoria, Kaskaskia, Miami, and Shawnee Indians. As one official noted, shipping this "abundance of flour" required "a great deal of tribute paying to the Illinois and Shawnee nations" so that the colonists could work "without any harassment of the French or the Negroes."[106] To make a slave economy, Illinois masters drew on different slaving practices, drawn from indigenous and Atlantic frameworks, to make a single localized slave system.

With indigenous- and African-descended slaves filling Illinois's labor pool, the region forged its own localized slave system. Two systems of bondage came into contact because French settlers exploited the region's fertile fields and participated in Indian diplomacy to secure their colony. The local demands of indigenous relations and alliance building drove the rise of Indian slavery in French Illinois while Atlantic systems of plantation production shaped the black experience in bondage. Despite those differences, Indian slaves in French Illinois often found themselves working alongside enslaved people of African descent in a variety of capacities. In time, the two groups of slaves shared a common space in colonial Illinois. They intermarried, raised families, and shared funeral rites. The export economy that provisioned New Orleans necessitated that masters accommodate Indian politics while also finding ways to keep coerced workers toiling in the fields and on the convoys. In time, those twin purposes comingled and took root in a single, adaptable slave system that came to be an important part of life in French Illinois. With scores of bateaux semiannually traversing the Mississippi, Illinois's small size would still have made a big impression on observers.

In Illinois, as elsewhere, enslaved people's experiences did not fall along institutional lines. Slavery operated according to local circumstances, and the two forms of bondage—Indian and Atlantic—did not diverge over time. Unlike other places in North America, attempts to force enslaved Indians to work in staple production succeeded.[107] This reality invites a reassessment of the idea that the two forms of bondage fell into separate frameworks. An institutional approach to understanding different forms of slavery cannot explain how for decades enslaved people of indigenous and African descent lived and labored alongside one another. Masters performed an alchemy of slavery as they drew from different slaving practices to make a colonial society and economy deep in the heart of North America. Into the 1740s, contrary to the institutional pressure of each form of bondage, native slaves were born into inheritable bondage, and black slaves were captives seized in distant lands and trafficked into the region.

Despite rough similarities to other places in the Atlantic, the early years of the attempted plantation revolution in Illinois took its own particular course that integrated diverse slaves into a single colonial economy. Through multinational relationships with various indigenous nations, French men and women secured a foothold in the heart of North America. Increasingly secure in their titles to land, *habitants* imported slaves from New Orleans in growing numbers. As these enslaved people of African descent toiled alongside enslaved Indians, the tiny colony created a lucrative slave economy that shipped grain across North America. In Illinois, farmers did not transition from relying on enslaved Indians to African slavery, as happened elsewhere. Instead, Indian and African slaves together helped drive a transition to colonial Illinois that made it a staple export economy. In time, these people would be known as "French Negroes," a term that concealed their diverse origins. Yet that lay in the distance. More immediately, when the French empire abandoned its claims to the region after the Seven Years' War in 1763, British colonizers would pick up where the French left off. They would learn, as the French had before, that a local history of slaveries would shape the course of empires.

CHAPTER 2

Another Law and Empire

As autumn leaves began to fall in 1767, settlers in the Illinois Country witnessed an unusual event. Roughly 200 enslaved men, women, and children, strangers to Illinois, were marched into Kaskaskia to be sold. Since Illinois's slave economy hosted fewer than a thousand bound workers, this group of slaves meant a marked increase in the enslaved labor force. Yet these individuals likely stood out for reasons other than their number relative to the rest of the population. Unlike the Indian- and African-descended slaves who had toiled in Illinois's grain economy during the previous decades, the workers for sale in 1767 came from within the British Empire. When Britain defeated France in the Seven Years' War, it won new domains in North America and incorporated Illinois into its empire. By terms of the treaty, the Mississippi River became a border, with all lands to the east belonging nominally to Britain and all lands to the west belonging nominally to Spain. With new lands to exploit, the Philadelphia-based trading firm of Baynton, Wharton, and Morgan began shipping black captives to the distant colony. Already a meeting ground for Indian slaves and Francophone slaves of African descent, Illinois became still more diverse when this third group of slaves arrived in the region.

The 1767 group came from two different regions within the British Empire. Baynton, Wharton, and Morgan purchased ninety slaves in Philadelphia and sent them down the Ohio River to the Illinois Country. These enslaved men and women probably spoke English, likely had been born in Pennsylvania, and no doubt had families they left behind in Pennsylvania.[1] Meanwhile, the firm had its agent, James Rumsey, send a second shipment of slaves from Jamaica to Illinois.[2] These slaves could have been born in Africa and were almost certainly accustomed to living in areas with black majorities and a high mortality rate.[3] The firm's partners congratulated Rumsey for "the inexpressible Fatigues that you have undergone with the Negroes." They cheered him for "the whole of your Conduct respecting them from the Time you bought them at Jamaica to your landing them at Kaskaskia."[4]

Perhaps surprisingly, French masters at first refused to buy these newly imported slaves. For more than a year after they arrived in Illinois, George Morgan, a partner in the firm, struggled to offload them. Writing his associates in December 1767, Morgan reported that the French *habitants* had not made "a single offer" to purchase slaves being sold by another British firm, "on Acc[ount] of his Negroes being, as they say, All English." He continued, "The Monsieurs declare against having any thing to do with his Negroes. Apprehending that as they have been so long among the English & some of them Country Born, they must have been Sent here for the Rogueries." Since the slave uprising in Jamaica dubbed Tacky's Rebellion had occurred only a few years earlier, it was not unreasonable to think that some of the captured rebels might have been shipped to remote places such as Illinois. Whatever French masters thought, their actions spoke volumes. The firm's slave sales for late 1767 and early 1768 indicate that at first, only English settlers or the occasional desperate Frenchmen were willing to buy. Yet as spring 1768 came and planters soberly assessed their need for labor, larger purchases began to pave the way for a rapid dispersal of the imported slaves. Wealthy French planters Antoine Bienvenu, Pierre Charleville, and a member of the Beauvais family purchased slaves in large numbers. Relieved, Morgan reported in November 1768 that he had sold "the two last Negroes" for a "very agreeable" price, observing that otherwise, "they would have been a Considerable Expense to keep."[5]

Pleased with his firm's efforts, George Morgan dreamed of bulging pockets and a monopoly on the Illinois trade. He accepted grain and other commodities as payment for slaves, hoping to use his human cargo to consolidate power over the provisioning economy. He declared, "We have it in our Power to make a Monopoly of all the Flour in the Country by purchasing it with Negroes."[6] A year later, he still believed that commerce in slaves was a means to consolidate the firm's power over the provisioning trade in Illinois: "slaves will always command what they Will—viz. Flour, Cattle & Salt Beef."[7] By some measures, Morgan won the day. In a single year, sales of slaves earned the firm the soaring sum of nearly £20,000. At this point, British capital and slave labor seemed poised to transform Illinois; helping his case, Morgan had the backing of many prominent British officials who wanted to expand British authority into the Mississippi Valley.

Morgan's successful sale was the result of a wider set of changes at work in the Illinois Country, and it heralded an attempt by British policy makers in London and merchants across Anglo North America to integrate Illinois into the British Empire, making it a provisioning colony for the Caribbean. After defeating France in the Seven Years' War, Britain acquired vast new territories in India, the Caribbean, and most of North America east of the Mississippi River. With backing from imperial officials, British firms began to incorporate Illinois into the existing Atlantic empire, and slaves and goods traveled between the Mississippi Valley and the rest of the empire. Despite various Native American nations and French settlers who contested the assertion of colonial power, British traders, British capital, and British goods began to remake the heart of the continent.[8] New sources of enslaved labor, new British consumer markets, and new sources of credit in London all facilitated an expansion of the small but lucrative slave economy in Illinois. Yet like the French, colonial claims to the region always remained tepid, and British settlers, merchants, and officials of various ranks would spend years attempting to turn nominal claims to this territory into a more durable sovereignty. They would have only modest success.

Illinois's localized slave system did not respect the boundaries forged at Europe's diplomatic tables, and the ability to manipulate the newly drawn border at the Mississippi River highlights how slaveholders could adapt the slave economy to meet new political circumstances. Just as French settlers had to reckon with the indigenous politics of slavery and captivity, they would now also have to work within the new political realities that came along with British settlement. French slaveholders who did not want to join the British Empire confronted their would-be rulers with a host of strategies intended to maintain their control over enslaved workers and keep the staple grain economy running to French markets in New Orleans. One strategy was simple: fleeing the colony. In 1763, rather than submitting to British rule, many French *habitants* relocated across the Mississippi to the newly erected village at St. Louis, nominally in Spanish territory. They hoped that the border at the Mississippi River would protect local control over the slave economy and fend off their would-be British governors. Yet many of these emigrants continued to maintain ties with French, Indian, and enslaved communities that spanned the Mississippi River. French and Indian settlers sustained a smuggling economy that brought goods from

British territory into St. Louis and then on to New Orleans, as they had done for decades. Even when they stayed put, masters improvised amid the political turmoil of the 1760s and 1770s, developing new strategies to keep the slave economy working much as it had before, oriented toward New Orleans, not to Philadelphia. The obstacles Morgan encountered as he attempted to sell his black captives signaled a larger set of problems that he and other British agents would grapple with for nearly another decade.

French slaveholders also tried to exert control over their homegrown system of slavery by manipulating British military officials and the local court. For most of the 1760s and 1770s, the British military ruled the region directly, and British officials steadfastly refused to extend civil jurisdiction to the region. To undercut local military power, French *habitants* appealed to British commanders all the way in New York to settle local disputes. This distant military power proved unwieldy, and British agents eventually formed a local civil court, hoping it would bring some order to Illinois's governance. Across the empire, British imperial policy allowed localities a measure of self-governance. Illinois was no different, and Frenchmen quickly co-opted this second source of authority to perpetuate their own local legal control in the region. Notably, no empire-wide system of slave laws like the *Code Noir* existed in the British Empire. Fractured imperial politics, French and Indian communities that defied international borders, and a slave economy with a diverse group of enslaved workers that did not fall into British orbit all explain how French masters found ways to keep the colony functioning much as it had for previous decades.

Over the course of the 1760s and 1770s, French *habitants* used local knowledge of the landscape and the economy to overcome British imperial designs.[9] In these years, they learned how to live under a new empire without changing the local economy and society. British settlers and officials spent considerable effort in making Illinois a colony of their own, by bringing new slaves to the region and attempting to create new trade patterns that would send wealth east to Philadelphia. Yet rather than seizing the colony and imposing their power over the local community, British attempts at empire only introduced more complexity to Illinois and made it more ungovernable. As a consequence, the fluidity that marked the region during the French period persisted into the 1770s.

British colonial rule added new dimensions to the adaptable forms of enslavement so prevalent in Illinois. Once again, slaving practices never operated in any one framework. Some Indians were born into inheritable slavery, despite the fact that indigenous bondage typically operated through systems of captive exchange. Meanwhile, hundreds of African-descended slaves had been taken from their homes in places around the British Empire and trafficked long distances to the Illinois Country, making them outsiders to the developing colonial society. Like before, masters had to accommodate imperial norms and customs surrounding slavery even as they worked with local forms of enslavement prevalent in Illinois. With the French *Code Noir* now defunct, masters had to find new ways to exercise legal authority, which meant dealing with their new British colonizers. Masters had to conform their slaving activities within new parameters, including new borders drawn at the Mississippi River and different forms of legality and governance in the new empire. Slaveholders had to accommodate, at least modestly, these new realities, and masters simultaneously drew on certain forms of indigenous bondage and European colonial slavery to make a colonial export economy. As it turned out, the British claims to the region would be short-lived. But the history of accommodating a new empire, deflecting its attempts at remaking the region, and erecting local control over the slave economy would act as a rehearsal for later, when in the 1780s, the U.S. government tried to seize the region and make it free soil.

During the 1750s and 1760s, Illinois's population continued to grow even as warring imperial powers carved up the region with new political borders.[10] In the first third of the eighteenth century, only five French villages dotted the landscape. By the 1760s, the number had grown to eight. The towns varied in size from French Kaskaskia, the largest village, which in 1770 had 500 Europeans and a similar number of enslaved Indians and Africans, to French Cahokia, 45 miles north with a few hundred Europeans and roughly 100 slaves.[11] The remaining towns ranged in size, some with only a few dozen inhabitants.[12] Fort Chartres, the French outpost on the east bank of the river, was falling into disrepair in this period, but it still provided an important camp for British officials, settlers, and soldiers. In addition to the European settlements, two major Indian villages sat along the east bank of the Mississippi River—Kaskaskia and Cahokia. The towns were situated near mills and along major roads, suggesting that the alliances and trade networks forged during the 1750s continued. Yet when the Seven Years' War came to an end, by the terms of the Treaty of Paris, France split its North American empire between Britain and Spain, and the Mississippi River suddenly became an international boundary between rival empires. The region's towns straddled this boundary: six villages were along the east

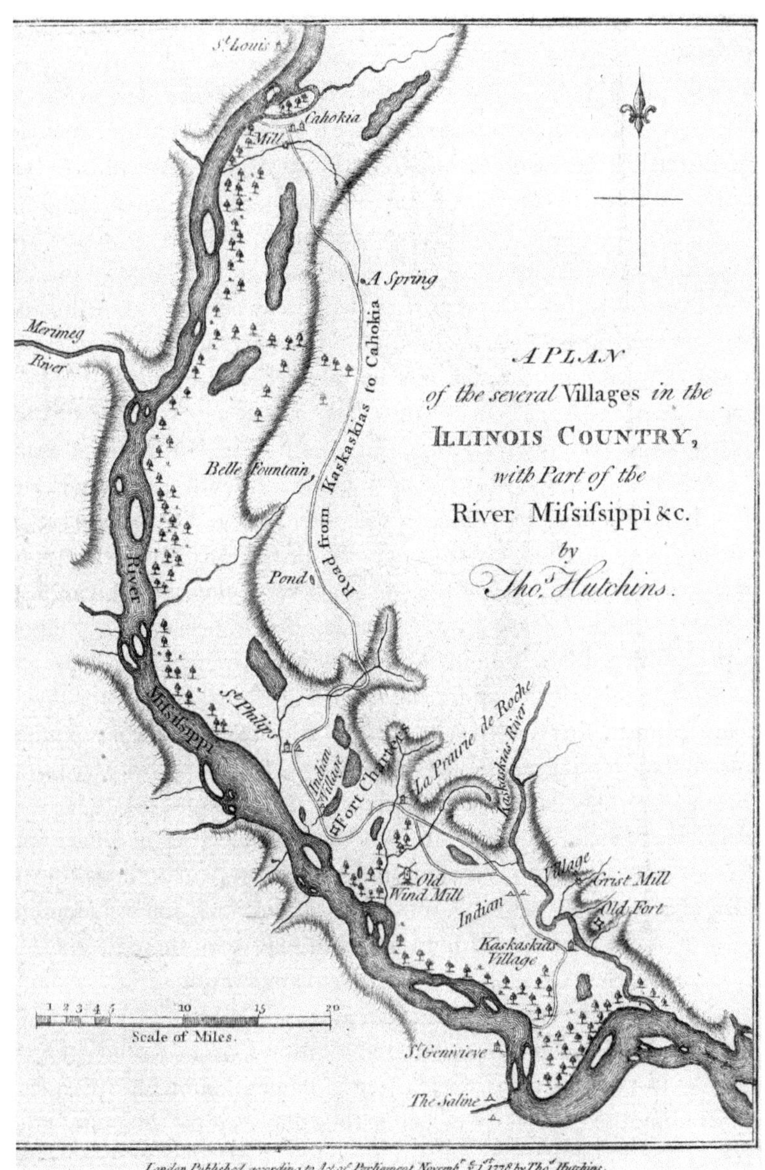

Figure 2. Plan of the several villages of the Illinois Country. Thomas Hutchins, *A Topographical Description of Virginia* (1778), RB 8410. Reproduced by permission of The Huntington Library, San Marino, Calif.

bank of the river and thus in British territory, and two towns were on the west bank that became Spanish territory.

By redrawing imperial borders, the 1763 treaty opened new markets to British merchants and businessmen. In 1763, Baynton, Wharton, and Morgan joined as partners who eagerly looked west from Philadelphia to build a fortune. Prior to the firm's formation, George Morgan, who was orphaned at a young age, had been apprenticed to John Baynton and Samuel Wharton. Morgan specialized in the fur trade and Indian relations during his apprenticeship—a focus that would direct his entire business career.[13] By the 1760s, when Baynton, Wharton, and Morgan began its venture, Morgan had been elevated to a full partner and controlled the firm's affairs in the trans-Appalachian West. The firm developed close ties with British officials, including Thomas Gage, commander-in-chief of British forces in North America; Sir William Johnson, the influential superintendent of Indian affairs; and Johnson's deputy, George Croghan. The firm was trusted with a monopoly to supply the British garrison with supplies. With access to powerful patrons, it quickly became the favored firm in the region, often receiving help from British military officials in carrying out its voyages between Pennsylvania and the Illinois Country.[14]

Officials in the British Empire and businessmen such as Baynton, Wharton, and Morgan formulated a potentially lucrative scheme for imperial expansion that would use Illinois as a breadbasket for other British colonies. Writing in 1766, William Johnson reported that Illinois was "one of the finest Corn countries in the World" and added that it "would have in its power not only to supply the different Posts in Indian Country, but the two *Floridas* with Provisions." Johnson also noted that many Frenchmen regarded it as the "*Granary* of Louisiana and that when there happened to be a scarcity at New Orleans the French Settlement at the Illinois, small as it then was, sent them upwards of 800,000 weight of Flour."[15]

Influential officials in London shared Johnson's vision. In the late 1760s, a pamphlet laid out the case for a "Strong Settlement" along the Mississippi. After detailing the possibility of cultivating staple crops, including wheat and corn, the pamphleteer assessed the impact of labor scarcity in the greater Mississippi Valley. With "very few laboring people there," he observed "the only method of Settling such hot Countrys is by Negroes, a Method that Experience has led every Nation of Europe into."[16] Others echoed these views. In 1770, the new president of the Board of Trade in London, Lord Hillsborough, wrote General Gage and remarked that "the great and solid Advantages arising . . . from . . . North American Colonies, depend principally upon giving proper Encouragement to . . . the Supply of the Sugar Islands with Lumber and Provisions." He continued, "The commercial Advantages which may be derived from these Possessions . . . render them an Object deserving the most serious Attention."[17] Like the French in earlier decades, British officials hoped to make Illinois a feeder colony for British Caribbean holdings. Just as before, enslaved people's labor was critical to this ambitious imperial plan.

British hopes of profiting from the new territory faced fierce French and Indian resistance that plunged the region into chaos. In 1763, the same year as the Treaty of Paris, an Ottawa chief named Pontiac helped lead a war that threatened Great Britain's viability in the trans-Appalachian West.[18] In two short years, Pontiac's Rebellion, as scholars subsequently called it, had razed or placed under siege most of the British forts west of the Appalachians. As the war went on, British officials watched their newly won dominion fall from their grasp. This was particularly true for the Illinois Country, where Pontiac's allies fought British expansion west.[19] Yet after a few key British victories, notably at Detroit, the war entered a long stalemate, and eventually both sides sued for peace. By 1765, the pan-tribal resistance had subsided, but the British learned important lessons. Just as the Fox Wars had forced accommodation on the French, this uprising compelled British officials into trade alliances with American Indian nations once the hostilities subsided.[20] Although the British eventually managed to overcome the resistance to their expansion, the rebellion had a major impact on the course of the British Empire. During the years of the rebellion, British officials could not physically travel to the Illinois Country, and without personnel on the ground, their claims to the region grew brittle.

As the British fumbled to find a way into the Illinois Country, French *habitants* fled their jurisdiction for St. Louis on the Mississippi's west bank, which was controlled but largely ignored by the Spanish.[21] The British viewed this development with alarm. Writing to London, George Croghan, deputy superintendent of Indian affairs, noted that "the French are forming an establishment about Sixty Miles from Fort Chartres." British officials immediately suspected that the rival Francophone settlements would funnel trade and people out of their newly won colony. "With this new outpost," Croghan noted, "they will again engross all the Traffic with the numerous Nations to the Westward of us, and thereby deprive us *of the present use* of our Canada Conquest."[22]

Even after major threats to British power subsided, including indigenous rebellion and settler migration west, quotidian forms of resistance continued to undercut their power over the Illinois Country. In particular, British merchants eyeing the region's grain economy knew that contraband trade from Illinois to St. Louis would deny them staples and other profitable goods coming out of the Upper Mississippi Valley. In particular, the emerging French smuggling economy across the Mississippi undercut Baynton, Wharton, and Morgan's venture. The firm looked to imperial officials to bring order to the local economy. Writing merchants in Jamaica in 1764, Morgan lamented "the unfounded trade that has been carried on between this Province and our ancient Enemies the French (for We still look at them in that light) has been of essential detriment to the commerce of our own." Morgan expected that "the Parliament that is now setting will put an interdiction to it." If the British could stem the tide of French smuggling from Illinois, Morgan expected "a commerce to be carried on beneficially between Jamaica & the Continent."[23]

Still, French settlers had to come to terms with new British claims to the region, which they sought to contest and disrupt seemingly at every turn. Eventually they would carve out a local control over the slave economy while selectively drawing on the British to prop up their societies. Yet that would take time to accomplish. At first, the scale of local resistance to British authority was on full display in 1765 when British officers Thomas Reid and John Wilkins landed at Fort Chartres. Upon arrival, Reid and Wilkins might have thought their quest for the Illinois Country was complete. In fact, it had only begun. Many French settlers had crossed the Mississippi to St. Louis, and those who remained were not tractable. After proclaiming British authority, Wilkins's deputy, Captain Thomas Sterling, required "the Inhabitants to take the Oath of Fidelity" to the king. Many French settlers refused. "The whole presented a memorial praying for Nine Months to Settle their Affairs" and leave the colony. Sterling refused any time for transition, and the colonists worked themselves into a frenzy: "they seemed resolved to go over [to Spanish Missouri] immediately." Sterling conceded and delayed administering the oath. "I imagine it would be a very great detriment to this Colony to have it depopulated—I at last agreed."[24]

Sterling cooled the immediate unrest, but he could not halt the steady migration to the Mississippi's west bank. French *habitants* moved "to the other Side of the River, where there is two Villages . . . established since the Cession of this Country to the English by those who did not like to be under our Government." In 1765, Sterling reported the colony in "ruinous condition, the Chief inhabitants having left it."[25] Observing the same situation in spring 1766, a traveler remarked that the *habitants* "are gone to the Spanish side with their Cattles & Corn, which makes provisions very scarce."[26] The French settlers easily subverted British regulations, and the British knew that "many of them [the French] drove off their cattle in the night and carried off their Effects and grain," reported Colonel Wilkins in 1767, "which I did everything in my power to prevent."[27] Amid the ongoing smuggling and outmigration, Gage wrote Lord Hillsborough, president of the Board of Trade, to seek a solution at the highest levels of the British state. Hillsborough assured Gage that the board would work "to give security to the Dominion of the Country" because it was "of very great importance" to the empire.[28]

The British were not the only newcomers who struggled to govern the Illinois Country. The clandestine trade across the Mississippi River also drew a response from Spanish imperial officials that had nominal claim over St. Louis. Contraband smuggling alarmed Don Antonio d'Ulloa, governor of Spanish Louisiana residing in New Orleans, who in response forbade any commerce across the Mississippi. In 1768, he ruled that he would "by no means permit the Spanish Subjects to pass to the English, nor to have any Commerce with them, except in particular cases of necessity." If such occasion arose, the trader would need "to have passports directed to the English Commander . . . under Penalty, that if they be found without one, they shall be entirely deprived of the rights of the Nation."[29] Like his British counterparts, d'Ulloa wanted to secure the empire's borders and avoid excessive entanglements that could cause conflict between the great powers. Given that the Seven Years' War between France and Britain had ignited because of skirmishes in the Ohio Country, perhaps his fears were well grounded.

Despite some attempt to reign in smugglers in the Upper Mississippi Valley, the Spanish had scant authority in St. Louis. Like the British, Spanish officials struggled to forge workable alliances with the French communities that populated their North American holdings. Just as it took Captain Sterling two years to make it to the Illinois Country, no Spanish officials arrived in New Orleans until 1766, a full three years after Spain took nominal control of the territory. What's more, the French Superior Council in New Orleans defied Spanish governance seemingly at every term, and d'Ulloa found he could not keep control over the French settlers. Tensions grew so bad that in 1768, armed French rebels rose up and expelled d'Ulloa from power. Nearly a year passed before his replacement, General Alejandro O'Reilly, arrived in New Orleans. Once on site, he mustered a show of force when 2,000 Spanish troops drilled in modern-day Jackson Square. He dissolved the Superior Council and installed the Cabildo, a Spanish city council, and began to govern. As this turmoil played out, French settlers in St. Louis continued to exercise local control over their economies and communities. Decrees banning trade across the Mississippi had little practical effect on the ground.[30] As one local observer remarked, "The Spaniards make but an indifferent appearance here."[31]

On both sides of the river, French masters sustained a local control over the slave economy and found ways to adjust to British or Spanish rule without restructuring their society. Through marriage, French *habitants* forged kin networks that spanned the Mississippi River, and these relations facilitated a covert economy that brought goods out of British Illinois. In this way, they managed to keep the export economy to New Orleans running as it had before. Enslaved people continued to marry in the Catholic Church and took Frenchmen and women as godparents for their children. As enslaved people of Indian and African descent turned to the church for social sanction, they, too, continued to live and labor in Illinois as they had before. Although the British Empire was hostile to Catholicism, enslaved families used the church to make a life in bondage, and these local arrangements continued in ways that ignored the new political realities. As British agents understood, migration offered French settlers and slaves a way to stymie British expansion.

Extended families lived on both sides of the Mississippi River and appear to have traversed the border with little impediment. Consider the Duclos family. Antoine Duclos and Marie Jeanne Saucier resided in British territory at Prairie du Rocher when they married in 1768. Duclos's father, Alexandre, lived in Spanish territory at Ste. Genevieve. But it was no great hurdle for Alexandre to cross the river in 1768 to sign the marriage documents, which he did along with nearly a dozen other members of the couple's extended family.[32] The Duclos-Saucier union was not unique. In 1770, Jacques LaSource, who ordinarily resided "on the Spanish side," lived in British-controlled Kaskaskia at the time he married Elenne Beauvais.[33] Marriages between families on opposite sides of the river further weakened the political boundary.

With so much mobility across the river, French settlers managed to keep control over their local slave economy despite the new political realities. Cross-river social relationships had commercial implications: they helped funnel goods out of British territory. Agreements between family members who resided on opposite banks illustrate how business and family relationships transcended imperial lines. For example, Jean Baptiste Beauvais of British Kaskaskia had commercial ties across the Mississippi through his brother, Raphael of Spanish St. Genevieve. In 1768, one Beauvais brother appears to have purchased slaves for another, and in 1773, Jean Baptiste sold grain from Kaskaskia to Raphael in St. Genevieve.[34] The Beauvais brothers owned scores of slaves, some of them purchased from Baynton, Wharton, and Morgan in spring 1768, as well as sufficient land and draft animals to export grain annually.[35] That such large French planters owned land and slaves on both sides of the river and used family ties to transfer land and wealth shows how cross-river kinship let *habitants* funnel wealth from British Illinois to Spanish Missouri.

As was common in slaveholding societies across the Americas, enslaved men and women participated in these French trade networks with their own economies. During slack labor seasons and on their own time, slaves grew modest amounts of grain, corn, and other provisions.[36] While most slaves probably relied on these crops to enhance their own subsistence, passing evidence suggests that at times, enslaved people sold their crops for profit. In one such case, the firm's partner George Morgan purchased a "quantity of Provisions at a very cheap Rate . . . from the French Negroes."[37] Morgan also saw an opportunity in selling goods to Illinois's bound population.[38] These local economies likely continued to thrive when a new political order arrived on the scene. It was one continuity of many.

Like their masters, slaves lived in communities that spanned the Mississippi River and frequently crossed that nominal dividing line. They continued to marry and baptize their children in the Catholic Church, occasionally traveling from the Spanish west bank of the Mississippi to the British east bank to participate in baptism ceremonies.[39] In this way enslaved people, both of Indian and African descent, forged kin networks in the Catholic Church. One crucial source of these ties came through the relationships of infant slaves to their godparents. Numerous Frenchmen and women stood in compaternity with enslaved infants at Kaskaskia's Catholic baptismal fount. Many of these godparents did not own slaves of their own. While at the church, slaves would have mingled not only with godparents and relatives but also with other inhabitants of British Illinois and Spanish Missouri—both slave and free. By traveling across the Mississippi, receiving Francophone *habitants* as godparents, and attending public rituals, slaves also formed social ties that spanned the Mississippi and sustained existing communities that predated British presence. Slaves' mobility was not uncommon, and the kin ties enacted in the Catholic Church crossed the boundaries between enslaved and free, Indian and African descended.

Indian slaves continued to live in French households, and Illinois Indians continued to have a place in colonial society. In a handful of cases, local priests buried enslaved Indian children, such as the 1761 case of an unnamed "little Indian boy belonging to Mr. la Bussier." His birth into bondage reflects that some Native American slaves experienced inheritable lifelong servitude, in an era when enslaved Africans were newcomers that had been trafficked into the region.[40] In other instances, enslaved Indians received baptismal sacraments as adults. The fact that they did not take these rites as children, which was common practice, may indicate that new enslaved Indians continued to arrive in Illinois and were incorporated into local French society as they had been for decades.[41] In 1771, the local priest buried Catherine, "an Indian slave belonging to Louis Cottineau," with full sacraments. Catherine was then laid to rest in the small churchyard alongside Illinois's local notables. It is not clear why she received such extraordinary treatment, but her fate speaks to the ways that enslaved Indians had a range of experiences in bondage and a lasting place in colonial Illinois.[42]

As was the case in the French period, enslaved people had diverse origins in the British period as well. No single enslaving practice brought people into bondage. Some Indian slaves were born unfree and took church rites with French godparents. At the same time, some enslaved people of African descent were trafficked into the region and were at first strangers in the land. Over time, enslaved people, no matter their experience with enslavement, found they had at least some things in common once in Illinois. During British occupation, enslaved people of Indian and African descent continued to intermarry and share households. In the 1760s, children born of enslaved black women and Indian men had their children baptized in French Kaskaskia.[43] Certain exemplary cases stand out. In one such case, the local priest baptized an unnamed "Illinois Savage" who was the son of Andre, an Illinois Indian man, and an enslaved woman of

African descent.[44] These mixed-race enslaved families were not numerous, but they enjoyed the sanction of the church and took free French godparents. At least some of the time, Indian- and African-descended slaves belonged to a slave community that, like before the British arrived, had origins in the diverse forms of slaveries. The different paths to enslavement and the differences between slaves did not keep people stuck in different institutions of slavery. Instead, masters owned indigenous slaves, Francophone Catholic slaves, and enslaved Anglophone newcomers. The heterogeneity within the slave community did not disappear when the British claimed the region. In fact, it only grew more diverse.

The enslaved men and women from Jamaica and Pennsylvania whom the British brought to Illinois likely did not join these Catholic communities, and they probably did not integrate easily into Illinois's existing slave population. Before the British period, slave shipments to Illinois had trickled to a halt.[45] Most slaves, then, had known Illinois from birth, belonged to relatively stable families, and probably spoke a version of French Creole. Moreover, most of them received sacraments in the Catholic Church and may have observed at least some tenets of the faith. But when the enslaved men and women from Jamaica and Philadelphia arrived in Illinois, they brought new languages, religions, and cultures, things many French masters were eager to avoid. Some went to extraordinary measures to bypass the new traders. "Many Frenchmen," according to Morgan, planned to "depart for New Orleans on no other Acc[ount] than to purchase slaves."[46] Given the reluctance with which Francophone masters purchased slaves from British merchants, it seems likely that slaves in Illinois belonged to two separate communities: Illinois-born slaves, whether African descended or indigenous, largely belonged to French masters, while slaves imported to Illinois during the 1760s mostly belonged to Anglo-American farmers. Slaves in French Illinois would have to accommodate to these strangers, and those changes took time to play out.

Meanwhile, however, work in the staple economy changed little. British migration to the region remained scarce, but British agents still worked to expand the local economy. British firms invested capital in the region, and during the 1760s, settlers formed new towns, improved more acreage, built new mills, carved out new roads, and continued to barge up and down the Mississippi. In 1770, writing an agent in New Orleans, Morgan boasted, "I have brought an experienced mill write [*sic*] with me from Pennsylvania. I shall have my Water Mill ready to grind 100 Bushels in 24 Hours and shall make as good Flour as ever was sent to you from Pennsylvania." He added proudly, "I have even been so particular as to bring two Pair Mill Stones With me from Pennsylvania at no small expense."[47] Keeping an eye on the region's connections to New Orleans, in one instance, Baynton, Wharton, and Morgan sent "three Negro men" to row a convoy of various goods up the Mississippi.[48] Slaves still worked grain fields, milled flour, packaged goods, worked river convoys, cleared land, and served in household economies. Notwithstanding the many obstacles to their success, British traders and officials worked to make Illinois part of their realm.

French masters, meanwhile, had maintained their ties to New Orleans, and by sending their goods to the west bank of the Mississippi, they could exclude British merchants from their trading ventures. Writing of the British presence in the Mississippi Valley more generally, one British official stressed the need for the "French Inhabitants with the Slaves, coming to settle on our side of the River."[49] He noted of the "Fur Trade at the Illinois" that "Furs are usually sent to Orleans, and fall into the hands of French Factors."[50] French masters also shipped grain south, such as Antoine Morrain "and his negro" who traveled from Illinois "to New Orleans" to "load and unload . . . *bateaux* with different merchandize."[51] The French commerce south diverted so much wealth from Illinois that British agents hoping to keep more of the trade to themselves welcomed attempts at "forbidding French Traders from going on the east side of the Mississippi."[52]

British settlers leaned on military authority to control the export economy because no civil jurisdiction existed. In the now-famous Proclamation Act of 1763, the British Crown forbade land sales and settlement west of the Appalachian Mountains. The settlements at Illinois, then, stood outside of British civil law. Several factors motivated this policy, but the desire to limit the cost and size of Britain's mainland empire stood chief among them. Some British policy makers assumed western settlement would undermine the maritime and commercial elements—the so-called Blue Water doctrine—that were the heart of the British Empire.[53] Already forced to garrison 10,000 soldiers in North America, faced with crippling war debts, and reeling from Pontiac's Rebellion, the government hoped to avoid the burdens of western expansion.[54]

Without a civil authority, the military had to fill the void and act as an arbiter of local affairs. This meant that despite his attempts to stay above day-to-day governance, General Thomas Gage found himself dragged into petty squabbles. In one case in 1767, Gage personally adjudicated a dispute between a French master, a slave, and the British commandant. According to the French slaveholder Paul Derisseaux, one of his slaves had begun a series of rebellious actions. First, the slave "Insulted [Derisseaux's] wife," then "refused doing his Duty."[55] More alarming still, this unnamed slave was accused of fomenting rebellion in the colony by "putting arms in the hands of the Slaves against the masters." This slave's actions would result in "dangerous consequence[s]" for the French population, but lacking civil authority and a slave code, Derisseaux felt he "could not obtain redress" and thus resorted to his "power to punish him at his own discretion."[56] It is not clear what happened next, but Thomas Reid, the commandant of British Illinois, confiscated the slave from Derisseaux. Perhaps Reid worried that Derisseaux's brutality would ignite the slave rebellion it was trying to prevent, or perhaps he saw an opportunity to seize property from a Francophone master and make an example of him to the French planters who resisted British rule. Regardless of his rationale, Derisseaux appealed to Reid's superior, General Thomas Gage, headquartered in New York. In his petition, Derisseaux requested that Gage nullify Reid's power to seize the enslaved man. Gage did, sanctioning Derisseaux's authority to punish his slave and immediately issuing an "order [that] his Negro to be returned to him," which he hoped would offer the slaveholder "Justice against the numerous Calamities" he suffered.[57] The legal structure of the British Empire made these sorts of adjudications a challenge. No empire-wide slave code existed akin to the French *Code Noir.* Without a local court and legislative assembly to create laws for slavery, cases like these had to appeal to far-off authorities, such as those in New York, who could act with a broad discretion. Unlike in the French period when locals conducted trials, such as the one for Marie Jean, who was accused of infanticide, by the 1760s, slaveholders had to appeal to military authority, sometimes a distant one, to settle disputes.

This case took years and more than one appeal, which underscored that military power proved too cumbersome a tool to govern the region. A diverse constituency of British and French settlers in Illinois and colonial officials in New York and London debated expanding civil authority to Illinois. Their chief objective was to find some way to wrest control back from the French communities that continued to evade their power. The British commandant of the colony concluded that "some Regulation of power is becoming absolutely necessary particularly with regard to the Slaves now become numerous by their Increase and late Importation."[58]

Reflecting on Illinois's absent civil authority, Gage reported to Lord Hillsborough, the president of the Board of Trade in London, that the region was "out of the Reach of Law and Government."[59] Despite a pressing, ongoing call for civil authority in Illinois, officials an ocean away in Whitehall argued over the proper course of action. In 1770, Lord Hillsborough informed Gage, "The Illinois affords a very large field of Discussion; And the King's Servants here [have] given the full attention & consideration to so important a subject." However, Hillsborough confessed that imperial policy toward the Illinois Country left him "in a state of perplexity [that] I am not able to get over."[60] A full year later, Hillsborough again reported that the Board of Trade has "weighted With Great Deliberation the different opinions & propositions that have been stated on the one hand & the other hand respecting those Establishments."[61]

While imperial officials dithered in London, a local legal culture filled the vacuum. Illinois boasted a small but lucrative slave economy, held strategic importance along one of North America's critical waterways, and offered a foothold into the interior Indian trade that could enrich merchants in the British Empire. It had a diverse local population of Indian- and African-descended slaves, free Frenchmen, and many indigenous nations who challenged British rule and made it difficult for the would-be rulers to tap Illinois's sources of wealth. Both the French and British yearned for political structures to smooth over these divisions. While General Gage had originally hoped not to extend civil jurisdiction into Illinois, he eventually relented and issued provisional orders to establish a civil court. Thinking that if settlers could act as their own arbiters, conflict between rival camps would subside, Gage instructed that the "commanding officer will, when disputes happen between the inhabitants, assemble arbitrators from amongst themselves." Going further, Gage ordered that "their differences be decided by Arbitration according to their own laws and customs."[62]

These instructions enabled Frenchmen to extend their existing control over the region and gain the upper hand over their British foes. The court had six magistrates and a president, all of whom took part in deliberations. While in the 1740s and 1750s, the French court had sat at Kaskaskia, the British relocated their court to Fort de Chartres, a couple dozen miles away. The court was at first staffed by six Frenchmen, with George Morgan acting as its president and only British member, and the business of the court appears to have been conducted mostly in English. Soon the French community in Illinois used the court—given that French settlers dominated its membership—to suppport their power in the colony. Hoping for peace, Gage unintentionally bolstered French local authority, which in turn stoked further conflict. His mistake was dealing with Illinois as if it were a single, stable community when the region hosted a diverse, fractious group of inhabitants who held onto their earlier histories, culture, and trading practices.

The court could create the kinds of legal transactions—recording bills of sale, executing deeds to human property, notarizing contracts, probating wills—that any economy, especially a slave economy, needed to thrive. It became a new venue for conflicts between Francophone and Anglophone settlers to play out. Inhabitants turned to the court to settle myriad property conflicts, but it failed to function as planned. Rather than cooling tensions, the court proceedings inflamed conflicts between British and French settlers. Nearly every case on the docket concerned debt litigation and detinue cases over disputed property, and the majority of cases had plaintiffs and defendants of different national origins.[63] To cite only one instance in 1771, a case concerned "a Quantity of Swine that were Stolen from the Said Dennis M. Crohan . . . part of which were found Concealed in the Negro House of [Mr.] Charlevile." The court ordered the defendant to pay 275 livres in damages.[64] However, settlers often disputed judgments like these; for instance, one plaintiff protested the outcome of his case, "alleging that for want of a proper Interpretor" his argument "was not fully explained" to the Anglophone judge.[65]

British merchants soon realized that the court could not extinguish simmering conflicts between French and British settlers. In particular, the court's president and only Anglophone magistrate, George Morgan, drew ire from local residents. Conflicts between the rival groups deteriorated to the point that, as one *habitant* observed, "Mr. George Morgan . . . has given great offence to all the French inhabitants in the Colonie, he being Universally hated by all those people, and indeed has but few friends of any other Nation here."[66] Frustrated with Morgan, French settlers turned once again to General Gage in New York, sending him a flood of complaints about British rule. With a growing dossier of appeals arriving at his New York headquarters, Gage found himself in an impossible situation. Far away in the east, he was in no position to get involved in land and labor disputes. Nor could he implement a cohesive slave code in light of London's refusal to extend full civil jurisdiction to Illinois. Moreover, French magistrates would not enforce any laws he hoped to impose. He also likely knew that many years of trying had done little to stop the local smuggling economy across the Mississippi. Without a way to resolve these tensions, Gage carped that he "received so many complaints of violence and injustice toward the inhabitants of Illinois."[67] Gage's frustration points to the success with which French habitants relied on a local legal culture to perpetuate their authority over the region.

Lacking any way to hold onto a lucrative enterprise in Illinois, Baynton, Wharton, and Morgan saw its fortunes collapse. By 1772, the firm had accumulated £71,000 of debt, and the partners believed the only practicable way to surmount these losses would be land sales. For a brief moment, however, it looked like their venture would be saved. Imperial officials had decided to make a new colony in Illinois and to offer Baynton, Wharton, and Morgan a sizable land grant. Closely tied to British agents, Morgan wrote Samuel Wharton to say he had "lately received a Copy of his Majesty's confirmation of the new Colony. Sir William Johnson forwarded it me." Wishing Wharton "joy on the Occasion," Morgan hoped proceeds from the sale of these freshly opened lands would halt "several suits" that "have been lately commenced against us" because the firm "shall make over to our Creditor or to Trustees for this use all our portions of the Western lands."[68] This brief hope of triumph soon faded, however. Although the King's Privy Council—a powerful group of advisers that shaped the Crown's opinions on matters of state—had backed their cause, the Board of Trade reversed its own decision under pressure from Prime Minister Lord North. Officials in London held onto the Blue Water doctrine of empire and nullified the land grant, hoping to limit British presence in interior North America. Disgusted, Morgan wrote Wharton, "I beg leave to urge as my Opinion that you should immediately return to America . . . leaving Authority with some Creature of Lord North's to solicit" on their behalf. "For my Part I think we shall hardly obtain a Charter worth accepting at this Time."[69] By the mid-1770s, the firm collapsed under its mounting debts. It would not be long before British authority also vanished from the region.

* * *

Great Britain was the second empire that hoped to create a colonial plantation economy in Illinois. It was the second to fall short. But the period of British rule saw an expansion of the region's slave economy. New towns, mills, and roads came into being, and new stretches of improved land came under cultivation. Already a meeting ground for enslaved Indians and captive Africans, Illinois now hosted a population of Anglophone slaves as well. Yet British settlers and military officials could not control the French slave economy that predated their arrival. The transition from the French empire to the British Empire revealed that colonial slave economies did not change with the scratch of a pen. Throughout the period, the river convoys continued their runs, and goods grown on both sides of the Mississippi flowed to New Orleans. Frenchmen and women found ways to use the border to subvert British authority and used the court to make a local legal culture.

French masters accommodated the new political reality and kept the local slave economy functioning much as it had before. The British ultimately lost the region in the 1780s, after the U.S. War for Independence, before finding a workable solution. Before long, a new kind of empire would try its hand at controlling Illinois's slave economy. During the 1780s, when another treaty transferred the territory to the United States, the mix of slaves would undergo a reworking. The 1760s and 1770s, then, proved to be a practice run at deflecting imperial authority and keeping local control over the slave economy. In time, the U.S. government would hope to wipe away the colonial history of slavery by abolishing human bondage in the region. Owing to the dexterity they gained under British rule, French masters managed to avoid this reality. U.S. settlers and officials, like the French and British before them, had to confront the reality that local arrangements could trump imperial declarations issued from distant cities, be it London or Washington, D.C.

CHAPTER 3

Remaking the French Negroes

On January 23, 1801, 270 "humble inhabitants" from the Illinois Country submitted a three-foot-long petition to the U.S. Congress.[1] The plea gathered signatures from a cross section of Illinois society. Pierre Menard, known as "the father of Illinois"; William Morrison, a recent migrant to the region and well-to-do slaveholder; and Therese Chouteau, the head of a major trading family, had all signed.[2] The petitioners requested that Article Six of the Northwest Territory Ordinance of 1787, which banned "slavery and involuntary servitude," be "modified as to admit the introduction of Slaves."[3] The signers informed Congress that they "owned a number of slaves" and requested a change to territorial laws to "permit the Introduction into the Territory of any of those who are Slaves in any of the United States."[4] The authors of the memorial had two goals: to attract slaveholders from the newly formed United States to Illinois and to exempt the slaves already in Illinois from emancipation. They hoped to incorporate their colonial slave economy into the new nation's expansion westward.

As this political conflict played out, it soon became apparent that the United States could not force Illinois to become free soil. With this petition, residents in Illinois contested the now-famous slavery prohibition found in the Northwest Territory Ordinance. Their appeal joined nearly a dozen others from Illinois constituencies, all asking for the same thing. These requests and the ban that inspired them belonged to the long national debate about freedom and slavery in the young republic. At the national level, Congress had hoped to eradicate human bondage from the Northwest Territory. The ordinance was part of a wider assault on slavery under way in the wake of U.S. Independence, which northern state legislatures led by passing gradual abolition laws. However, countless planters in the South were hoping to forge an empire for slavery in the trans-Appalachian West. These proslavery voices had the upper hand over events in Illinois. Just as they had in the French and British periods, the U.S. period saw wealthy inhabitants and slaveholding migrants into Illinois make a local slaveholding economy that in part ignored the legal decrees that distant colonial authorities projected on the region. By dodging legal prohibitions on human bondage, settlers in Illinois used slave labor to open up the economies of the Upper Mississippi Valley to the new nation. Significantly, between 1780 and 1810, virtually no free people in Illinois fought for slavery's abolition, and many worked to keep it. With so many local inhabitants pushing for slavery's survival, political leaders in the United States could not wipe away the region's colonial history or set it on a path toward emancipation, and the power relationships over slaves forged in earlier colonial times continued to shape the history of the nineteenth century.

Due to the Northwest Territory Ordinance in 1787, the Mississippi and Ohio Rivers became a supposed dividing line between slavery and freedom, although the ban on slavery faced stiff resistance on the ground. As in previous decades, politicians in distant cities worked to carve clear borders around Illinois. And as before, local residents worked, traded, and traveled in expansive ways that did not respect those borders. Although the region's geographic form underwent important changes in this period, colonial systems of slave production still spanned the Mississippi and Ohio Rivers. Between the 1780s and the 1810s, masters displayed a resilient ability to adapt, changing slavery's legal basis and its local operations in order to keep people in bondage. Just as the British could not draw and enforce a border along the Mississippi River, U.S. officials also failed at this task. Instead, the local settlers controlled slavery's fate, and at the turn of the nineteenth century, Illinois's settler population underwent important changes. Two key factors would transform how slavery functioned and give enslaved labor new opportunities to expand: Virginian migrants and the state's newly discovered salt mines.

Virginia migrants streamed into the region, and they helped shape much of the local history of slavery and freedom. After the 1780s, Illinois attracted Virginians and their slaves, introducing another new group of bound workers to the region. Virginians had eyed lands in the trans-Appalachian West for decades, and they hoped to build slave economies in the greater Ohio and Mississippi River Valleys. Some Virginian migrants sought out these lands hoping to build a life in free territory, but in the early years, very few settlers fit this description. Before 1800, many Virginian settlers brought slaves into Illinois and undertook new ventures that changed the nature of the region's economy. Large landed holdings gradually disappeared, but slavery did not, as a new commodity emerged that used slave labor. The salt marshes of southeastern Illinois, which eventually produced nearly 15 percent of the nation's salt, relied on slave labor. In these ways, migrants into the state reformed how slavery operated even as they did little to upend the existing economy.

New migrants, new mining economies, and a new legal environment in the Early Republic combined to trigger a new category of slaves in the Illinois Country: the "French Negroes." With so many U.S. citizens surging into the region, settlers in the Illinois Country did not need to participate in captive exchange to maintain control over the land through alliances with indigenous nations. As a consequence, by the turn of the nineteenth century, Indian slavery no longer served the political functions it had for European colonizers in earlier decades. Amid this new political reality, new forms of racial hierarchy took root. In particular, U.S. law and U.S. settlers tried to conceal the history of Indian slavery: the racial basis of U.S. slavery equated blackness with bondage and whiteness with superiority. By creating "French Negroes" as a category of slaves, American settlers innovated to make slavery synonymous with blackness, putting all slaves, regardless of their true origins, into an invented legal category of people that could be exempted from the emancipation laws. As happened in previous decades when different forms of slavery met on the ground, the alchemy of slavery was on full display as enslaved people of diverse origins all became "French Negroes."

With "French Negroes" lawfully remaining in Illinois, the entangled forms of human bondage that had marked Illinois became one part of the broader landscape of slavery and freedom in the early United States. Bound labor adapted to meet new legal realities, and much of Illinois's colonial society and economy continued as it had before. Even as many residents in Illinois adopted new national allegiances, they did not let go of a long history of Indian and African bondage. Slaves of diverse origins who came out of different slaving practices coexisted alongside one another. To accomplish this trick, masters reinvented how enslavement would work in the early nineteenth century in ways that enabled human bondage to survive its legal abolition. Kin networks, local geographies, and regional economies mediated the force of law, and the U.S. empire, much as the French and British empires before it, could not draw firm boundaries between slavery and freedom or break slaveholders' power over their captive workers.

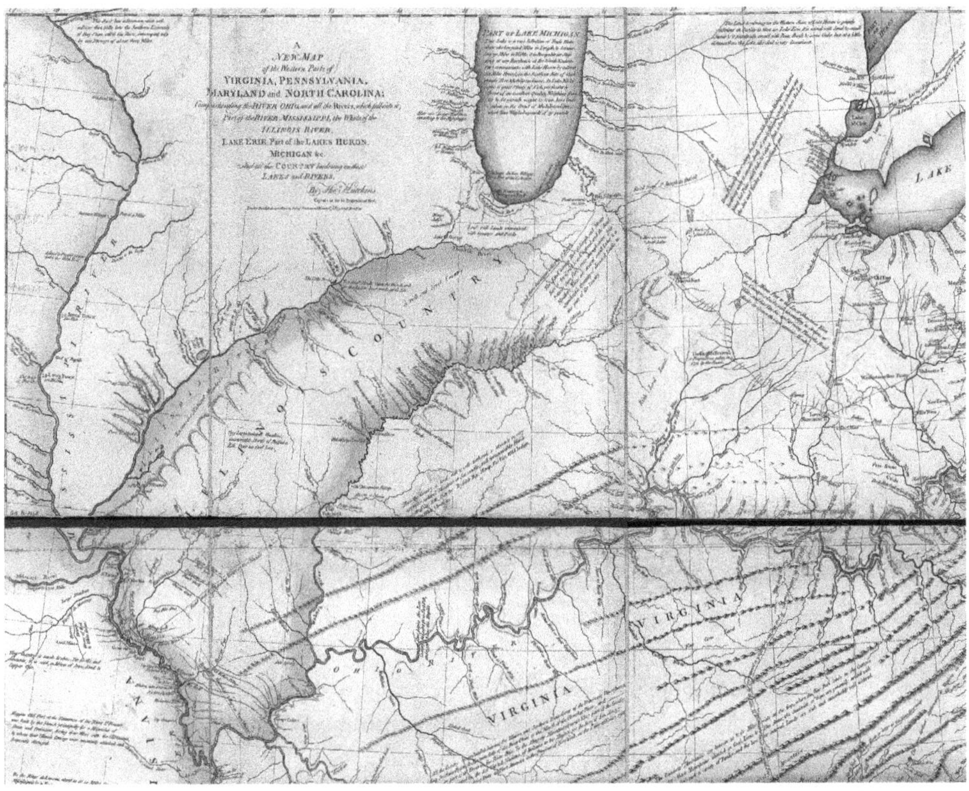

Figure 3. This 1778 map reflects Illinois as part of the trans-Appalachian West. Virginia's claims to the region appear as stark black lines extending westward into the Illinois Country. Thomas Hutchins, *A new map of the western parts of Virginia, Pennsylvania, Maryland, and North Carolina; comprehending the River Ohio, and all the rivers, which fall into it; part of the River Mississippi, the whole of the Illinois River, Lake Erie; part of the Lakes Huron, Michigan &c. and all the country bordering on these lakes and rivers* (London, 1778). Retrieved from the Library of Congress, https://www.loc.gov/item/gm71002165/. (Accessed June 14, 2017.)

* * *

During the 1780s, for a third time in the century, a distant imperial power claimed Illinois. This time it was the United States of America, and its control over the Illinois Country would provide a new legal and political context for slavery in the region. Anglo-American settlers living along the eastern seaboard had long eyed the trans-Appalachian West with desire. Although expansion had been stymied under British rule, the success of the U.S. Independence movement offered settlers a chance to migrate west. During and after the U.S. War for Independence, residents in Virginia and Pennsylvania went deep into Indian Country and wrested huge swaths of land from its indigenous inhabitants. While much of the most intense fighting of the U.S Revolutionary War played out along the eastern seaboard, the creation of the United States also triggered continental transformations that would in time change the terms of encounter in native North America.[5]

With an eye to the profits that could be wrought from the trans-Appalachian West, during the U.S. War for Independence, Virginian authorities commissioned Colonel George Rogers Clark to conquer the Illinois Country. In his instructions to Clark, Virginia Governor Patrick Henry charged him to "take every possible measure to secure the Artillery & Slaves & whatever else may advantage the state."[6] In 1778, Clark left from western Virginia. His "expedition was made in barges on the Ohio River" and made landfall "five leagues above the confluence . . . with the Mississippi." His nearly 300 troops began "marching five days through the woods, [and] reached the post of Kaskaskia." He easily overwhelmed the British garrison at Fort Chartres—a mere thirty-five soldiers—and took the fort "without firing a shot."[7] At "two in the morning," Clark and his men captured Phillippe Rocheblave, "the commanding colonel," who was "barefooted, barelegged and with his . . . equipment and musket on his back." Despite being placed in "leg irons and handcuffs," Rocheblave refused to capitulate, declaring, "The King of Great Britain is my sovereign." He continued, "I have only one regret, and my regret is now that it should not lie within my power to destroy you."[8] After capturing the commanding officers, "a great confusion arose among the inhabitants who decided . . . to surrender." Clark thought the settlers in Illinois would "become as good citizens as anyone can imagine," and he immediately "caused the oath of allegiance to the United States to be administered to them."[9]

Once Clark secured Illinois, he issued a proclamation asserting Virginia's authority over the newly won territory. Both French and British settlers cheered Clark's assertion of power, unlike the episode in 1765 when British declarations inspired an exodus. In addition to creating a district of Virginia in Kaskaskia, the proclamation permitted a free election for civil officials. The new Virginian authority assured the citizens of Illinois that they would be secure in their lands and other property. Before Clark left Illinois for Vincennes, he appointed Captain John Todd as magistrate in chief—or head civil officer—for the colony. Todd established two civil courts, one at Prairie du Rocher and the other at St. Philippe, and he announced a protocol for electing judges, stating that "every person who has the right to a vote may give . . . his preference for the election of him who you shall choose."[10] Clark instructed Todd "to inculcate in the people the value of liberty and the difference between the state of Free Citizens of this Commonwealth and that Slavery to which the Illinois was distened."[11] More a transition than a conquest, Clark did not displace or subdue the French and English settlers, instead collaborating with them to secure Virginian authority.[12] He informed the *habitants* that the "Republic of the Virginians" claimed the territory "to invite you to participate with them in the blessing of a free and equal independence and to be governed and judged by officers who shall be placed in power by the people."[13] In short order, Virginia claimed Illinois as one of its western provinces and began to construct authority over the distant colony.

Despite the revolutionary ideas about equality articulated in the Declaration of Independence, Virginians secured and protected the slave economy of the Upper Mississippi River Valley. Shortly after issuing the declaration of civil authority, Clark created a slave code. Responding to "the complaints, which have been addressed to us by several inhabitants . . . through their petitions," Clark established laws to "remedy the disorders, abuses and brigandage that for such a longtime has been caused by the too great liberty enjoyed by the red and black slaves."[14] He indicated that such "liberty" prevented slaves "from accomplishing the different pieces of work in which their masters employ them, thus causing the total loss of this colony." Clark went on to bar the slaves' access to liquor and to ban them from meeting "after sunset or for the night, for the purpose of dancing, feasting, or holding nocturnal assemblies." He forbade "all persons to buy from or exchange with the said . . . slaves any goods, commodities, pigs, wood or other things whatsoever, unless the said slaves are furnished with a permit from their masters." Slaves caught violating this code would be "beaten with thirty-nine strokes of the whip at their master's expense." The code empowered all "captains, officers of the militia and all other persons to enforce the execution of the present proclamation."[15] In their solicitation of a slave code, masters wanted to make the new Virginian regime work for them, and they found a friend in George Rogers Clark.

The slave code, together with Virginian assertions of power, erected a new political reality that slaveholders would have to accommodate. The slave code was only suggestive, but by treating "red and black slaves" as one group, it pointed toward a shift in categorization that in time remade Illinois's heterogeneous forms of bondage into a homogeneous category called "French Negroes." Rather than issuing separate regulations, this one slave code treated enslaved people of diverse origins with a broad brush. Despite the apparent diversity of Illinois's enslaved population, Clark issued one law for all slaveries, and he collapsed diverse forms of bondage into a single category. Unlike French slave codes, which treated indigenous- and African-descended slaves with different legal norms, Clark's slave code seemingly reckoned with the fact that slaves of diverse origins lived and labored alongside one another. Into the 1780s, Indian slaves continued to live in Illinois, and U.S. officials beside Clark noted their presence. The French and British had grappled with competing definitions of slavery and an enslaved community that at times was fractured along linguistic, religious, and national divisions. Clark did not parse slavery's definition as others had before, perhaps in part because divisions between slaves subsided over time as diverse people increasingly became one community.

Despite Clark's code, enslaved people continued to have diverse experiences in bondage, and a slave trial confirms that many slaveries did not easily become one. In 1779, two slaves, Manuel and Moreau, were sentenced to be executed after having been convicted of a series of poisonings that killed "several of the good subjects of their Republic and soldiers of the garrison."[16] Colonial officials thought they had uncovered a murder spree that no fewer than a dozen witnesses confirmed existed. In June 1779, six months after Manuel and Moreau had arrived as enslaved captives from the Caribbean, the attorney general for the Illinois Country secured a death warrant that found "the manner of execution cannot be too cruel for criminals who have committed deeds so extraordinarily horrible and frightful."

The evidence in the trial documents three distinct attacks and the divisions in the slave community that had emerged from decades of colonial history. In the wake of the supposed poisonings, nine enslaved men and women belonging to seven masters testified to the string of murders they claimed to have witnessed. Coerced testimony from enslaved men and women is, by its nature, unreliable, and slaves had incentives to obfuscate the facts of the case.[17] As one slave stated, "Some masters said to their Negros not to confess anything or you will be hanged." Another enslaved woman reported she heard the same instruction against confession "said at the Court House" while still other slaves "confirmed they heard a master tell a slave not to confess." Presumably they gave this instruction in an attempt to spare their slaves from execution.[18] Despite this reality, it appears that the two enslaved men played some role in concocting potions and elixirs and that several inhabitants died of mysterious causes.[19] Moreover, the trial documents mobility patterns, communication networks, and relationships in the slave quarter that shed light on the divisions among enslaved people that could have sustained Manuel and Moreau's attacks.

One detail that emerged at the trial involved Moreau conversing with two other slaves about their harsh and cruel master. Moreau had asked two people owned by Madame and Monsieur Nicolle for a favor. After some back and forth, one of the Nicolles' slaves "complained to" Moreau that her mistress was "very bad." Moreau "promised that if she granted it [the favor] to him, he would give her medicine to make her mistress gentle." Bartering over this unnamed favor, they forged relationships that helped slaves find some freedoms in bondage. However, the Nicolles' slaves may have gotten more freedom than they bargained for—the Nicolles quickly died. Hearing news of their death, Moreau said, "You ought to be content now. There are your master and mistress dead and you can take a walk and go where you wish." Yet the two unnamed slaves later insisted, "We did not ask . . . to make them die. We wished only . . . [to] make them a little gentler." Regardless of the slaves' intentions—which never fully emerged—they used their social ties to make their masters "a little gentler" and to secure their mobility, which Moreau called "taking a walk."[20]

Two other episodes offer a glimpse of life in bondage in Illinois, and they shed light on mobility and communication networks. One afternoon in 1779, Sasa, an enslaved man, went to a neighboring farm owned by Monsieur Martin looking for Janette "to ask for a pipeful of tobacco." While in the farmhouse, Janette "told him to go to the head of her bed . . . he looked and found a horn in which there was boiling blood [*une Corne dans laquelle il y a avoit du Sang qui Bouillet*]." Recognizing it, the "negress told him not to touch that, and that it was Manuel who had given it to put her master and mistress to death." Another slave, Samba, "took this horn and had shown it to Moreau . . . [who] said it was the same horn that Manuel had given him to put to death Monsieur and Madame Nicolle." Alarmed that another attack was under way and perhaps concerned that blame would fall on them, one of the slaves threatened to "denounce them, which caused them to dig up [another] poison, which they had buried under the threshold of the door," seemingly saving his master's life.

In a third case, Manuel and Moreau targeted an enslaved man of African descent living near St. Louis. Although the Mississippi River supposedly acted as an international border, they crossed it without their master's permission. It appears that this attack followed a "quarrell" over Manuel's wife. Shortly after the fight, this enslaved man was "attacked . . . from a violent poison." His master called a doctor when his slave's "body was in convulsions and his limbs rigid on account of the corrosive poison which had insinuated itself into all parts of his body." Even if the particulars of this attack are unclear, it is apparent that enslaved people had access to an array of consumer goods, had access to information about these attacks, and could travel somewhat freely across the Mississippi. Slaves mingled in Martin's cabin, trading tobacco and perhaps gossiping about Manuel and Moreau's past and future victims. Some members of the community called on Manuel and Moreau for potions to make their mistress a little gentler. Others denounced and quarreled with the two newcomers—and suffered for it. Ultimately, a string of witnesses blamed the two newly arrived men for engineering a killing spree.[21]

The Virginian response to Manuel and Moreau's purported poisoning streak shows that they governed the region with at least some power on the ground. After slaves denounced Manuel and Moreau, the two men fled to St. Louis. They tried to manipulate the river as an international boundary to evade the Virginians, much as French masters had done with British authorities, but they soon discovered that the new American state observed no such boundaries. General Clark crossed the river to capture deserting soldiers and fugitive slaves.[22] Requesting and receiving extradition from the Spanish authorities in St. Louis, Clark brought the two men back into Virginia's territory, where they stood trial.

This long and tumultuous case not only offers a unique portrait on life in bondage but also shows how Virginians wielded their power. After convicting Manuel and Moreau, the newly arrived Virginia officials meted out punishments. One slave referred to public displays where "the negroes were punished" while "at the Court House."[23] Another mentioned an instance when "the negro of La Croix was whipped." Manuel and Moreau faced execution as part of the crackdown. After the Virginia district attorney issued a death warrant, Clark's deputy ordered a party of his soldiers "to guard Moreau" while he awaited execution. On the fifteenth of June, he was hanged in Cahokia while bystanders looked on.[24] Manuel faced a crueler fate: Captain Todd ordered him "to be chained to a post at the Water Side, and there to be burnt alive and his ashes scattered."[25] U.S. Independence, which transferred the region into Virginia's control, did very little to threaten slavery in the region. To the contrary, the Virginia militia issued slave codes, sought out and extradited slaves accused of crimes, and executed these enslaved men in the public square.

Along with the new slave code, Virginians brought trade and fresh sources of capital that helped prop up the slave economy. Richard Winston, Virginia's deputy governor of Illinois, repeatedly sold horses, oxen, ploughs, and yokes in Kaskaskia. He also sold at least two slaves, perhaps people that he had brought west as part of his own migration.[26] Another deputy governor, Lieutenant Girault, acting on behalf of the Commonwealth of Virginia's public accounts, bought goods from several prominent *habitants* of the Illinois Country. He purchased horses, skins, beef, clothing, and other provisions and employed men in a convoy to deliver the goods across the colony.[27]

In sharp contrast to the British period, Virginia's civil authority worked alongside Clark's military authority, which slaveholders used to their advantage. In the first years after Colonel Clark's arrival, Virginian authorities reinforced slaveholders' power in Illinois, affording them new legislative resources to punish slaves, contract labor, sell goods into the Virginia economy, make voyages to the eastern seaboard, and settle property disputes. In several instances, French masters petitioned the Virginia authority in Kaskaskia and the Virginia Assembly in Richmond to assert their rights over land, slaves, and access to trade routes. Several pleas about the resolution of trade disputes, application for trade licenses, permission to marry, or securing title to land appeared throughout the 1780s.[28] On one such occasion, Pierre Langlois petitioned the district court at Kaskaskia to reclaim his slave, Pompe, who had been seized as part of a dispute over Langlois's inheritance. The court ordered Pompe returned, and Langlois likely put him back to work on his midsized estate.

As the colony's inhabitants began to work with Virginians, a larger set of political changes unfolded. In 1781, Virginia ceded Illinois to the U.S. government, but the commonwealth's short-lived control bolstered slaveholders' power in ways that had lasting effects. Virginia transferred authority over the territory to the U.S. Continental Congress. By the terms of its Act of Cession, Virginia relinquished its claim over the Illinois Country in an attempt to protect its most valued western lands in present-day Kentucky. The terms of Virginia's cession protected the citizens' property rights by specifying "that the French and Canadian inhabitants, and other settlers of the Kaskaskies . . . who have professed themselves citizens of Virginia, shall have their possessions and titles confirmed to them, and be protected in the enjoyment of their rights and liberties."[29] For decades, Illinois planters and politicians pointed to this language to insist that U.S. control of the region was predicated on masters' control over land and enslaved labor, which in turn trapped "French Negroes" in bondage.

Having won control over vast lands, the new nation began to try and govern them, and slavery featured prominently in those national discussions about controlling the interior of the continent. Between 1775 and 1789, the Continental Congress ruled the new, fragile nation. With no president to conduct international affairs or to coordinate relations with the many nations of native North America, the United States' unicameral legislature set its hand to the important tasks of territorial administration. Despite many obstacles to the Congress's leadership, they erected a system of governance to manage far-flung reaches of the continent they hoped to claim as their own. The Northwest Territory Ordinance of 1787 stood out as the most important of these acts. It identified five potential states to create out of the Northwest Territory and divided each state into townships. Making provisions for schools, churches, and local governance, the congress's plan was that inhabitants would populate territories and then petition for statehood once they had 60,000 residents. In this way, the land in the Northwest Territory Ordinance forged an empire that linked western migration and democratic governance by letting territories become states as their population grew.[30]

The transition to U.S. control presaged migration and a major demographic boom for the Illinois Country. When Clark arrived in the Illinois Country, its population and economy had shrunk considerably. In 1780, probably only 1,500 people remained east of the Mississippi. The population grew in fits and starts before 1800. However, as the turn of the century approached, the population began to grow. In 1800, close to 5,000 people resided in Illinois, and by 1810, just over 12,000 inhabitants had settled in the Illinois territory.

Migrants often brought slaves and ideas about slavery with them. For example, Ichabod Camp, a Protestant minister, sold a twelve-year-old enslaved "Virginia Creole" girl named File.[31] Camp had recently relocated from Virginia and brought File with him. Amid this growth in the free population, the size of the enslaved population remained constant at roughly 1,000, even though the number of Indian slaves dwindled while the population of African American slaves grew. With U.S. settlers refusing to participate in indigenous captive exchange networks, fresh sources of Indian slaves dried up.[32] French and British settlers had to accommodate the politics of slavery in the United States, and the politics of alliance that once injected indigenous captives into colonial society ceased to be a driving force in the region.

With a growing settler population carving out control over the Illinois Country, the new U.S. government reorganized the region to its liking, which in this case meant banning slavery. "There shall be neither slavery nor involuntary servitude in the said territory," stated Article Six of the Ordinance of 1787.[33] Some have pointed to this language to indicate that U.S. independence helped to inaugurate a long process of emancipation.[34] And in fact, the territorial governor of the region, Arthur St. Clair, noted that inhabitants were "apprehensive that the slaves . . . are free according to the Act of Congress."[35] Yet St. Clair offered an interpretation of this law that undermined its effects. In 1790, in a letter to Secretary of State Thomas Jefferson, St. Clair added a postscript that said he "thought it proper to explain the Article respecting slaves as a prohibition to any future introduction of them." He continued that it would "not . . . extend to the liberation of those the people were already possessed of." Concluding, he remarked, "I have given them [the *habitants*] the understanding that steps would probably be taken for the gradual abolition of slavery with which they seem perfectly satisfied."[36] Yet he made no mention of any particular system, and no trend toward gradual emancipation appeared. While legislatures in the East worked to dismantle colonial systems of human bondage, officials in the West worked to blunt the impact of that work.

Disputes over emancipating the "French Negroes" would simmer for decades, but in the short term, St. Clair deflected the language of the Northwest Territory Ordinance and continued Clark's practice of allowing slaveholders to control the region. Congress thought it had the power to define Illinois as a free territory and make the Mississippi a boundary between slavery and freedom. Yet congressmen failed to appreciate the ways that established economies created first in French and native North America, and then later under British rule, crossed that boundary. Virginians collaborated with slaveholders in Illinois, enabling inhabitants to protect slavery in the earliest years after U.S. Independence. By creating a category of "French Negroes," St. Clair strategically adapted to the abolition laws, and he made a single legal category of people exempted from abolition, despite the apparent diversity of those bondsmen and women. By lumping all of the region's diverse slaves into this single legal category, the conniving adaptations that stood out as a hallmark of enslaving practices in the early eighteenth century continued unabated after the United States claimed the region. St. Clair included all of the region's slaves, regardless of their circumstances, into his interpretation of the law and in that way responded to the new legal and political realities as slaveholders always had by reinventing their enslaving practices to sustain their power over their coerced workers.

During the 1790s, slavery in Illinois was not on a path toward gradual abolition. Masters were not freeing the children of their slaves at birth or creating arrangements to free them after a certain period. The baptisms and burials of enslaved African American children confirm that inheritable bondage survived. Between 1787 and 1800, masters in two Catholic parishes along the Mississippi River—Immaculate Conception of Notre Dame in Kaskaskia and Holy Family in Cahokia—oversaw more than twenty-four enslaved children's baptisms. In this period, these baptized children were called the "slave," "negro of," or "black slave belonging to" their master.[37] In one such instance, in 1796, a one-year-old named Antoine received burial rights, and the priest identified him as a "black slave of Mons[ieur] Bienvenu."[38] In another case, in 1801, Marie, a black slave of William Morrison's, received the baptism sacraments.[39] The life cycle of the parish confirmed slavery's survival from ashes to ashes—slaveholding families baptized and buried dozens of enslaved infants who had inherited their mother's enslaved status.[40] In these years, other records of Indian slaves became increasingly rare, perhaps because priests identified them as "French Negroes" despite their true family origins or perhaps because there were simply fewer enslaved Indians.

Another sign of continuity in this period was that the region in many respects remained Indian Country, and enslaved indigenous people continued to have a place in Illinois. Although Indian control over the region waned, the United States did not fully displace them as powerbrokers. As local customs and economies continued, federal power was brittle at the margins of its territory. Across the region, the ordinary work of traveling the waterways of North America, securing treaties to land, exploiting natural resources, and selling goods at market required accommodating Indians. Francophone masters and "French Negroes" had decades of experience with this kind of diplomacy, affording French inhabitants leverage over U.S. inhabitants who had more recently arrived in Illinois. Significantly, settlers from the United States had to continue to forge limited alliances with the local Indian powerbrokers in order to secure access to land. Yet unlike French colonizers of fifty years earlier, U.S. officials did not appear to participate in the Indian slave trade. Instead, Indian diplomacy revolved around the U.S. agents dispatching trade goods. For instance, Captain John Todd noted that "a small tribe of the Wabash" arrived at his post "imploring the paternal succor." Todd offered them "six bushels of Indian corn, fifty pounds of bread, four pounds of Gun Powder, Ten Pounds of ball and One Gallon of Taffia."[41]

Like the French before them, U.S. migrants learned from experience that creating a colony and protecting its economy required an able diplomatic hand. Even when the Treaty of Paris in 1783 ended the political revolution against Great Britain, violence and turmoil continued to stalk the trans-Appalachian West, as the U.S. War for Independence evolved into a series of Indian wars.[42] To bring an end to these conflicts, the U.S. government began to erect a method of Indian diplomacy that favored trade and treaty systems. While many of the nations of native North America hoped for a form of working interdependence with the new nation that would leave them on their lands and forge trade alliances with the new nation, in the 1780s and 1790s, the U.S. government signed a series of treaties with different Indian nations, snatching up millions of acres of land. In return, U.S. officials promised steady payments of trade goods. This system was always fraught with deceptions and evasions, but across the region, local officials brokered an uneasy peace by directing trade and commerce and forging sovereignty over indigenous people's land.[43] Far from a workable interdependence that respected indigenous sovereignty, which is what Indian leaders sought, the U.S. government offered up money and goods in exchange for land and peace.

Virginian officials in the Illinois Country often bought peace with local Indians by exchanging commodities. In the 1780s, Captain John Todd recorded, as he often did, that a "Deputy of the Delawares, Shawnees, and Cherokee Nations" had arrived "begging that the Americans would grant the Peace." Todd said that "after smoking the pipe of peace and friendship with them," he distributed "10 bushells of Indian corn, 100 pounds flour, 10 pounds tobacco, 5 belts of Wampum, and a canoe which cost . . . 20 dollars."[44]

Other American sojourners also recognized that Illinois remained Indian Country. Writing General Josiah Harmar, the U.S. commanding officer in the Northwest Territory, a subordinate reported that when he "was in the Shawney Town . . . [a soldier] saw the Cherokee Indians bring in Seven Scalps, some Horses . . . [and] other plunder." Observing the potency of these warriors, the soldier reported that "several people has been killed lately."[45]

Migrants and traders who sought to expand Illinois's slave economy had to navigate indigenous power, just as they had to duck national legal decrees. In 1789, George Morgan, formerly of Baynton, Wharton, and Morgan, drew on his deep history with Illinois to undertake a second economic venture that brought settlers and slaves to the region. By this time, Morgan knew that his economic fortune would rise or fall based on local arrangements, and perhaps for that reason he made little effort to rely on U.S. patronage or military protection. One of his workers, Israel Shreeve, reported that Illinois—far from being a federal territory—remained largely beyond U.S. control. Shreeve observed in his diary that members of his surveying team had to "leave . . . Christian Principles behind and take upon [themselves] that of a savage."[46] An American "must have little or no feeling of humanity, if he sees a Savage with Human blood Braking from this hands."[47] Appealing to the native inhabitants was so fundamental to the surveying venture that when they learned of a "Murder just committed on the opposing shore he must justify his land and laugh at the Crulety."[48] And "if he should see an American prisoner tied to a stake . . . surrounded with faggots ready for a savage torture, he must . . . dance round and join with the savages."[49] As far as Shreeve was concerned, it was Indian authority, not that of the United States, that controlled the region.

With such weak federal control over Illinois, it is no wonder that a congressional ban on slavery had little effect. Shreeve recognized that the local societies and economies of North America did not conform to the boundaries that Congress drew. While encamped at Fort Massac in southern Illinois, for instance, Shreeve remarked on French hunters who arrived from New Orleans and pirogues departing from Illinois for the Lower Mississippi River Valley. He even noted "a Number of American Families came too at this place, from Illonois [*sic*] Bound to the Natches."[50] Previously, on his journey toward the fort, Shreeve encountered the forced migration of African Americans into the region. He "saw another doomed person," a "Negro Woman" who was part of "a new settlement [that] is forming." Shreeve went on to say that "the people informed me the afore mentioned doomed persons were one Negro Boy & 2 women the property of a Mr. Wood." These enslaved convoys consisted of people who were "completely catched in a mouse trap to satisfy some designing wicked man that wishes to get money by selling his fellow creatures."[51]

Settlers like Morgan and Shreeve came west to Illinois, but they did not respect the boundaries between slave country and free soil set out in U.S. law. In fact, western migrations allowed planters and merchants in Illinois to expand the scale and scope of their economic ventures while affording them the ability to purchase slaves from American migrants, despite the ordinance.[52] Slaves arrived from neighboring territories, and masters bought enslaved men and women from west of the Mississippi River and south of the Ohio. By purchasing these slaves, local planters defined the region in ways that defied state and national boundaries. Bills of sale described settlements on the west bank of the Mississippi—technically part of Spanish Missouri—as "the western district of Illinois."[53] In 1784, François Charleville, the son of one of the largest slaveholders in Kaskaskia, sold a slave to Louis Bolduc "St. Genevieve, of the Illinois country," though it lay in Missouri.[54] In more than one case, masters recorded other sales in "St. Louis of the Illinois Country," reflecting the way that local economic ties spanned the Mississippi and afforded avenues to introduce slaves into territory claimed by the United States.[55] These cross-river sales blurred the boundary between U.S. territory and Spanish territory—between societies with slaves and nominally free soil.[56]

Throughout the 1790s, slaveholders in Spanish-controlled Missouri routinely sold slaves into Illinois. In 1793, John Edgar, a justice of the peace for the Illinois territory, purchased a slave from Jean Cons, who resided in "St. Genevieve, of the Illinois Country," on the west bank of the Mississippi River, in present-day Missouri.[57] Three years later, a resident in Illinois purchased Betsy, an enslaved woman, in Missouri and brought her "into the state of Illinois" where she was "sold as a slave."[58] Similarly, in 1798, Antoine la Chance bought a slave from the wife of Antoine Louvien dit Amour. Again, this sale meant that a slave crossed the Mississippi River from territory identified as "St. Genevieve of the Illinois Country" to

Kaskaskia on the east bank of the river.[59] A legal dispute over a single slave sale reveals how weak boundaries supported the spread of slavery throughout Illinois. In 1792, Jean Boyce of Missouri sold a nineteen-year-old enslaved man named Ben to Jonathan Ously, a resident of St. Clair County, Illinois. The sale gave Ously one year to secure the cash needed to pay the purchase price. Although Ously ended up defaulting on the payment, during the year he owned Ben, he often used Ben's labor as part of his business voyages to the falls of the Ohio, near present-day Louisville. Many slaves, like Ben, moved into and out of free territories with ease, and their masters seemingly did not fear that their slaves would win freedom by virtue of crossing these borders.

The business and political fortunes of one prominent settler, Pierre Menard, illustrate the ways in which local inhabitants kept the slave economy afloat. Born in Montreal in 1766, as an adolescent, Menard participated in fur trade voyages that took him through Prairie du Chien and into the Illinois Country. During the 1780s, he made several voyages in the Great Lakes region, including, in 1786, at least one venture to Detroit. In 1790, he began a partnership with Barthelemi Tardiveau, and they resettled in Kaskaskia. Tardiveau was several years Menard's senior and provided both personal connections and access to capital, while Menard's decade of travel in the region meant that the firm had experience executing long-distance voyages. Throughout the 1790s, Menard sent convoys of goods to Philadelphia and New Orleans—voyages that often relied on slave labor. Menard used slaves in every component of his business, including loading goods, clearing land, building structures, milling raw materials, and tending to livestock.[60] And like many Francophone settlers had done before, he relied on slaves to work the convoys to New Orleans that connected Illinois's goods with larger markets.

While plantation agriculture, never vast, was slowly disappearing, slaves continued to be important to wide swaths of the economy. Like Menard, Francois Vallé, a prominent settler who lived on the west bank of the Mississippi, employed his slaves to ferry goods across the Mississippi.[61] He, too, never attempted to build a grain farm. In fact, many of the new merchants in Illinois broke up older grain farms, and although it could be difficult to discern at any given moment which direction the economy would go, one indication came when large planters died and their estates were disbursed. Pierre Charleville, who resided near Kaskaskia, operated a grain plantation, and his estate, including nearly two dozen slaves, was sold at his death. In

1782, the executor of his estate sold the enslaved men and women at public auction to a long list of buyers.[62] Of the twenty-two men and women sold, no one individual, with the exception of Charleville's children, purchased more than two. The buyers at this auction did not have major landed interests; they did not purchase his other movable goods—such as farm equipment—that would have been valuable in plantation production. In short, the Charleville auction suggests what Menard's and Vallé's practices reveal: slavery was crucial to the economy, even as staple agriculture slowly declined.

If some sectors of the economy underwent slow changes, in the state's salt mines, slave labor took off and gave the slave economy a new opportunity to expand. Under the leadership of territorial Governor William Henry Harrison and U.S. Secretary of War Henry Dearborn, the United States secured congressional appropriations to purchase the land surrounding Illinois's Saline Creeks, including the land at the "Shawnese Town," on the Wabash River.[63] The Delaware, Shawnee, Kickapoo, Potawatomi, Miami, and Kaskaskia Indians who claimed this land had proposed leasing it to the United States, but U.S. negotiators rebuffed them, saying, "We wish nothing without a price."[64] By 1803, with the Treaty of Fort Wayne, the United States had acquired 2 million acres, including the salt springs. Hoping to secure ready access to salt for the military, Congress designated the area public land and forbade any private ownership of the territory now called the U.S. Saline. The mining economy, which required dangerous, backbreaking work, met its labor demands via surplus slave labor transferred from Illinois's dwindling grain plantations. Masters residing along the Mississippi would hire their slaves east for limited terms, and slaveholders in present-day Kentucky did the same.

With so many inhabitants relying on slave labor, between the 1796 and 1807, masters used their political resources and petitioned Congress to repeal Article Six of the Northwest Territory Ordinance. The petitioners presented evidence of a long history of local legal control over Illinois's slave populations and asserted that slavery had played a fundamental role in the region's economy before 1787, when the ordinance went into effect. Consequently, the signatories on each of the nearly dozen extant memorials asked Congress to suspend Article Six, even if only temporarily, to afford them clear claims to their "French Negroes." Residents also hoped to create laws that would allow them to continue to import enslaved people from eastern states. Taking part in a domestic slave trade, they argued, would not increase the number of enslaved African Americans in the United States. Instead, such trade dispersed the enslaved population, which, they claimed, would make gradual abolition more practicable in the East.[65] Quite cleverly, slaveholders sought to protect and expand slavery in Illinois while appealing to gradual emancipationists in the eastern states at the same time.

For the more than two decades that the petitions dragged on, settlers stressed that slavery predated the creation of the United States, which, they said, compelled Congress to respect its place in the region.[66] In one early effort, four prominent slaveholders—John Edgar, William Morrison, William St. Clair, and John Dumoulin—appealed to the Virginian Act of Cession of 1784 to claim legal title to their slaves.[67] Article Six stood "contrary to the assurances" that had been made to them by "George Rogers Clark on his taking possession of this country," they asserted.[68] They were "then and now in possession of a number of slaves."[69] In succeeding years, such as in one 1805 petition, inhabitants in Illinois presented at least six memorials with similar arguments. In one, they contended that the Ordinance of 1787 left them with "certain heavy grievances," the ban on slavery in Article Six chief among them. As a memorial from twenty-two Randolph County citizens stated, residents "almost universally desired" a suspension of Article Six.[70] An 1806 plea stated that "domestic servitude" is "immovably established" in the territory.[71] And an 1807 petition from the Territorial Assembly asserted that "at the time of the adoption of the Ordinance of 1787 slavery was tolerated, and slaves generally possessed by the citizens then inhabiting the country, amounting to at least one-half of the present population."[72] The Territorial Assembly joined William Henry Harrison, the new territorial governor, in attempting to legalize slavery in the entire territory, what amounted to present-day Indiana and Illinois. Far from a fringe element, powerful political figures and institutions tried to reverse the 1787 emancipation provision.

In addition to protecting slavery as it existed, applicants urged Congress to allow immigrants to relocate to the territory with their human property. In all the various memorials, inhabitants stressed that they were not asking to introduce new slaves to the United States, only to transport African Americans already enslaved in eastern states.[73] One solicitation reassured Congress that the Illinois residents' only "desire is that inhabitants may be permitted to introduce from any of the United States such persons . . . as by the laws of such states are slaves therein."[74] The petitioners informed Congress that they had no interest in participating in the international slave trade and no plans to increase "the number of slaves already in the dominions of the United States."[75] Another application pressed this point by asserting that the eastern states were "overburdened with negroes . . . which they cannot comfortably support," and the western migration of slavery would create a "situation which admits not the most distant prospect of emancipation."[76] These proslavery advocates argued that slavery's expansion into the West allowed for its gradual abolition in the United States. In this way, Illinois residents appealed to southerners hoping to move west and to those factions of the nation that wanted gradual emancipation, insisting a domestic slave trade and gradual emancipation could coexist in Illinois.

After receiving several appeals, each from a broader, more powerful constituency, in 1803, Congress began to discuss the suspension of Article Six. Congressman John Randolph of Virginia chaired the select committee that received these requests. Although a Virginian, the chairman and the rest of the committee did not grant the petitioners' request. The committee observed that the abolition of slavery did not hamper western settlement, as "the rapid population of the State of Ohio sufficiently evinces."[77] Three years later, Congress again considered these memorials and again declared "that it is not expedient at this time to suspend the sixth article" of the 1787 ordinance.[78]

Even though Congress denied various attempts to legalize slavery, they did not take any direct steps to enforce the 1787 ban on human bondage in the region.[79] The pleas forced Congress to revisit its ban on slavery in Illinois and to confront the fact that a gradual, inevitable emancipation was not under way in Illinois. Through these solicitations, easterners became increasingly aware that slavery had found a way to survive its legal emancipation. Like the British and French empires that tried to regulate Illinois society, the U.S. Congress found that its power to draw boundaries and abolish slavery could not overcome local power to sustain human bondage in the economies. The law acted as one of many forces that could sustain or abolish slavery, and masters found ways to keep the slave economy alive even when the law was not on their side. Having learned how to undercut British legal proclamations in the decades before, settlers in Illinois continued to undermine U.S. laws.

Moving to St. Louis offered slaveholders an opportunity to avoid American decrees, just as French settlers had done during the 1760s. The various memorialists also argued that without an operating slave economy, Illinois residents would relocate to other regions where they could hold men and women in bondage. Several tracts discussed slaveholders' intentions to move from Illinois into Spanish Missouri if they could not retain title to their slaves. One plea reported that they "can not well reconcile the laws of the land" as it pertained to their slaves and their land. Declaring, "there is an Ordinance of Congress, an Ex Post Facto law, of April 1787 which declares that slavery shall not take place in the Western Territory," continuing, "many of the inhabitants of these districts have slaves and some have no other property but slaves. If they wish to preserve their property they must transport themselves to the Spanish side of the Mississippi; but if they do they shall lose lands granted them by congress." Identifying the conflict they faced, the petitioners concluded that "one law tells them: leave the country or ye shall forfeit your Negroes: the other saith; stay in the country or your lands shall be taken from you."[80] Reminding Congress of the porous border they lived along, the inhabitants suggested that the ban on slavery would depopulate the territory because settlers might "remove to the Spanish dominions where slavery is permitted."[81]

Taken as a whole, the several petitions reveal a local cross-cultural collaboration to protect slavery.[82] New migrants worked with French slaveholders to beg Congress for new laws, and Francophone and Anglophone names appeared on the same documents. The names of French families that had been prominent slaveholders as early as the 1760s appear on an 1801 memorial. These French residents include Antoine Bienvenu, whose relative was among the largest slaveholders in Illinois in the 1750s, and Etiene Langlois, who bought slaves from Baynton, Wharton, and Morgan in the 1760s.[83] Newer arrivals like Schadrach Bond—who would become Illinois's first governor in 1818—also signed the appeal. The Illinois Country still bore the imprint of French colonization, which survived the U.S. arrival in part because a diverse cast of inhabitants collaborated in the politics of protecting slavery.

The creation of the U.S. government did not inaugurate radical changes for either masters or slaves in the Upper Mississippi River Valley. Between 1780 and 1810, there was hardly any attempt by free inhabitants to end slavery in Illinois. During British rule, slaveholders had grown accustomed to circumventing imperial authority, with inhabitants expanding on a local legal culture that in part controlled how slavery functioned in Illinois. And even decades after the creation of the United States, local residents had little or no impetus to change their attitudes or their laws. Masters at first relied on Clark's slave code, and when it was voided, they continued to trade and move across the waterways of the continent. The border at the Mississippi featured prominently in their maneuvers. Recognizing that it acted as a legal but not physical boundary between slavery and freedom, they exploited it as part of their political and economic strategies. Time and again, they threatened to abandon U.S. territory in order to pursue their interests. Moreover, slaveholders petitioned Congress and controlled local governance to shape their own laws regarding slavery.

In this way, the multi-imperial history of slavery in Illinois defined the contours of bondage in the United States. Slaveholders in Illinois had ample experience defying legal decrees from distant seats of power, be it Versailles, London, or New York. They had regularly adapted to changing legal climates, reckoning with indigenous politics of captivity and British politics of imperial expansion. With such a long history of changing and adapting the slaving practices to meet new legal conditions, it is perhaps little surprise that the polyglot "French Negroes" who arrived in Illinois during the 1720s survived as a protected category of slavery into the nineteenth century. U.S. Independence and the transfer of the region into U.S. hands did not begin a process of emancipation or a radically new chapter for the region. Instead, the colonialism that brought diverse enslaved people into the region conditioned masters and slaves to change and adapt their societies when yet another colonizing empire arrived on the scene.

When all their efforts to convince Congress to suspend Article Six failed, slaveholders turned their attention to the territorial legislature to protect bound labor in the region, this time by creating a system of indentured servitude. In 1807, the Territorial Assembly passed An Act Concerning the Introduction of Negroes and Mulattoes into This Territory.[84] This territorial law provided a legal framework for slavery and servitude in Illinois until it became a state in 1818.[85] Any immigrant who was "the owner or possessor of any negroes or mulattoes" over the age of fifteen had to sign them into a servitude contract within thirty days of taking up residence in the state. Commonly, masters secured contracts that forced African Americans to a lifetime of unpaid service. Importantly, slaves were not entitled to any new freedoms when they came into Illinois; they remained slaves during their initial few months in the state. Consequently, at the time that they signed these servitude contracts, African Americans were legally enslaved, despite the fact that they had to sign contracts that converted them into indentured servants. Those contracts then had to be recorded at the Court of Common

Pleas and notarized by a local clerk. The contract system allowed slaveholders to convert their slaves into indentured servants—without sacrificing title to those slaves.[86] Children younger than fifteen years of age and any children born to indentured servants during their term of service became free once they reached the age of majority—age twenty-eight for women and age thirty for men. If masters failed to secure these contracts, they had an additional sixty days, after the thirty-day window expired, to leave the territory.

While the majority of Illinois's free inhabitants championed the servitude system, a small group of critics complained that abolition in Illinois was neither gradual nor even particularly likely. These opponents tended to be migrants from Kentucky or Virginia who moved to Illinois in part to escape slavery's presence. In one territorial representative's understanding of the Act Concerning Negroes, the law allowed for "evasion . . . [and] violation of said Ordinance" because it allowed for "a quallified species of slavery" in Illinois.[87] One settler lamented that the territorial assembly had "sanctioned a law permitting the Master of a slave who may be brought into the said territory" to retain his property rights in that African American. Another inhabitant satirically suggested that the "law . . . may be properly entitled 'A Law for the Establishment of Disguised Slavery in Opposition to the National Will.'"[88] In his mind, the territorial assembly had "passed several laws in open violation of the Ordinance of 1787," especially "a law authorizing the indenting of servants for an [unusual] length of time."[89] These critics objected to the law that allowed Virginians to migrate into Illinois and hold slaves as uncompensated servants for life.

* * *

Slaveholders in Illinois availed themselves of the tools of self-government to cement their position in Illinois's social hierarchy. During the 1780s, the United States proved incapable of controlling this region and impotent to break masters' power to hold African Americans in slavery. By 1810, the United States had secured dominion over the region, but it had also empowered local powerbrokers to shape the polity they had created. From George Rogers Clark's slave code to the Territorial Assembly's Act Concerning Negroes, slaveholders found ample means to create a local legal basis for their power that in some cases defied national laws. In response, U.S. authorities had to confront a central tension of imperial expansion. The

United States successfully asserted some control over the region because it empowered local planters and merchants. However, by empowering masters on the ground, they also afforded settlers in Illinois avenues to continue their economic ventures into slave country and to undermine national laws where they saw fit. As the United States haltingly moved into the Mississippi River Valley, slaveholders refashioned slave economies and adapted how slavery functioned to accommodate this new empire without sacrificing their claims to Indian- and African-descended slaves.

Local inhabitants deflected the impact of the Northwest Territory Ordinance, which meant that slavery knew no sectional boundaries in the Mississippi River Valley. As a consequence, U.S. independence and the assertion of U.S. power in the region did not mark a new epoch in the region. U.S. Independence did not signal a watershed for antislavery movements in the Upper Mississippi Valley. Instead, it was simply another chapter in the entangled history of empires and slaveries in the Mississippi River Valley. Rather than bowing to abolition decrees, masters evaded emancipation and Americanized slavery in this period. Once again, slavery had no one legal or institutional cast, and "French Negroes" lived and labored alongside slaves from Virginia who had been made lifelong uncompensated servants.

Although masters created a system that perpetuated bound labor in the aftermath of its legal abolition, that system was not airtight. As time went on, slaveholders faced challenges to their authority from a small but growing cohort of antislavery settlers and the slaves themselves. By the early nineteenth century, the battle over slavery's emancipation changed venues from national politics, territorial legislatures, and local laws to the fields, salt mines, and slave quarters where daily negotiations between slaves and masters threatened to upend the system. Masters subverted the will of the U.S. Congress, but as they at last set up a local framework for evading emancipation, they would in time find that another struggle over slavery was already playing out much closer to home.

CHAPTER 4

Contesting Bondage in the Slave North

On November 19, 1811, Dunky, a sixteen-year-old "colored woman" who resided in Kaskaskia, signed an indentured servitude contract for a term of forty years with her master, William Morrison. This was just one part of her harrowing journey into bondage. Dunky was not born into slavery, and Illinois was not her native land. According to testimony given some years later, Dunky "was born in Africa from which place she was shipped by persons unknown to her and landed at Charleston in the State of South Carolina." Arriving in Charleston was only a midway point on her journey. "She remained but few days," she later testified, "after which she was convoyed from there to Kaskaskia in the Illinois country."[1] Once in Illinois, Morrison, a merchant who had himself migrated west from Philadelphia, converted her from a slave into an unpaid servant. Lost and almost certainly disoriented, this adolescent woman entered new terms of subordination and began the painful work of rebuilding her life in Illinois. By purchasing this African captive as a slave and having her sign a servitude contract, Morrison managed to negotiate Illinois law and keep Dunky in a state of slavery.

Although consigned to servitude, Dunky did not resign herself to unfreedom. Instead, she learned to make the servitude contract work for her. Over time, she tried to enforce specific terms of the contract and use its violation to gain her freedom. In 1831, long before her term was due to expire, Morrison hired Dunky out to another slaveholder, Andrew Hay, in neighboring St. Louis. According to one account, Dunky did not consent to go into Missouri. Instead, Hay "with great force and violence pulled and dragged" her to go and struck her with "a great many violent blows and strokes and then and there imprisoned her." Dunky sued Hay in the Missouri courts, arguing that she was "justly entitled to her freedom" because the servitude law mandated she could only be sent out of Illinois with her consent. Dunky did not win this case, but the lawsuit, which sought to hold Morrison accountable to the contract's provisions, reveals that keeping men and women in servitude was no simple task.[2]

Dunky's master, William Morrison, like so many other slaveholders who resettled in Illinois, used the servitude system to remake slavery.[3] In the opening decades of the nineteenth century, Illinois witnessed a demographic explosion, with the state's population jumping tenfold. Most of these migrants hailed from Kentucky, Tennessee, Virginia, and the Upper South, and hundreds of them brought their slaves with them. By terms of the Act Concerning Negroes and Mulattoes, these slaves had to be converted to servants before being put to work in the rural economy. Illinois resembled many other states in the trans-Appalachian West, including Ohio, Indiana, and Kentucky, which all witnessed booming migration in these decades. The movement of migrants into the interior of the continent helped secure U.S. control over Indian lands and ushered in the first wave of national expansion. Yet unlike Ohio, which received migrants from New England and the mid-Atlantic, Illinois was at first populated as part of a southern diaspora. Confronted with the 1787 ordinance that abolished slavery in the Northwest Territory, masters who had migrated to Illinois turned their slaves into servants, thereby keeping title over their human property.

Converting a slave into a lifelong servant prolonged slavery, but at the same time, it gave bound workers an opportunity to disrupt this reclassification.[4] This dynamic challenges the notion that servitude simply re-created bondage, and the servitude system allowed some African Americans a pathway that brought them closer to freedom. Although there was nothing inherent in Illinois's system of contract bondage that encouraged this, African Americans seized on tiny openings in the indenture system to inch closer to freedom. Some enslaved persons used the negotiations of a servitude contract as an opportunity to strike bargains for shorter terms and compensation for their labor. And over decades, a sizable minority, roughly a third, of slaves won the promise of payment for their labor or even freedom. The outcomes, however, hinged on a host of circumstances particular to any given case, with masters and slaves endlessly jockeying for advantage.

With masters using servitude systems to adapt to the state's abolition laws, different kinds of enslaved people lived in the same small communities. Even as the servitude system took hold, a grandfather clause allowed masters to keep "French Negroes" in bondage, and the state continued to have a patchwork system of slaveries. Into the 1840s, inheritable bondage remained, and hundreds of African Americans were born into slavery in Illinois, under the premise that they descended from "French Negroes." Into the opening decade of the nineteenth century, Indian slaves lived alongside enslaved African Americans. Lifelong uncompensated indentured servants, servants with shorter terms of service, and children held in bondage until they reached the age of majority all lived beside one another.[5] In still other instances, masters from Kentucky sold their slaves into the salt marshes, where they became slaves for a term, working for a few months or even one year, before returning them to the neighboring slave state. The many differences in enslavement existed in part because masters so often adapted to the changing legal and political realities in Illinois. In previous decades, they had navigated the indigenous politics of slavery, while in the early nineteenth century, they found ways to make slavery work in light of abolition laws on the books. As had always been the case, slavery took no single, fixed, or institutional form. Reinvention was its hallmark.

Amid this jumbled landscape of lifelong inheritable slavery, term slavery, contract bondage, and degrees of unfreedom, African Americans challenged their masters by haggling over contracts and attempting to use the servitude system against their masters. Amid this ceaseless negotiation, Illinois's courts became involved in adjudicating the limits and possible abolition of servitude laws. In particular, they parsed the language of Illinois's 1818 state constitution, which both protected these various forms of slavery and gave antislavery politicians a footing to attack them. By grandfathering Illinois's systems of unfree labor into the state while simultaneously barring future introduction of slavery, Illinois's politics left the state suspended between slave and free. In 1828, two cases that challenged slavery's place in the state made their way to the Illinois Supreme Court, forcing judges to grapple with slavery's place in a nominally free state. These cases were part of a long antislavery struggle under way, one that began in the slave quarter with the conflicts between masters and slaves. Ironically, the adaptations that allowed slavery to survive in Illinois also helped begin a struggle that would in time bring about its demise.

In the first three decades of the nineteenth century, U.S. settlers poured into Illinois. For most of the preceding century, the state had been home to a few thousand European settlers and many more powerful indigenous inhabitants. In two short decades, those proportions reversed: in 1810, the free population hovered around 12,000, and by 1830, it had surpassed

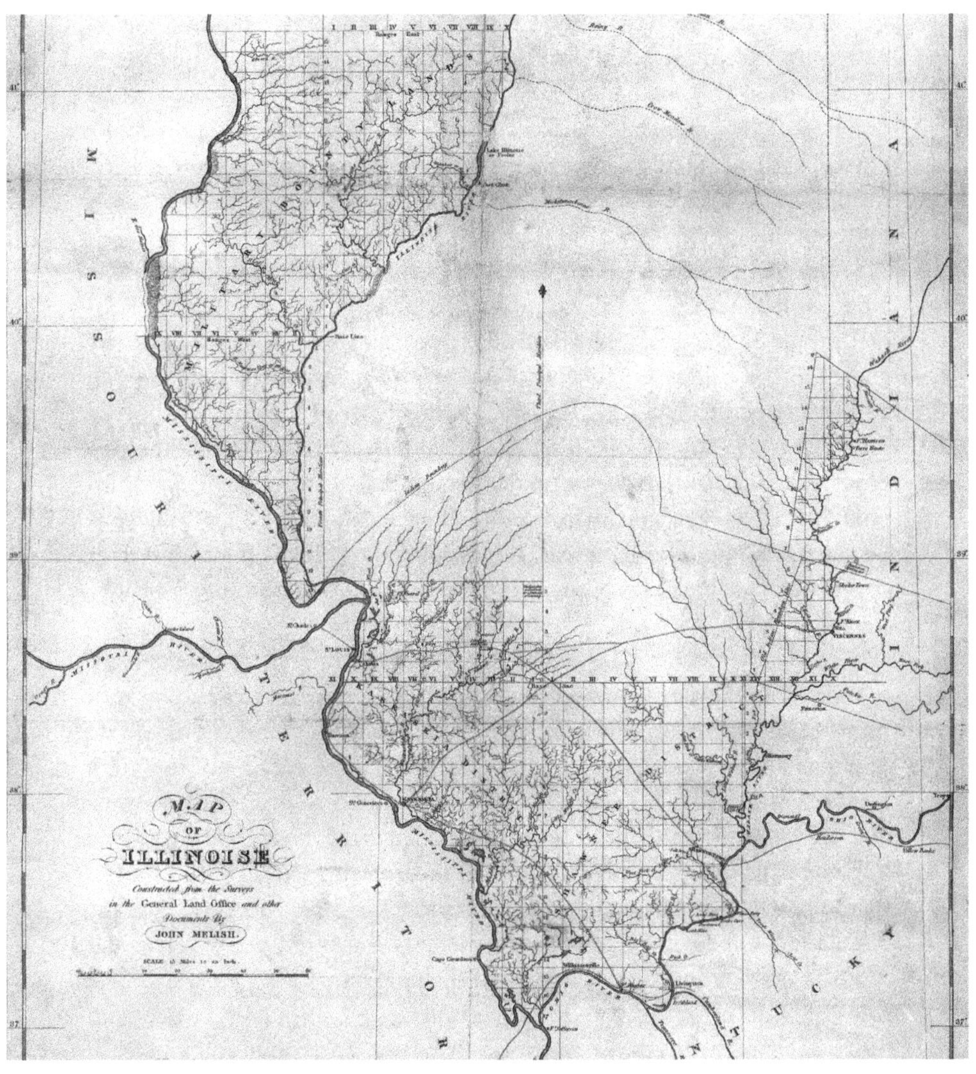

Figure 4. This 1818 map depicts Gallatin and Pope Counties, in the easternmost portion of the state, home to Illinois's salt marshes. It also shows Randolph and St. Clair Counties, along the Mississippi River. John Melish, *Map of Illinoise* (Philadelphia: John Melish, 1818). Retrieved from the Library of Congress, https://www.loc.gov/item/2003627085/. (Accessed June 14, 2017.)

150,000. In the eighteenth century, various competing communities of natives and newcomers had jostled to control the region. By the nineteenth century, those contests had largely subsided. The change in population was dramatic. One observer remarked on the "rapid increase. . . . So rapid, indeed, has been their advancement," he continued, "that it is quite natural for those who are accustomed to the more tardy progress of the older states to doubt the reality of ours."[6]

An influx of settlers ended the region's colonial history of overlapping empires, as the new U.S. inhabitants wiped away Indian titles to land, colonial export economies, and the divided loyalties that for nearly a century had been the hallmark of the Illinois Country. Once antagonists, French and British settlers worked alongside the new cast of U.S. migrants. "The inhabitants are Americans, French, Canadians, Negroes," remarked one observer of the state's polyglot population.[7] Notably, many migrants to Illinois learned French and married into French families. To cite only one instance, in 1800, John Reynolds, who migrated to Illinois from Tennessee and would eventually become governor of Illinois, married into a prominent French family.[8]

These collaborations helped ensure continuities within Illinois's slave economy. By the early nineteenth century, white slaveholders had lived in Illinois for nearly a century. They welcomed southern slaveholding migrants and kept slavery intact. Over the first three decades of the nineteenth century, anywhere between several hundred to over 1,000 servants and slaves resided in Illinois, a number that held mostly steady over a thirty-year period.[9] Census data offer an incomplete picture, but in 1820 in Randolph County, slaves and servants represented nearly 10 percent of the population. On the opposite side of the state in Gallatin County, slaves and servants stood at just over 8 percent of the population but played a critical role in the local economy.[10] These percentages were roughly in line with other societies with slaves in North America, including colonial New England, the mid-Atlantic, and parts of the upcountry South. Certain pockets of southern Illinois along the Mississippi and Ohio Rivers hosted a slave economy that, in terms of proportion of the larger population, looked much like western North Carolina, western Maryland, or parts of colonial New York.[11]

Illinois's status as part slave and part free was not entirely unique in the wider nation. During the early nineteenth century, various northern states passed a series of gradual emancipation statutes that blurred the boundaries between slavery and freedom for African Americans.[12] Generally, these laws freed all children after a given date and in this way set slavery on a path to destruction. In New England, court rulings and state constitutions abolished slavery, but systems of indentured servitude persisted, and workers found themselves trapped in unfree labor.[13] Meanwhile, in the mid-Atlantic, states passed gradual emancipation statutes that took years to play out. In New York, Pennsylvania, and New Jersey, children born to slaves lived in servitude until they reached the age of majority. Former slaves also commonly entered servitude contracts and labored for former masters, albeit under new terms.[14] These arrangements at times allowed masters to define the meaning of freedom and to exploit African Americans and their supposedly free-born children. New Jersey's system stood out for its tendency to force African Americans into a chattel status and render them "slaves for a term."[15] In the neighboring Upper South, systems of term slavery that promised freedom after a period of service became an increasingly common way to extend slavery's slow demise in places where it had ceased to be profitable.[16] In Indiana and Ohio, enslaved African Americans carried into the region often labored as indentured servants before winning their manumission.[17] These servitude arrangements recast the terms of subordination, rendering African Americans outside of the plantation economy neither slave nor free. The servitude system in Illinois had much in common with other jurisdictions, but Illinois differed in part because it set no fixed date after which children would be born free, and the principle of *post-nati* emancipation did not find its way into Illinois law.

The particular history of migration into Illinois also set it apart from other states in the Old Northwest, which in the early nineteenth century experienced dynamic population growth that affected the politics of slavery. Indiana and Ohio attracted migrants from New England into their borders, and state leaders stamped out slavery in those communities. In 1803, the Ohio state constitution barred slavery in absolute terms. Masters who arrived with enslaved African Americans could convert them into indentured servants, as in Illinois, with the key difference that the Ohio statute limited terms of servitude to one year, which helped to expedite slavery's demise. Meanwhile, in neighboring Indiana, a servitude system that trapped African Americans in bound labor for long terms took root. The territorial legislature, led by territorial Governor William Henry Harrison, contrived this means of sanctioning bondage in the state as part of a larger proslavery politics. Yet by 1810, a cast of upcoming politicians had adopted antislavery platforms—some out of genuine principle, others in an attempt to overthrow Harrison and the rest of the ruling territorial party. In short order, abolition laws and court rulings dispatched with the system of servitude in Indiana.[18] The migrant populations in these states stood in stark contrast to the settlers arriving in Illinois who hoped to join the ranks of the region's slaveholders.[19] The indentured servitude system let them do just that.

Hundreds of slaveholders arrived in Illinois. In Randolph County, the largest slaveholding district in the state, roughly 70 percent of masters were recent migrants to Illinois.[20] Once in Illinois, slaveholders had to convert their slaves into servants within thirty days or forfeit title to their human property sixty days later. Slaves younger than fifteen who entered the state could not sign an indenture contract, owing to their status as minors. They were recorded at the courthouse to become registered servants bound to labor until they reached the age of majority—twenty-eight for women and thirty for men.[21] During that initial month after arriving in the state, African Americans remained slaves and could not petition for freedom. Once signed onto contracts, African American servants became chattel subject to their master's will. Given that slaves had no free volition to sign contracts, the servitude system could allow masters to coerce lifelong unpaid labor from servants, and children of servants would be held to decades of service. For this reason, the state's system of contract bondage gave masters new resources to reduce people to slavery. By moving into a new jurisdiction in Illinois, migrant slaveholders changed the legal status of their enslaved workers without sacrificing an ability to coerce labor from them.[22]

Just as bondage took many different forms in the eighteenth century, slavery underwent important changes in this period. Using the servitude system, masters could hold their former slaves as lifelong uncompensated servants. Approximately 620 extant contracts that African Americans signed between 1807 and 1840 show that this system perpetuated slavery across large sections of Illinois. Native Americans appear not to have signed any servitude contracts, and African Americans made up the entire population of these lifelong servants. In roughly a dozen cases, masters secured indenture contracts for ninety years or longer and included no payment for the worker.[23] Roughly one-quarter of the indenture contracts compelled African Americans to labor for their natural lives without compensation. Even when masters promised to pay their workers after the terms expired, often the servants did not live to claim the money. To cite only one example, in 1818, William Wilson migrated from Missouri to Illinois with two slaves. He then secured

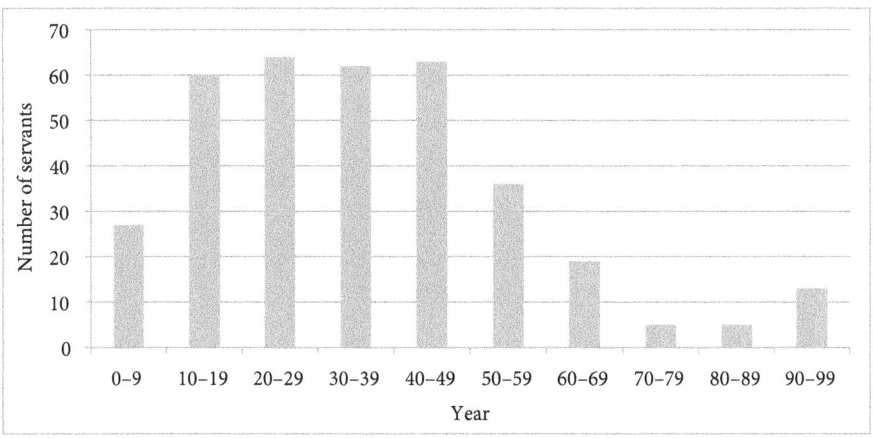

Figure 5. Terms of service and number of servants.

ninety-nine-year indentureships, offering the slaves $400 compensation at the expiration of the term of service.[24] Far from beginning a system of gradual emancipation, the servitude system kept slavery alive in Illinois.

The servitude system was intended to re-create slavery, but masters did not go unchallenged. Time and again, some African Americans succeeded in subverting the system. Although contract bondage hardly relied on slaves' consent, bound workers relied on the contestations inherent in signing a contract to fight their subordination. Some contracts offered slaves the promise of freedom. Tracking the variations in terms of service over time confirms that the servitude system was dynamic, not static. A sizable minority of African Americans struck bargains and entered indentures both to receive compensation for their labor and to inch closer to freedom. In total, roughly a third of the extant indenture contracts would emancipate workers before the age of sixty.[25] For instance, in 1818, James Nelson agreed to serve his master for one year and twenty-three days.[26] Other servants labored for less than a year.[27]

In still other cases, the amount of compensation varied even when the same master indentured two servants at the same time. William and Ned, both in their early twenties, each agreed to serve Nathaniel Anderson for thirty years. William was to receive $400 compensation, Ned, $350.[28] This discrepancy hints that perhaps William haggled with Anderson and won a larger sum. Over the 1810s, variations like these were common, and the

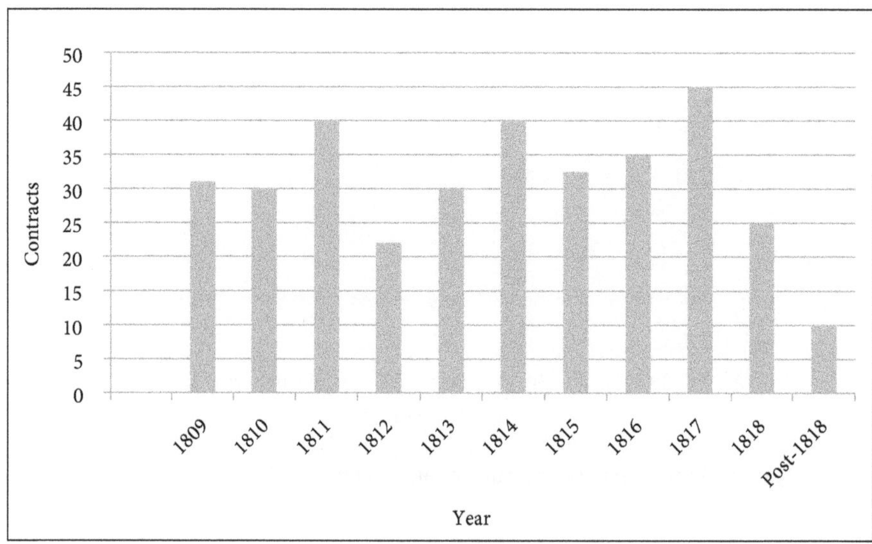

Figure 6. Median length of servitude contracts over time.

median length of contracts changed from year to year: in some cases, the median term exceeded forty years of service, but in other instances, the median term dipped to roughly twenty years of service. The fluctuations in the length of service reveal that no gradual trend toward freedom developed.

In addition to haggling over servitude contracts, some African Americans went further and brought legal action against their masters. In these suits, they endeavored to prove that their bondage violated key provisions of state law and was thus invalid. In one early case in 1810, Bob and Lydia took their master, Jincy Mitchel, to court for holding them in slavery without first securing an indentured servitude contract. Mitchell had owned Bob and Lydia in Kentucky and brought them into Illinois to labor in St. Clair County. He failed to sign an indenture for them within thirty days of arriving. The two slaves wisely waited several months before filing their suits for freedom because their master had a sixty-day window during which he could return them to Kentucky without forfeiting his title. By timing their suit correctly, Bob and Lydia won their freedom.[29]

Although some African Americans found their way into freedom, masters still held "French Negroes" as inheritable slaves. Slaveholders regularly bought and sold slaves who were supposedly descended from bondmen and women brought to the region during the French period. They then recorded these sales at their local courthouses. William Morrison was one such slaveholder. Born in Philadelphia in the 1760s, Morrison moved to Kaskaskia, Illinois, in 1790. A prominent slaveholder who enjoyed unrivaled success in Illinois's shipping economy, Morrison spent years amassing a bound labor force. In 1805, he paid nearly $800 at public auction to purchase two African Americans.[30] Two years later, Morrison purchased "a certain mulatto slave girl" from a middling farmer.[31] A few years after that, Morrison purchased an enslaved woman named Molly from John Kinzie, "of Chicagou."[32] In 1814, Thomas Cox sold Morrison a family of four bound workers.[33] And in 1815, Morrison talked of purchasing a "slave . . . perhaps (Mary) Michel Beauvais' Girl."[34] He remarked that he hoped to purchase her because she "will be considered a slave under the law of the Territory."[35] Morrison's accounts laid bare the open secret that slaves could be legally bought and sold nearly three decades after the Northwest Territory Ordinance supposedly made Illinois a free state.

This was possible in part because key civic institutions, most notably the Catholic Church, supported slavery's survival. Between 1800 and 1845, priests baptized nearly 200 African American infants as slaves in the local Catholic churches. Along the Mississippi River near St. Louis, in the parishes of the Immaculate Conception in Kaskaskia and Holy Family parish in Cahokia, parish priests registered a majority of African American children as "slave," "negro slave," or "negro child belonging to."[36] In these parishes, masters did not abide by any system of gradual emancipation or freedom at birth—no priest reported baptizing the child of a slave as a "free negro."

Slavery was no mere colonial vestige, and inheritable bondage was visible to the local community that observed baptism ceremonies. Priests recorded black children's servile status with remarkable consistency, indicating that local officials knew and sanctioned slavery's place in Illinois. In 1838, Cynthia Ann, "slave of Judge Pope," received the sacrament of baptism. With the local judge holding slaves, the wider society surely knew about slavery's existence. What's more, in these ceremonies, enslaved African Americans took godparents who rarely held slaves of their own. None of these godparents seemed to object to inheritable bondage continuing in their parishes. In one case of several in Kaskaskia, Baptiste and Elizabeth LaChapelle—who did not hold any slaves or servants—acted as godparents

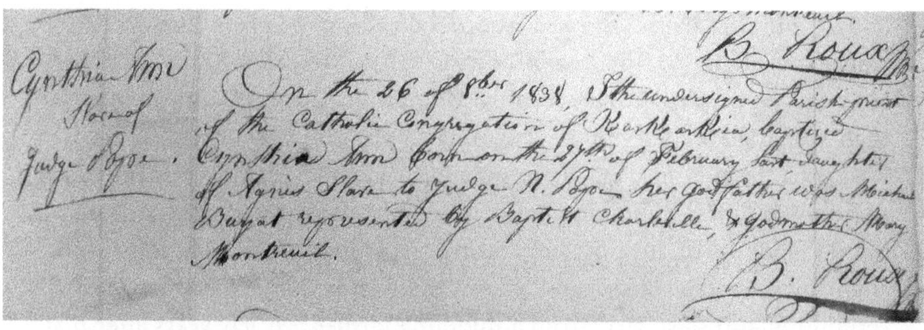

Cynthia Ann Slave of Judge Pope.

On the 26 of 8ber 1838, I the undersigned Parish priest of the Catholic Congregation of Kaskaskia, baptized Cynthia Ann born on the 27th of February last daughter of Agnis Slave to Judge N. Pope her godfather was Michael Bayat represented by Baptist Charleville, & godmother Mary Montreuil.

B. Roux

Figure 7. This entry made on August 26, 1838, was for "Cynthia Ann slave of Judge Pope." She was the "daughter of Agnis, Slave to Judge N. [Nathaniel] Pope." Baptism entry from Registry of Baptisms, 1759–1815, Parish of the Immaculate Conception of Notre Dame, DAB, p. 201.

to "Marie, an enslaved woman, aged about 7 years old, born of a slave."[37] In another such case, Pierre Derousse—who also did not own any African Americans—served as godfather to Virginie, an enslaved infant.[38] For these communities in southern Illinois, it appeared that very little had changed since the late eighteenth century.

Still, by the early nineteenth century, black slavery became the exclusive form of human bondage, with Indian slavery slowly receding. The new nation was committed to black subordination, white supremacy, and, increasingly, Indian removal. Owing to the centuries of human bondage that marked the region, it seems likely that some people of Indian descent remained in the enslaved community. Many Native Americans had married into the slave community and therefore their presence likely persisted. Still, diverse racial origins collapsed into a single, invented racial label. In 1806, when Marie, an Indian slave belonging to Louis Pensoneau, was laid to final rest, it marked the twilight of indigenous slavery among Euro-American settlers and the rise of a culture that exclusively equated blackness and bondage.[39] These "French Negroes," so called regardless of their racial makeup, emerged from the initial two slave systems in Illinois, systems that, in the eyes of many local residents, had now become one.

The continued presence of "French Negroes" shows how the long history of bondage in French North America shaped the state. The Bienvenu, Beauvais, and Charleville families, who had first lived in Illinois during the 1750s and 1760s, continued to hold slaves into the 1830s. In exceptional cases, enslaved people brought to Illinois in the eighteenth century still resided along the banks of the Mississippi. In 1815, Francois, a black slave aged about eighty who belonged to Louis Pensoneau, died and received funeral rites. Not long after, Catharine, a slave to Jean Baptist Saucier "aged about one hundred years," was laid to rest. These two enslaved people may have lived in the region in the day when an export staple–dominated economy made Illinois the breadbasket for empires. By the nineteenth century, it is likely that their children or members of their extended family were still toiling along the banks of the Mississippi.

Masters still advertised enslaved African Americans for sale or hire in the state's newspapers. In this way, slaveholders relied on print as a way to make slavery public and show that they would not respect abolition laws the U.S. government imposed on them. In 1815, Ninian Edwards, the territorial governor, advertised "22 slaves for sale. Between Ages 10 & 17," although Congress had banned slavery from the region almost a decade before their birth.[40] Edwards was no stranger to slave sales. A few years earlier, he had sold Sam, "a negro boy" who was "now at St. Louis," to Pierre Menard.[41] Others followed Edwards's lead. In 1820, a freeman in Kaskaskia announced that he "will sell a negro girl and will rent out a negro man."[42] A few years later, a master advertised an entire family of "negroes . . . for sale," and another announced "a likely Negro woman for sale," along with her two children.[43] Meanwhile, a prospective purchaser posted a newspaper notice reading, "Wanted to Hire: a Negro Boy or Girl."[44]

Masters frequently recorded their slaves in deed books to ensure they had an enforceable legal title. In each case, county and circuit clerks aided masters as they registered title to their human property. In 1820 in Randolph County, Francois Menard purchased Felicia, a "little slave," for $400 and Brazile, a "mulatto slave," for $200.[45] In 1822, Joseph Cornelius, a resident of St. Clair County, sold Ben, "an 18 year old negro boy slave," for $500.[46] In Pope County, John Henry sold "a negro slave" to a relative in Kentucky.[47] In Johnson County, near the Kentucky border, Josh Fisher settled a debt to John McIntire by transferring "5 good negro boys" to him.[48] Into the 1820s, these transactions were public, with one man purchasing a newspaper notice reading, "A family of Negroes for Sale."[49]

Slaveholders also passed bound workers to their kin and recorded their human property in wills and probate inventories, which meant that courts and probate judges sanctioned these practices. In 1820 in Randolph County, to cite one case, Pierre Lasonde's heirs inherited a "Negro woman" and three "negro boys." These four slaves, presumably a family, had a recorded value of nearly $2,000.[50] In another Randolph County case, Jack was listed as part of his masters' estate and was eventually transferred to his master's heirs.[51] These probate practices continued uninterrupted over decades. Given these realities, it seems that slaveholders were not worried that laws and legal officials would jeopardize their claims to human property. Each of these proceedings, transactions, or sales, from the church house to the courthouse, required a wider community of clerks, church officials, and newspaper editors to make them possible. In each instance, it appears that slaveholders had little fear that local officials would undermine their control over their slaves, even if, as one master knew, slaves "could get free if they stayed in the state."[52]

Masters who bought, sold, and hired African Americans worked their servants and slaves in an array of industries. Slavery and servitude in Illinois varied by region. Along the Mississippi River, farming and shipping predominated. Along the Wabash River, Illinois's great salt marshes always needed bound labor, and Kentucky slaveholders commonly leased workers into the salines. Similarly, masters in Illinois's agrarian districts along the Mississippi River trafficked their workers across the state to work in the booming mining industry along the Ohio River. The dangers of working in salt mines, the travails of rowing on convoys, and the long history of slave labor in the farming economy acted as a disincentive for free workers to move into these industries, creating a demand labor that servants and slaves met.

By the nineteenth century, with access to fertile lands in the greater Ohio River Valley, U.S. officials no longer looked to Illinois as the nation's breadbasket. The nearby Ohio economy boomed, and freeholders exported their agricultural surplus into the wider nation, which meant the relative importance of Illinois's grain economy shrank.[53] Staple export agriculture thus ceased to dominate Illinois. Many settlers established small or mid-sized farms, some of which relied on enslaved labor. Along the Mississippi River, slaveholders used bound workers to grow grain, hemp, and other crops that they shipped to Missouri and Kentucky.[54] Few slaveholders owned more than a handful of bound workers, and outside of growing season, many used or hired them out to do an array of odd jobs.[55]

Servants and slaves were frequently hired out to clear land, chop wood, or work in artisanal roles. Sometimes they earned wages and retained some of their income, which they used to purchase goods in local stores, paying with cash. In a Cahokia shop, a slave named Antoine bought "sundry goods." At times he bartered for objects, and in other instances, he paid "by work," revealing that he hired out his own labor at least in limited circumstances. On occasion, he paid "by cash."[56] Antoine was not unique. A slave named Jarrot maintained an account at the local store and seemingly paid for his goods by hiring out his labor.[57] Meanwhile, a slave named Pet Pet paid for goods with corn, and a fourth slave named Harry paid for goods in cash no fewer than seven times.[58] It seems that small freedoms to hire out labor and keep some earnings could add up.

Slaves in Randolph and St. Clair Counties also worked as domestic labor, serving as cooks, seamstresses, laundresses, and in various other household roles, often for the state's most prominent citizens. Ninian Edwards, the territorial governor, boasted of his slave that she "deserves to be considered, in this part of the world, at least, as a first-class cook." He added that "the ladies insist upon it that she is an excellent seamstress, and I know she has made and ruffled my shirts as well as I have ever been able to find any other person capable of doing. . . . She has done almost all kinds of fine work, and that she can cut out and make her own dresses as well as any lady in this part of the country."[59] Edwards was far from the only slaveholder to have domestic slaves. Another master advertised that "a strong healthy negro man, [and] his wife" were "for sale" and that "the woman is a first rate cook."[60] Still another master simply stated, "I will sell a negro woman, suitable for a family."[61] Political leaders and other local notables in Illinois had slaves in their homes, making slavery a highly visible part of the state's local culture.

Since Illinois settlers maintained their ties to the Lower Mississippi Valley, other slaves worked in shipping economies. Over the first three decades of the nineteenth century, the port of New Orleans grew steadily, and goods from across the interior of North America funneled down the Mississippi to its parts. Randolph County's location on the Mississippi made Illinois's merchants key players in the transportation economy. They frequently brought on additional enslaved workers during peak seasons. William Morrison paid local slaveholders for use of their bound workers on "sundry voyages."[62] In one instance, Morrison's firm paid cash to a slaveholder "for his negre at New Orleans."[63] In another, Morrison hired three African Americans who belonged to Michel Beauvais and Pierre Menard to work on a convoy that exported goods to New Orleans.[64] On a separate voyage, Menard took out "provisions for two negroes for one month."[65] Another master sent "cash to Francois Menard for the use of his Negro, Congo."[66] This same master hired black labor into the mid-1820s, when he rented "Ned the Negro" to labor on the ferries between Illinois and St. Louis.[67]

Slaves working river-going vessels had considerable mobility, earning potential, and even some autonomy on long river voyages. On the other hand, the work posed the threats of injury and capsizing. Rowing against the current also demanded exhausting around-the-clock labor. At each outpost, slaves loaded and unloaded cargo, often in sweltering heat. Once at the final destination, the full convoy required offloading and immediate reloading for the return trip.[68] Still, the work afforded servants and slaves a respite from their masters and the opportunity to make connections with a range of black southerners and to exchange information about slavery and freedom in the Mississippi Valley.[69]

As the shipping economy grew, so did the salt marshes along the Wabash River. In 1803, the U.S. government took title to the salt marshes from the Shawnee Indians. Making salt was difficult: it required digging wells some 20 feet in diameter and 60 feet or more deep to reach subterranean salt creeks.[70] In the mid-nineteenth century, there were reports that people went "down the mine"—that is, the well collapsed on them—indicating the risky nature of a job free laborers preferred to avoid.[71] To harvest the salt, workers hauled water through the wells and into a series of crude pipes that sent the brine to furnaces for processing. The brine exited the pipes in the furnace room into a large central kettle. Workers had to ladle the brine from the first kettle down the line into other containers that sat over a furnace pit, skimming impurities as they worked. Frank, a slave who ran away from the salines, reported that he was "scalded at the salt works," likely from transferring blistering water.[72] Boiling the brine took enormous amounts of energy, and on a daily basis, workers had to fell wood, dry it, and haul it to the factory. Slaves continually stoked the fires. Once the water evaporated and the crystals cooled, skilled workers constructed barrels and prepared the salt for export.

Testifying to the importance slave labor played in the state, during the first two decades after the salt marshes opened, the annual salt tax revenue comprised nearly 20 percent of Illinois's revenue.[73] In the 1820s, the salt works produced nearly 160,000 bushels annually, generating nearly $30,000 in state tax revenue for Illinois's meager coffers.[74] It took 300 gallons of brine, on average, to create one bushel of salt. By the 1810s, the salines had been producing 500 bushels of salt per day, nearly 12 percent of total U.S.

production.[75] Slaves and servants met labor demands of this lucrative industry. Writing to a territorial governor in 1812, one of the salt makers reported that his workers were "mostly negroes."[76] In Gallatin County, the largest salt firm, Taylor Wilkins & Company, employed forty-five white men and 175 African Americans.[77]

This expanding local economy attracted labor and capital from neighboring regions. Illinois law allowed masters to send slaves from neighboring states into the salt marshes for up to one year without sacrificing title to them. However, Kentucky masters frequently relocated to Illinois and converted their slaves into lifelong uncompensated indentured servants, avoiding the trouble of annually sending slaves into the state. In August 1819, John Posey, son of Indiana's former slaveholding governor, secured a sixty-year indenture for Phillis, a fifteen-year-old woman, in exchange for one dollar due at the expiration of her term.[78] In the same month, William Bowles indentured a fifteen-year-old woman named Winney for seventy-five years without compensation, keeping many of the essential dimensions of slavery intact.[79]

Slaves from Kentucky and agrarian districts on the Mississippi worked in the salines, experiencing at least some freedom away from their masters. In the 1810s, Milly claimed that her owner had brought her into Illinois from Kentucky and "held [her] as a slave" while she worked in the salt marshes.[80] Another slaveholder brought Jack "some distance into the interior of the State of Illinois," where he was "held as a slave" and hired out "to work by the day."[81] Masters did not always accompany their slaves into Illinois; sometimes they simply demanded monthly remittances. In 1815, Vincent, a slave, was sent from Kentucky to Illinois, where his master "hired him out there to labor." Vincent had to "pay his master" from his earnings but was also permitted to retain a share.[82] Yet his owner complained that he was "disobedient" and frequently had to pressure Vincent to "collect his money" and "settle his business."[83] While the distinction between slavery and servitude may seem insignificant for the men and women toiling in the salt mines, the status they held as servants offered some workers tiny spaces to negotiate the terms of their subordination.

All of these labor arrangements afforded African Americans resources that helped them contest their bondage. No matter how grueling their labor, elements of life in the agrarian, shipping, and mining industries offered slaves ways to improve their condition. In the farms along the Mississippi, some slaves appeared to hire their labor or sell their own goods and keep some earnings. This cash, which allowed them to buy goods in local stores, could be saved to purchase freedom or pay legal fees associated with using the courts to win emancipation. Travel along the Mississippi exposed slaves to a wider world that could have helped them conceive of ways to live in freedom—either in Illinois or by running away. Last, in the salt marshes, slaves worked alongside white workers, possibly meeting people who could have acted as witnesses or provided other evidence in lawsuits for emancipation.

With slaves playing a role in so many different industries, masters were keen to keep their workers in bondage as time went on and Illinois became a state. Migrations that brought slaveholders into Illinois had acute political dimensions: after the territory reached 60,000 inhabitants, the territorial assembly could petition for statehood. The state constitutional convention convened in the summer of 1818, and slaveholders and their allies fashioned a constitution that protected existing slaveholding practices. But this was no simple task: masters and their backers had to find a way to protect slavery without alienating the rest of the state or enraging the U.S. Congress. Many of the delegates at the convention opposed the further introduction of slaves to Illinois.[84] Moreover, proslavery advocates confronted a stark reality: the U.S. Congress would likely never assent to a proslavery constitution. Matthew Lyon, a former congressman, warned, "I am alarmed" that the convention works "under the expectation of bringing congress to terms of the subject of Slavery." He reminded the delegate that "all of the States as far as Pennsylvania have long been unanimous on this subject. Four senators from Ohio and Indiana are added to this force." He concluded by saying, "Such a course would be unwise as there is not the least probability that congress will ever comply."[85]

As the convention grappled with slavery's divisive politics, a patchwork plan to protect slaveholders' power emerged. The constitution declared that "slavery and involuntary servitude shall not be hereafter introduced" into Illinois, while exempting all slaves and servants already in the state. The constitution also stated that all servitude contracts would remain in force and that African Americans would be held to specific performance of their terms of service. Last, Kentucky masters could continue to bring slaves into the state to work in the salt marshes for up to one year, but only until 1825. "The question of slavery is settled," one press account noted. It continued, "The slaves belonging to the French are secured. . . . The indentures of negroes brought into the state previous to this period are made good."[86]

Notably, the constitution protected the three major sources of bound labor and organized them into three legal categories: "French Negroes" born into bondage, servants held to lifelong contracts, and slaves annually trafficked into Illinois.[87]

When Illinois presented its constitution to Congress for ratification, antislavery members in the chamber seized on its proslavery provisions. Congressman James Tallmadge of New York asserted that "the principle of slavery, if not adopted in the constitution, was at least not sufficiently prohibited."[88] He reminded his colleagues that the Northwest Ordinance barred slavery from the region. According to his reading of the constitution, it "contravened" the exclusion of slaves from Illinois "either in the letter or the spirit." Ratification of the constitution, he continued, "embraced a complete recognition of existing slavery . . . particularly the passage wherein they permit the hiring of slaves [from Kentucky into Illinois] . . . for any number of consecutive years."[89] Tallmadge's speech aroused a very brief debate in the chamber, and George Poindexter of Mississippi asserted that Illinois had "virtually complied" with the Northwest Ordinance, just as Ohio and Indiana had.[90] Others insisted that Congress had no power to alter or amend a state constitution, only to accept or reject it. In short order, Congress quickly adopted the constitution: only thirty-four congressmen, all from northern states, voted against statehood. The congressmen did not record why they objected, but given the regional opposition, it may have been because Tallmadge persuaded them that slavery would live on in Illinois. Whatever their motivations, their opposition was not strong enough, and slaveholders in Illinois had succeeded in circumventing a ban on slavery in Illinois.[91]

Having achieved statehood without abolishing slavery, Illinois residents promptly elected slaveholders to statewide offices. Shadrach Bond, the first governor, had moved to Illinois from Maryland and in 1820 had at least a dozen servants and slaves. Pierre Menard, the lieutenant governor, was a prominent French trader who owned just over a dozen bondsmen at the time of his election. Menard's place in statewide office reflects the ways French Illinois communities found entry into the new political landscape. No obvious antagonism existed between the French and Anglophone politicians, and collaboration at the local and statewide levels appeared to be the norm. The first two U.S. senators, Ninian Edwards and Jesse Thomas, both had migrated to Illinois from the Upper South, and each owned a few slaves. Edwards had previously served as chief judge on Kentucky's

Supreme Court and in that capacity had beaten back a 1799 attempt to pass an antislavery constitution in the bluegrass state. Illinois's first slate of elected officials reflected a larger reality about the state: newcomers and French inhabitants worked side by side to keep slavery alive, and slaveholders had a broad authority over the state's politics.[92]

Given the cast of proslavery statewide officeholders, it is perhaps not surprising that they quickly passed a set of restrictive Black Laws that denied black citizenship in the state. While several other states had a set of Black Laws, the ones on Illinois's books were among the most restrictive set of antiblack legislation in the antebellum nation. Passed in 1819 and revised in 1853, the Black Laws limited black citizenship, denying African Americans the vote and the ability to testify in court. They restricted the mobility of African Americans and barred them from militia service and gun ownership.[93] Other states passed Black Laws that included similar provisions. Illinois's laws went further in their restrictions on black people's liberty and required all African Americans to record their manumission documents at the county courthouse and pay a bond of $500, later raised to $1,000, to obtain a certificate of freedom. If a fully legal system of slavery became untenable in the wake of Illinois's statehood in 1818, state lawmakers found ways to shore up racial hierarchy and exclude freed men and women from full citizenship.

Illinois's statehood in 1818 and its first elections played out amid a national crisis over slavery, national expansion, and statehood. In the same session of Congress in which James Tallmadge sparked a debate over Illinois's constitution, he also helped ignite a controversy over Missouri's statehood. Although Missouri had proposed entering the union without banning slavery, segments of Congress hoped to stop this. In March 1819, Tallmadge offered an amendment to the Missouri constitution that banned slavery in the state, triggering a political firestorm that pitted southern and northern constituencies against each other. No less a figure than former President Thomas Jefferson advocated against the Tallmadge Amendment. For two years, Congress and the nation remained deadlocked. Eventually, Jesse Thomas, one of Illinois's senators, and others brokered a complicated compromise.[94] In 1821, Maine would enter the union as a free state, and slavery would be banned north of the 36′ 60″ parallel. In exchange, Missouri entered the union with slavery intact, and the principle that states would be on equal footing with each other and not subject to congressional interference in their constitutions won the day.[95] Throughout the long turmoil,

Ninian Edwards and Jesse Thomas, Illinois's two senators, consistently voted against the Tallmadge Amendment to the Missouri constitution. This national political reality helped to frame statewide debates over slavery, as it appeared that Illinois consistently sided with southern slaveholders.

The 1822 governor's race turned into a testing ground of proslavery politics in Illinois. While many of the southern migrants to the state advocated for a slave economy, some southern migrants had left their homes to escape slavery's influence on their lives. What's more, many of these migrants into the state hoped to exclude African Americans from Illinois entirely. They cheered on the state's Black Codes, and they extolled the advantages of free labor and yeoman farming. A sizable block of migrants into the state subscribed to this strain of antislavery and antiblack thinking, which believed in the superiority of free labor and the inferiority of African Americans.[96] In time, they found a leader in Edward Coles. Coles had been private secretary to President James Madison, and he moved to Illinois from Virginia in 1808, thinking his ambitions for office would fare better in the Prairie State. Like fellow Virginians, he brought slaves with him, but he saw no place for slavery in Illinois and freed all ten of them on arrival. Coles made slavery a cornerstone issue in his campaign, and he garnered support for his position, winning a third of the popular vote in the three-way race of 1822. He took the governorship with just 200 more votes than his closest rival, a former chief justice of the Illinois Supreme Court who ran on permitting slavery's further introduction into Illinois. After eking out his win, Coles demanded that the legislature abolish slavery in Illinois.[97]

Proslavery forces refused to accede to Coles's ultimatum. They quickly began a campaign to amend the state constitution so that it legalized the future introduction of slavery, and they called for a convention to rework the state charter. This attempt to amend the constitution to permit slavery's future introduction threatened to upend the uneasy balance of power that stood in the wake of the Missouri crisis. Notwithstanding the national political implications, proslavery figures pressed their case. In Randolph County, proslavery residents circulated petitions across the rural landscape.[98] Several prominent citizens joined in this campaign, including the wealthy merchant John Edgar and future senator Elias Kent Kane. Alongside these well-to-do citizens were signatures of modest landholders who may have had only a single servant.[99] The proconvention forces pushed for slavery's total legalization, but they were defeated at the polls, with 57 percent voting against a constitutional convention (6,650 to 4,997). According to John Reynolds—

who would become governor in the 1830s—during "the elections through the State, the utmost exertions prevailed, but no riots. The aged and crippled were carried to the polls, and men voted on this occasion that had not seen the ballot box before in twenty years."[100] The intense political campaigns led to high turnout—in excess of 80 percent statewide. The voting broke along regional lines, with the southern segments of the state voting decisively to amend the constitution. In Gallatin County, a majority of nearly 80 percent voted for the convention, while in the central portions of the state, where Coles had won his support the previous year, opposition to the convention ran nearly as strong.[101]

Amid the extended campaign, a few sources of opposition to the convention came to the fore. First, some of this resistance to the convention came from a tiny cadre of abolitionists who sought to see the nation abolish slavery writ large. Yet during the 1820s, very few people in the state counted themselves among the ranks of abolitionists. Most of the opposition to slavery's full legalization came from settlers who believed in the superiority of free soil and free labor, embracing those tenets decades before leaders of the Republican Party advanced their version of free labor ideology.[102] A final strain of opposition emerged from the factions that formed around leading political figures in the state.[103] As had happened in Indiana, some support for antislavery politics came from segments of voters who wanted to topple the state's leaders from power. In the convention movement, they hit their mark. Proslavery leaders who had long wielded influence over territorial and state politics faced defeat.

Despite the outcome of Illinois's convention movement, slaveholders and nonslaveholders alike suspected that the issue would continue as a source of political conflict for years to come. "There was a great fuss about slavery . . . at our next election it will be revived I expect," one farmer wrote in 1824, immediately after the convention movement failed.[104] Others agreed that the future was uncertain. In 1822, Benjamin Farmer, a freeholder in Sangamon County, put specific provisions on what to do with his slaves in his will. He directed that "a negro boy named Tom and a negro girl named Franky" were to be "hired out until it is ascertained whether slavery will be admitted in this state." He continued if it is "not admitted . . . I wish the two negroes to be sold by my wife" into a slave state. "But if slavery is admitted . . . I wish the two negroes to be kept in the family."[105]

Confronting threats to their power from enslaved African Americans and their small but growing constituency of antislavery allies, people like

Edward Coles and his supporters, masters turned to the press to articulate a defense for the jerry-rigged system of slavery and servitude in the state. Ninian Edwards emerged as the most vocal advocate for Illinois's system of bondage. Born in Maryland, Edwards had relocated to Kentucky in the 1790s. In 1809, President James Madison appointed him the first and only governor of the Illinois territory, at which time he fended off criticism of Illinois's servitude laws. After statehood, Edwards became one of Illinois's first U.S. senators. In 1824, he resigned from the Senate and accepted a diplomatic appointment to Mexico. Two years later, at the expiration of his service, Edwards returned to Illinois and won the governorship.[106] During the 1820s—while still a U.S. senator—Edwards took to the press defend the voluntary nature of the state's indenture system. Aware that national laws barred involuntary servitude, he asserted that legal prohibitions on "involuntary servitude . . . must have a limited construction" to include only "outright slavery." He continued that indentureship was a "benefit to slaves, and not repugnant to the public interest." Consequently, Edwards saw "no evil in allow[ing] them to be made."[107] For Edwards, slaves who were coerced to sign a lifelong uncompensated indenture contract fell within the broad scope of free and voluntary labor because they had supposedly consented to their servitude.

Edwards insisted that no gradual emancipation laws applied to Illinois and argued for slavery's legality in light of its long history of French colonialism and its slave economy. He asserted that it was "erroneous" to claim that "our negroes are all entitled to their freedom."[108] According to Edwards, "Slavery existed under the Governments of France & England and was permitted by Congress" under the terms of the cession of Virginia, which stipulated, as Edward quoted, that "settlers &c. should have their possession & titles confirmed to them and be protected in the enjoyment of their rights & of which right that to hold their slaves was as perfect . . . as to hold any other species of property."[109] He continued by saying that the "conclusion is irresistible that . . . Congress intended to protect the inhabitants of their Territory in the enjoyment of their rights to their slaves."[110] Edwards insisted that "Congress has never freed a single slave, and never even intended to."[111] He concluded that state and national law had "done nothing to change the common law principle *partus sequiter ventrem*," which held that children's condition of servitude followed their mother. As Edwards pointed out, "The posterity of slaves born since the Ordinance [is] completely subject to [its] operation."[112] Slavery was legal in

Illinois, Edwards insisted, because of French colonialism in earlier generations.

Repeatedly, proslavery advocates advanced Edwards's arguments and rejected any claims that Congress had fully banned slavery and servitude from Illinois. In various opinion pieces, authors of both sides conceded Edwards's point: that Virginia ceded the territory on the condition that citizens would be "protected in the enjoyment of their rights and liberties."[113] An anonymous author asserted in the Kaskaskia *Republican Advocate* that most masters "hold wat are called French Slaves, (which were, by the laws of France and Virginia, *property*, rightfully acquired) . . . as much property in the eye of the law as land or any thing else."[114] Still another defended the lawfulness of the servitude system by asserting that "many negroes bound themselves to serve" and that "the people have the indisputable right to permit blacks voluntarily to indenture themselves for such time as they may elect."[115] These authors maintained that state law protected "French Negroes" as human property and sanctioned indentured servants as another form of chattel. They emphasized that enslaved African Americans signed voluntary agreements, and therefore indentureship could not be construed as involuntary.

These justifications for slavery's continued presence in Illinois were put to the test. Notably, bound African Americans initiated the early assault on proslavery politics. Across the state, slaves tried an array of legal tactics in their suits for freedom. Eventually, some of their strategies worked. In 1820, an adept enslaved litigator sued her master. Amy had been sold from Kentucky into Illinois, where she was kept in slavery for years. When her master attempted to sell her out of the salt marshes into the counties that bordered the Mississippi River, she sued for her freedom, asserting that her master had failed to sign her to a servitude contract when he relocated from Kentucky. Amy argued that the failure voided her subsequent sale. It is not clear why Amy delayed in bringing her suit, but her timing—like Bob and Lydia's a decade before her—worked to her advantage. At the time she began litigation, Amy had been passed from a petty farmer to Ettienne Pensoneau, one of Illinois's wealthy French businessmen: when she sued for damages, she collected more than $400 along with her freedom.[116]

Before long, challenges to slavery came to the Illinois Supreme Court, which in 1828 heard two cases that posed profound threats to contract bondage. In *Nance v. Howard* (1828) and *Phoebe v. William Jay* (1828), indentured servants, with the help of local attorneys, petitioned the court to invalidate their indentures by arguing that slaves could not sign contracts. Consequently, servitude could only be understood as involuntary labor. This argument faced daunting odds. The state supreme court, like so much of the state's political leadership, comprised justices with clear proslavery politics. For instance, in 1822, Joseph Philips, the first chief justice of Illinois, joined the proconvention forces that proposed legalizing slavery in the state. Philips had stepped down by 1828, but the bench was still proslavery. Theophius Smith, who served from the 1820s to the 1840s, edited a proslavery newspaper and also had joined the proconvention movement. The justices had to answer questions about slavery and servitude under unique legal circumstances. The 1787 Northwest Territory Ordinance and the 1818 Illinois state constitution barred bound labor from the state while also sanctioning voluntary servitude. Consequently, a slave's will, always a conundrum for jurists, became doubly confounding. In Illinois, slaves had to consent voluntarily to becoming servants, which in turn would make them property without volition.

The first case, *Nance, a Negro Girl v. John Howard* (1828), began when Nance, an indentured servant, was sold at auction, clapped in chains, and delivered to another owner. On July 12, 1827, Thomas Cox, a middling farmer in Springfield, Illinois, had his "goods and chattels [and] lands" sold at public auction to cover a debt. Two servants, Nance and Dice, were among the property put up for sale.[117] Cox held Nance under a servitude contract that bound her to Cox until she reached age twenty-eight. At auction, Nathan Cromwell "became the highest and best bidder and the purchaser of Nance." He settled the sale and "the said Coroner in pursuance of said sale did deliver said Nance to the said Cromwell . . . [and] the said Nance voluntarily and of her own free will and consent did agree to go with the said Cromwell to his place of residence in Sangamo."[118]

Witnesses of the sale, including Cox's wife Jane, disputed this version of events. According to Jane Cox, during the sale, "she saw said Nance . . . confined with chains; that said Nance became very sick . . . thus confined."[119] After seeing the coroner "sell said Nance," she overheard Cromwell ask "Nance if she would go and live with him and said Nance refused and presented she would not." The county official then "tied her and took her back to the old salt house. That after this . . . Cromwell took her off."[120] Within a year of sale, Nance filed a freedom suit, petitioning the circuit court in Sangamon County to compel her manumission. She asserted her sale "was forced against her will and consent" and that she was "restrained of her said personal liberty by said Cromwell."[121] At trial, Nance's suit for freedom failed, and the circuit court upheld her sale to Cromwell as a simple property transfer.[122] She appealed her decision to the state supreme court, where Nance insisted she did not consent to her sale and deserved her freedom. The case compelled the justices to explore if an unfree worker could consent to being sold as property.

After dissecting Illinois law—in particular the 1807 Act Concerning the Introduction of Negroes and Mulattos—the supreme court found that "the time of service of such [indentured] negroes and mulattos may be sold on execution."[123] The court went on to declare that "the legislature have always regarded them as property" such that "indentured and registered servants must be regarded as goods and chattels, and liable to be taken and sold."[124] They added an important qualifying remark to this decision: "service may be assigned . . . [to another] master, with the consent of the servant."[125] The supreme court of Illinois upheld Nance's sale to Cromwell and concluded that Nance freely consented to be sold at public auction as chattel. In sanctioning Nance's status as human property, the court ignored the coercion—the chains and threat of violence—that compelled her submission. In light of this ruling, bound labor's survival in Illinois relied on African Americans' extorted consent.

In the same term, the justices heard another challenge to bondage in the state. In *Phoebe v. William Jay* (1828), they had to consider if the newly minted constitution, along with the ordinance of 1787, invalidated her servitude in absolute terms.[126] Specifically, the court had to consider if the act of transforming a slave into a servant violated the ban on involuntary servitude. In 1814, Joseph Jay migrated into Illinois with his slave Phoebe and signed her to a forty-year indentureship, which he properly recorded with the county clerk. When Jay died in 1827, Phoebe entered his estate as movable property, and Jay's son, William, took possession of her. Phoebe appears to have resisted this transfer, and William Jay "had necessarily to use a little force and beating" to compel her "to attend to and to perform the duties of an indentured servant." Phoebe brought a suit against her master for trespass and false imprisonment and demanded her freedom.[127] Her case asserted that masters could not coerce consent to create property in people. The suit challenged masters' ability to translate social power over African Americans into legal authority to hold servants in Illinois.

The court at first signaled that Phoebe deserved her freedom. Asking if a slave could consent to a servitude contract, it reached a sweeping conclusion, asserting any claim that her contract was voluntary servitude constituted an "insult to common sense."[128] According to the majority opinion, "If the only question to be decided was, whether this law of the territory of Illinois conflicted with the Ordinance," the court "should have no hesitation saying it did." The opinion continued, "Nothing can be conceived farther from the truth than the idea that there could be a voluntary contract between the negro and his master." The decision rejected any claim that slaves had "free agency" to sign servitude contracts. In short, the court concluded "the indenturing was in effect an involuntary servitude for a period of years and was void being in violation of the Ordinance."[129] In its ruling, the court acknowledged what the uneven terrain of freedom in Illinois made manifest—African Americans did not voluntarily consent to their servitude and the state's servitude system violated the state constitution and the federal ban.

Notwithstanding this sweeping language, the ruling kept Phoebe in servitude. Using a finely parsed reading of the laws, the court held that when Congress accepted Illinois's 1818 constitution—which mandated the validity of all existing servitude contracts—it unknowingly revised the state's prohibitions on unfree labor. Although the 1818 constitution prohibited involuntary servitude, the court found that its provisions did not protect Phoebe from serving out her contract. The chief judge asserted, "Had the plaintiff asserted her right to freedom previous to the adoption of the constitution of this state, she would, in my opinion have been entitled to it. When the constitution of this state was presented to Congress in order to [secure] our admission into the Union, the attention of that body was called to that clause of our Constitution," and by accepting the constitution, they "gave their consent to the abrogation of so much of the Ordinance" as was necessary to uphold contract bondage in Illinois.[130] In short, Phoebe's indenture was a form of involuntary servitude prohibited by one portion of the state constitution, yet, because of another provision, she was not entitled to her freedom. The court held that Phoebe was chattel without a will, but it also maintained in the same term that Nance was a voluntary servant consenting her subordination. In the court's own words, contract bondage relied on a legal foundation that insulted common sense. These rulings meant that attempts to end slavery and servitude had to proceed in an incremental, case-by-case manner, since the high court refused to interpret the laws in a way that would do away with bound labor in one sweeping ruling.

* * *

This legal and political climate stood in stark contrast to the thinking of statewide officials in northern states along the eastern seaboard. Across the mid-Atlantic, various state legislatures had passed gradual emancipation laws that freed all slaves born after a particular date. These antislavery laws had support among leaders in Pennsylvania and New York. In time, some elected officials concluded that abolition's glacial pace had to accelerate and that any loopholes for emancipation had to end. The New York State Supreme Court invalidated long-term uncompensated indentures, and in 1827, the legislature issued a general emancipation law just as Ninian Edwards put forth his broad defense of slavery and servitude in his state.[131] The New York act freed roughly 20,000 African Americans in a single instance, making it the largest general emancipation up to that point in the nation's history. This trend toward abolition extended even to neighboring New Jersey, where slavery had been more intractable. Although thousands of African Americans remained in bondage and many thousands more labored as term slaves, the state did host an abolition society, and in 1820, its legislature reaffirmed the gradual emancipation statute that had passed over a decade before. By the 1830s, the efforts to stymie emancipation in New Jersey, like other places in the mid-Atlantic, had faltered in the wake of growing antislavery forces.[132] Antislavery laws and their broad construction were becoming the norm in other northern states. Illinois's political leaders, in contrast, insisted on construing congressional and state prohibitions against slavery as narrowly as possible.

Even with the servitude system intact and the "French Negroes" remaining in the state, things would not stay as they were. Illinois masters increasingly had to reinvent unfree labor. While servitude contracts introduced a façade of freedom, they also retained most of the characteristics of bondage. Workers like Nance and Phoebe could be clapped in chains and sold at auction owing to the pretext that they consented to bondage. Still, no matter the skill with which masters navigated the new legal landscape, by the late 1820s, a growing number of Illinois's bound workers had escaped their masters' grasp; ironically, this was possible because of the very servitude system that had been designed to perpetuate bondage. But progress toward emancipation was halting and uneven, which meant that African Americans and their white allies would have to adopt new antislavery tactics. Women like Nance, Phoebe, Dunky, and Cynthia Ann would need new allies in their struggle, and the antislavery movement in Illinois was small. That would change in a few short years.

CHAPTER 5

Paths to Independence

John and Priscilla Baltimore faced an uncertain future when they migrated to Illinois. Born slaves in Missouri, by the 1820s, they had managed to scrape together $1,100 and purchase their freedom. They wanted to live in a free state and build a new life, which in part motivated their migration across the Mississippi. In 1829, they settled in St. Clair County, Illinois, along with a dozen other free black families who had made the migration together. Together they founded Brooklyn, an all-black town. By the 1840s, John and Priscilla had become landowners, and their families enjoyed a growing civic life in Brooklyn. With leadership from the Rev. William Paul Quinn, the African Methodist Episcopal Church opened a congregation there. By owning land, protecting their families, and building black institutions, John and Priscilla Baltimore forged a secure freedom.

Yet that freedom stood always in the shadow of slavery. When the Baltimore family arrived in Illinois, human bondage clung to life in St. Clair County, where Brooklyn was located. The growing free black community in the town lived alongside the state's remaining population of "French Negroes," descendants of the original African and Indian slaves that French settlers held in the Illinois Country. By the 1830s, the number of "French Negroes" had dropped to a few hundred. Their masters were a familiar cast: the Bienvenu, Beauvais, Menard, and Pensoneau families, which had all lived in Illinois since the late eighteenth century. Deep in southern Illinois, "French Negroes" continued to be born into slavery, to work in the agrarian economy and the salt marshes, and to be bought and sold as chattel. It would not be long before the black community in Brooklyn set its sights on at last freeing the slaves in rural Illinois. Together with enslaved men and women, the residents of black towns waged an assault on slavery in Illinois.[1]

These residents offered critical support in the attack on the pockets of human bondage that existed in Illinois. Brooklyn was one of many black towns that fostered a deep hatred for slavery and helped push forward the state's emancipation process. During the 1830s and 1840s, black migration into Illinois helped remake the state's rural landscape. Between 1829 and 1840, migrants founded four black towns, all in the counties where slavery persisted—not just St. Clair County along the Mississippi River but Pope County along the Ohio River, as well. Free African Americans living in these towns could offer enslaved people the resources they needed to escape bondage: knowledge of the law, ties to antislavery attorneys, relationships with witnesses who could help provide evidence in courts, and some money to pay legal costs. Residents in black towns did not simply retreat to Illinois from neighboring slave states and isolate themselves from the hostile white community in the Upper South. Instead, they planted their communities where slaves needed them the most.[2]

In Illinois's freedom villages, a sophisticated use of the law became commonplace, and that legal knowledge and skill proved to be an existential threat to slavery in the state. African Americans used their experience with the law, which included self-purchase, signing servitude contracts, selling their labor, and even litigation, to craft local legal strategies that helped support legal emancipation.[3] All African Americans, no matter their circumstances, had to undergo a legal process to live in freedom in Illinois. This was especially true because Illinois's Black Laws required African Americans to register proof of their freedom at the courthouses. Most commonly this involved showing a will, an expired servitude contract, or a receipt for self-purchase. Similarly, all masters had to register servants and slaves with local officials. Building on their earlier history of contesting—albeit often in small ways—Illinois's uneven servitude regime, African Americans pieced together a knowledge of the law that they then wielded in their daily quests for freedom.

Besides a working knowledge of the law, African Americans hoping to exit bondage needed to assemble freedom networks comprising a broad cast of allies. To use the courts, they needed help from attorneys, witnesses, judges, clerks, and juries. Lifelong servants had to find specific violations of contract law, and "French Negroes" had to prove some technical legal violation to win their freedom. While several northern states had passed emancipation statutes and expansive antikidnapping laws, as well as created manumission societies to enforce those provisions, Illinois lagged behind.

African Americans in Illinois could not rely on an antislavery committee, enforce an emancipation law, draw on a ready corpus of antislavery attorneys, summon black urban institutions to their cases, or call on a sympathetic press to publicize their cause. Before the 1830s, Illinois hosted no major urban black population, had no statewide abolition society, and chartered no abolitionist newspapers, and the legislature had little interest in hastening slavery's abolition. In the absence of these resources, finding freedom was a daunting task, and though there were some willing allies, support from the state's white population was intermittent. Lawyers could be hired and fired, and some white attorneys hostile toward slavery accepted slaveholders as clients based on their ability to pay rather than out of principle.[4]

Initially in short supply, white allies became more numerous as new migrants flooded into the state. By the 1830s, Illinois had attracted a new set of settlers, and the state was a crossroads for domestic and international immigrants who found themselves drawn into the freedom campaigns that African Americans initiated. From the late 1820s on, migrants from New England, the mid-Atlantic region, and Western Europe poured into Illinois. They tended to settle in the state's northern districts, especially Chicago, and their presence offered African Americans new resources in their campaigns against bondage. With a rapidly changing population, the state's laws and politics also underwent broad shifts. The state's judges, clerks, prosecutors, and juries all drew from these new immigrant populations, and an increasing number of attorneys hostile to slavery arrived on the scene. Elected political leaders used their appointment powers to staff the judiciary with Yankee and mid-Atlantic migrants hostile to slavery.

Illinois had long been a meeting ground of diverse slaveries and conflicting empires, and by the 1830s, a new set of migrants had reshaped the conflicts over slavery and freedom. "French Negroes" pushed forward a long process of emancipation that brought them through various stages of unfreedom, including term slavery, provisional emancipation, captivity, and, finally, freedom. African Americans drew on the community's legal knowledge to use local courts to their advantage, and they enlisted the state's new migrants to help them prevail in their cause. Relying on the newly arrived black and white migrants to serve as witnesses and lawyers, unfree African Americans stitched together a team of allies that supported their quest for freedom. Because Illinois's statutes targeted freed African Americans with burdensome registration requirements, they gained

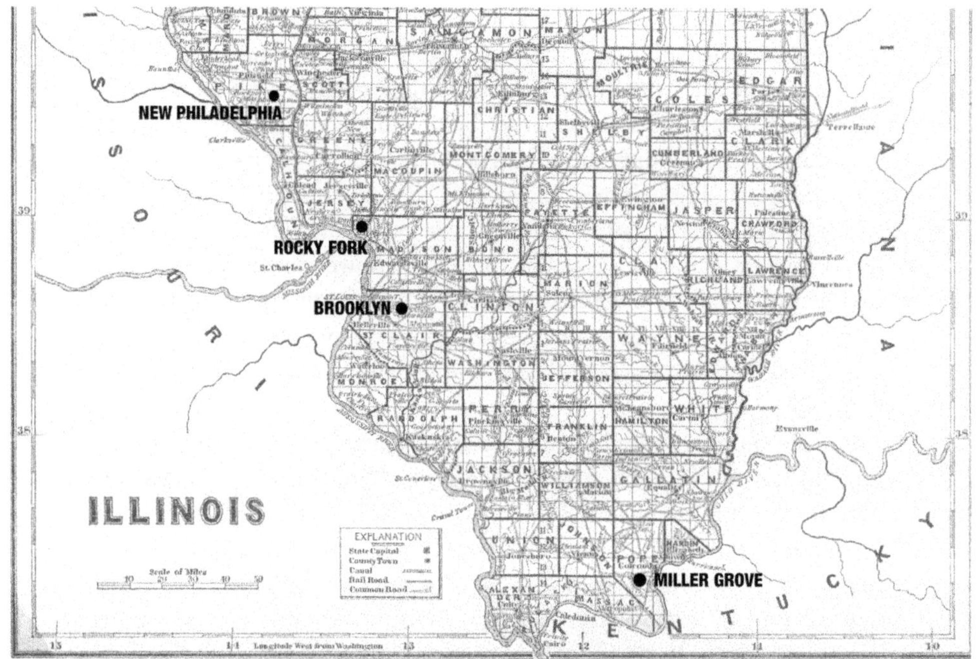

Figure 8. Location of black freedom villages in Illinois. Map created by Christopher Richmond.

exposure to the law and skill in navigating legal processes. In time, African Americans leaving slavery and servitude built networks of allies who helped free the last population of enslaved people, often one case at a time. The campaigns for freedom took this arduous path because African Americans had to combat the shape-shifting slave systems that trapped them in bondage. Freedom was a process of struggle and work that did not come simply from passing and enforcing an emancipation law.

* * *

In Illinois, as elsewhere, emancipation did not happen at a given moment but played out as a protracted, contested, and costly process. In light of the state's Black Laws, which mandated that freed men and women post emancipation bonds at local courthouses, a wide cast of African Americans spent months or even years moving between a state of slavery and a condition of freedom. This was in part true because meeting the registration requirements spelled out in the Black Laws was no simple task. Free African Americans could record their master's will, an expired servitude contract, manumission papers, or other legal proof of freedom at the county clerk's office. African Americans who lacked these documents had to find two witnesses who would swear to their free status. All of this was required to show that freed men and women would not become public charges, as stipulated by the statute. And as they went about assembling this evidence, they remained in limbo: slaves no more but not yet secure in their legal freedom.

Slaves could spend years suspended between slavery and freedom, and the process of emancipation could bring people from slavery to freedom, into captivity, and back into freedom, as happened to John Merry. An Illinois "French Negro," Merry traveled through degrees of unfreedom as part of a long process of emancipation. He was born in Cahokia around 1790 "of a black mother who was claimed and held as a slave."[5] At birth, both his "father and mother were slaves."[6] The child of slaves, Merry faced a grim future when Illinois lawmakers exempted "French Negroes" from abolition laws, leaving him living "in servitude, in the character of a slave."[7] But by the 1820s, Merry had become "desirous of obtaining his natural freedom."[8] To effect his manumission, he "entered into a verbal agreement with" his owner, Louis Pensoneau, to "obtain his natural liberty." Pensoneau was a French slaveholder whose family had migrated to the region at the turn of the nineteenth century. He owned several slaves, and into the 1830s, his slaves received baptismal sacraments in the local church. After some negotiation, "it was agreed that the said Louis Pensinno should liberate and discharge . . . [him] from servitude as a slave, for the consideration of the sum of four hundred and fifty dollars." Two years later, Merry paid half of his price and won conditional emancipation when Pensoneau "did liberate and discharge" Merry from servitude.[9] In the years he spent working to earn the final installment on his purchase price, Merry, like many in Illinois, remained in a tenuous limbo between slavery and freedom.

Merry appeared to be on a path toward full emancipation, but Pensoneau adapted and forced Merry into captivity to extract yet more profit. Facing the prospect of Merry's emancipation, Pensoneau "intended to cheat and defraud" Merry "out of the sum of money paid" and reduce him "to a state of slavery and servitude for life."[10] Pensoneau tracked down Merry in

St. Louis, where he had hired himself out and "seized . . . [Merry] by force and put . . . [him] into the common jail, as his slave." Clapping Merry into "chains and manacles," Pensoneau placed him "on board a certain steam boat bound for the City of New Orleans," consigning him to "John G. Stephenson, then a commission merchant in the City of New Orleans with order to sell . . . [him] as a slave."[11] In New Orleans, Merry stood for sale at public auction, and the highest bidder sent him to a nearby plantation.

Even in the depths of the plantation South, Merry had ties with Illinois residents who might help him escape. He had a knowledge of Illinois law, likely gleaned from his own bartering over self-purchase, and a resilient drive to live in freedom. While in Mississippi, he "absconded from the possession" of his new owner and "after many hardships reached Cahokia in the County of St. Clair in the State of Illinois."[12] Relying on runaway networks and help from strangers across North America, Merry "again was in the possession of his natural and legal liberty." Merry likely knew he needed proof of his legal freedom, and he quickly began a lawsuit against his former master. William Carr, a white attorney, undertook his case. Together, Merry and Carr summoned several residents of St. Clair County to support his "application for freedom."[13] In one deposition, August Trottier testified that he had known Merry from "his birth about thirty five or thirty six" years ago. In another affidavit, Pierre Bennet testified he knew that "Louis Pencenneau" had sent Merry "to New Orleans," and he urged that the court "give him his freedom." In light of this evidence, John Merry won both freedom and financial compensation.[14] Merry then would have had to register proof of his freedom at the local courthouse and post an emancipation bond in order to live in a secure freedom. The long process of emancipation Merry experienced—self-purchase, captivity, escape and clandestine migration north, litigation, and registration—required him to piece together legal knowledge and assemble a cast of allies, including witnesses and attorneys, running from bondage, and navigating local legal bureaucracy.

Merry's case was exceptional for its complexity, but all African Americans had some exposure to the law as they went through processes of emancipation. They had four major ways to prove their freedom. First, migrants into Illinois had to show evidence that they had been free in their native state. Second, freed men and women already residing in the state had to provide documents—such as wills or self-purchase agreements—that included a sworn affidavit from a municipal official testifying to their

Table 1. Emancipation Bonds Posted in Illinois by Freed Slaves

Year	*Emancipation in Illinois*	*Migration into Illinois*	*Total*
Pre-1800	5	2	7
1800–1814	0	2	2
1815–19	49	12	61
1820–24	28	25	53
1825–29	65	76	141
1830–34	63	37	100
1835–39	86	90	176
1840–44	69	133	202
1845–49	106	128	234
1850–54	68	76	144
Post-1855	16	7	23
Total	555	588	1,143

authenticity. Alternatively, two witnesses could certify an African American man or woman's free status.[15] The third and fourth—much less common—routes to emancipation were runaway slaves who petitioned for freedom and unfree African Americans who sued their masters. Runaways who sheriffs captured in Illinois could earn a legal freedom. After their capture and jailing, the local official would hire them out to an overseer to work for one year, and notice of their capture and auction had to be posted in the local newspapers. At the end of that year, if nobody had claimed them, runaway slaves could petition for freedom papers. To earn a freedom certificate, convicted runaways had to produce proof of faithful service for one year and had to show that their capture had been advertised in a local paper and that no one had attempted to claim them as a slave in Illinois courts. Dozens of runaways completed this process and obtained their legal freedom. And, just as rarely, men and women at times sued their masters for freedom. Mounting a freedom suit brought enormous risks of retaliation and required African Americans to have access to capital, witnesses, and, if possible, an attorney. Despite these high barriers, African Americans litigated on their own behalf, discovered technical legal violations, and prosecuted cases successfully.[16]

Leaving servitude or slavery, proving lawful freedom at local courthouses, posting emancipation bonds, at times resisting captivity and reenslavement, and retaining freedom papers constituted the long process of emancipation. By the 1820s, a small but growing number of people had walked these paths out of bondage. Masters began to free children born in Illinois who by law exited term slavery when they reached the age of majority.[17] In other cases, African Americans bound to shorter and compensated indentures found their freedom. For instance, in 1831, Charles and Maria Adams completed their twenty- and sixteen-year indentureships and posted emancipation bonds at the courthouse. The Adams family had been servants to former governor Ninian Edwards and had skills they could hire out, including domestic labor and farming. They relocated to Gallatin County with their children and began a prosperous life in freedom.[18] For many African Americans, freedom came late, as some manumissions came after servants were past their productive years. For example, three different masters freed John Morrison, Elizabeth Jones, and Elizabeth as they approached the end of their lives. Aged sixty-eight, seventy-eight, and eighty-eight, respectively, these free people nearing the end of their lives received no compensation for a lifetime of work and likely lived out their final days in grinding poverty.[19] Yet other freed men and women left slavery early and found ways to buy land that would help secure their future. For instance, in 1818, Maria, "a free black woman," bought a parcel of land in Randolph County for $66.[20] In 1829, Therese, "a free woman," bought a tract of land in Randolph County for $25.[21]

African Americans traversing the long process of emancipation found new allies among the migrants from New England who populated the state. One ally was Henry Eddy, who migrated to Illinois from Vermont in the 1820s. After settling in Gallatin County, on the banks of the Ohio River bordering Kentucky, he founded *The Illinois Emigrant*, one of the state's earliest newspapers. Soon thereafter, he joined the Illinois state bar and began a private law practice, routinely taking on freedom suits and winning important victories. In 1826, Eddy won election to the state assembly. After serving one term, he returned to private life and became one of Illinois's most distinguished lawyers, serving as counsel for the Illinois state bank.[22] During his ascent, he filed several suits for freedom and repeatedly acted as a witness for people in pursuit of freedom. Before long, the state's bound population considered him a powerful ally.[23]

In the 1820s, Eddy began taking on freedom suits that African Americans initiated. In 1828, Lucinda, who "worked in the salt works in or near Shawneetown," was "stolen and run off" and "sold into slavery" in Tennessee.[24] She convinced a sympathetic Tennessee resident to reach out to allies in Shawneetown and ask for evidence of her freedom. According to the correspondent, Lucinda thought there was an Illinois attorney who would help win her freedom. She insisted that "a man by the name of Champ or Carr" and also a "lawyer by the name of Eddy . . . and one by the name of Green also know her to be a free woman."[25] It is not known if Lucinda won her freedom. However, she knew Eddy by name, and that knowledge enabled legal action. Moreover, her case underlines the reality that African Americans working toward freedom always faced the risk of being kidnapped and sold into slavery in a neighboring state.

In case after case, relationships between black and white opponents of slavery sustained the struggle against human bondage in Illinois. In one case in 1829, Eddy "commenced a suit in the Jackson circuit court against Mr. Linn and others" on behalf of "Sukey, a woman of color." He "undertook the plaintiff's case" in "hopes she will ultimately have justice done her and obtain freedom." While prosecuting the case, Eddy and another attorney argued that "that the Defend[ants]s have no more right to hold the pl[ainti]ff in slavery according to the laws of Ill[inois]."[26] The outcome of this case is not known, but it underscores the legal networks that African Americans assembled to climb out of bondage. Sukey lived in Jackson County—on the opposite side of the state from Eddy, but his reputation as a skilled, sympathetic attorney traveled around the state, perhaps carried by bound workers hired out in different sections of the state.

The networks between slaves and free white allies, like those that Sukey and Lucinda mobilized, enabled successful emancipation lawsuits. In 1828, a slaveholder kidnapped Frank Granger, a black resident of Gallatin County, and carried him into slavery in Tennessee. Granger convinced a Tennessee-based opponent of slavery to write Eddy asking him "to establish the Freedom of Frank."[27] Eddy assembled the necessary papers and dispatched them to Tennessee. In the next term of the circuit court of Tipton County, Tennessee, Frank won his freedom. Frank's relationship with this attorney helped him use the courts to secure his freedom—Frank Granger knew whom to contact to win his case.

Bound workers had to initiate contact and persuade lawyers like Henry Eddy to take their case. At a minimum, this process required paying Eddy's legal fees, which in protracted cases could be substantial. Unlike in some northern states, there was no cadre of lawyers willing to take these cases for free. One of Eddy's acquaintances wrote asking him to take on a new suit for freedom, and although he did "not know what agreement you have made for a fee," he "believe[d] the Plff will do all she can to pay you what she promises." He urged Eddy to take the case and "promise[d] to be security for the plff in the amount of [a] reasonable fee to you." Eddy's colleague acknowledged that litigating against slavery was also a business: "I believe your humanity would incline you to defend the rights of the oppressed how degraded so ever their condition. But it is right you should be paid for the trouble."[28] In myriad ways, Henry Eddy helped African Americans use the courts to win their freedom, but bound workers needed capital, knowledge of the law, and a network of family members to incorporate Eddy into their freedom campaigns. His skills might have been invaluable to the enslaved, but he nevertheless put a price on them.

Before long, people like Eddy became more numerous in southern Illinois. In the 1830s, just as African Americans began exiting bondage in growing numbers, a broad demographic transformation dramatically changed the state's population. In 1810, the free white population had hovered around 12,000; in 1840, it surpassed 475,000 settlers.[29] Migration from the U.S. South had long dominated the state's population growth, and Illinois's capitals had always been placed in the south of the state. But by the 1830s, that had begun to change. Chicago's 1837 founding attracted migrants from Europe, New England, and the mid-Atlantic region. The city's potential as a trade hub attracted settlement, and between 1830 and 1850, nearly 25,000 settlers arrived in Illinois just from Germany and the British Isles. By 1850, half of the city's population was foreign born.[30] As Chicago took off, the state's capital shifted northward to Springfield, and a new crop of statewide leaders stood poised to win elected office. A regional divide came into being as new immigrants who abhorred human bondage made slavery's place in the state a political issue.[31] In time, those migrants would play a host of roles in enslaved people's freedom networks.

Domestic migration also began populating the state with people who did not want slavery in their communities. Beginning in the early nineteenth century, migrants from New England and the mid-Atlantic region trekked into southern Illinois. Between 1830 and 1850, hundreds of thousands of migrants from these regions made their way to every corner of the state.[32] For example, the population in Randolph and St. Clair Counties, adjacent to St. Louis, increased by nearly 50 percent.[33] As one historian has argued, New England migrants relocated to Illinois hoping to live "entirely clear of the evil of slavery."[34] Upon arriving in southern Illinois, they became an antislavery constituency and were joined by second-generation

German Americans from Pennsylvania who carried what one scholar has called a "hatred of slavery."[35]

Some migrants to Illinois may have opposed slavery because they themselves were not wholly free, and they worked alongside bound African Americans. Some settlers entered short servitude contracts to earn limited amounts of capital upon their arrival.[36] In some counties, white children—orphans and those with destitute parents—also entered servitude contracts, where they remained until they reached the age of majority. These contracts differed in key ways from the system of black contract bondage; notably, they did not compel white servants to work for life, and they often offered some form of monetary consideration for their labor. In Pope County, the only locality with a substantial number of extant contracts, roughly eighty children entered this system, sometimes comingling with bound black workers. During the 1830s and 1840s, eleven African American children served alongside white children in contracts that held them until the age of majority. In some cases, masters held both black and white children in servitude over a number of years.[37] Similarly, in Sangamon County, children of both races in dire situations entered servitude.[38] Not only black children entered these systems of poor relief: in Randolph County near St. Louis, Dick, "a negro about 65 . . . former servant of John Edgar," entered the rolls.[39] These relationships had the potential to make poor white residents in Illinois more sympathetic to bound African Americans.

Within the state's booming migrant populations, servants and slaves found new assistance from within the legal profession. Besides acting as lawyers, some white migrants to Illinois took on roles in the local courts that gave them the power to shape the terms by which enslaved people pursued freedom. Though clerks may have had a minor role in the larger legal system, they judged the validity of a person's freedom and issued certificates of emancipation. A hostile clerk could pose substantial obstacles to freed men and women hoping to register manumission records at the courthouse, and a sympathetic one could make things easier. For instance, an enslaved man in St. Clair County hoped to document his legal freedom by submitting manumission papers. At first, the clerk accepted evidence of his freedom and issued papers. Later, however, the clerk reversed himself, deeming the evidence insufficient and fraudulent and rescinding the emancipation documents.[40] In Pope County, however, John Raum, an antislavery man, acted as both county and circuit clerk for three and a half decades. Raum migrated from Pennsylvania in the late 1820s; in 1833, he won elected office as a state senator, and he also served as the county and circuit clerk.[41] He used his position in small but significant ways to help African Americans live in freedom. To cite just one such case, when four free African American children were kidnapped in 1841, Raum contributed to a fund for their return and joined public pleas for justice.[42]

The process of emancipation required not only lawyers and clerks but also a range of witnesses to provide evidence in their case files. In suits across the state, African Americans seeking their freedom relied on recent white migrants in this important capacity. In Gallatin County, Venus Davenport sued her master to prove she was a "free black woman of color." Born in slavery in North Carolina, she resided in Illinois as a free woman for over twenty years. Yet when her master died, she was taken to New Orleans and "claimed as a slave." Managing to assemble several witnesses who submitted testimony to certify "she was set free" by her former master, she won and returned to Illinois.[43] In another case in 1835, Aelsey sued to contest her servitude. Her master brought her into Illinois from Kentucky but had never properly registered her indenture contract. To win her case, she relied on the testimony of a white man who swore "she was held to service as a slave" and that "Aelsey has not been registered . . . [or] entered or otherwise bound to perform labor." The witness added that "she lived in the . . . State of Illinois for a long and uninterplaced term of years" and was "to all interest and purpose a free woman." Aelsey won her freedom.[44]

The law also played important administrative functions, and white witnesses extended aid beyond the courtroom, often testifying to the free status of African Americans. In 1828 in Gallatin County, Joe Allen, a formerly indentured man, relied on the testimony of white residents to prove his freedom.[45] Two years later in the same county, Clara Robertson posted her emancipation bond and relied on two white men to swear oaths on her behalf.[46] In another case, Henry Eddy and Ephraim Gatewood "being duly sworn, declared and said that . . . [they] were acquainted with Nelly a black woman . . . [who] always claimed to be free by virtue of her former master's will made verbally on his death bed." Lacking any papers to document her emancipation, Nelly relied on Eddy's and Gatewood's testimony, and the court granted her freedom. Nelly was not alone: in Gallatin County between 1815 and 1839, African Americans called on white witnesses to testify on their behalf in roughly 70 percent of all cases.[47]

Free African Americans also provided vital assistance to unfree persons working toward emancipation. In 1822, Pelagie, an enslaved child, filed a suit in St. Louis, claiming that her residence in a small settlement known as the "French Village" in St. Clair County on the Mississippi's eastern banks entitled her to manumission. Because of her age, she had to rely on David Jack, a free black man, to initiate the suit. Jack's exact role in the suit, as well as his relationship with Pelagie, does not survive in the slender case file. Neither does the verdict in the case. Still, Jack's actions reveal that free African Americans served crucial roles in the quest for emancipation.[48]

In the long emancipation process, instituting a suit for freedom via a petition for a writ of habeas corpus or a civil suit for trespass and false imprisonment was a risky tactic, carrying enormous perils of kidnapping in retaliation and substantial financial burden.[49] In many counties, as well as before the Illinois Supreme Court, it was female slaves who availed themselves of this dangerous option.[50] Across the state, records of roughly two-dozen suits survive. Consequently, the numbers are too small to establish any firm statistical trend. Still, statewide it appears that men outnumbered women in the overall population but that women outnumbered men among those suing for freedom.[51] In Randolph County, women comprised the slight majority of petitions for freedom.[52] On the eastern side of the state in Pope County, there were only two suits for freedom, both initiated by women. And in the cases that came before the state's supreme court, women appeared more often than men.[53]

Regardless of the statistical data, the arguments advanced in these freedom suits illuminate the powerful ways women shaped the movement to freedom.[54] Women's experiences in bondage may explain why they chose this hazardous path. The sparse case files typically include very little about the life circumstances that led enslaved people to use the courts, but in Illinois, as elsewhere in the United States, women had more limited access to wage labor in bondage. They less commonly worked the Mississippi River economies or hired themselves out in field labor. Consequently, self-purchase remained out of reach for many unfree African American women.[55] Women who turned to the courts made a strategic decision that reflected a shrewd calculus about the nature of slavery, servitude, and freedom in Illinois.

In case after case, black women sought emancipation in part so their children could be freed. When an enslaved woman established her freedom, her children commonly left bondage along with her. For instance, in 1827, Mary sued her master, linking her three children's fate to hers. She claimed to "have been brought up in a state of slavery in Kaskaskia," where she lived for many years, but at her master's death, she was sold into St. Louis.[56] While in Missouri, she went before the local court to claim that "she and her three infant children are . . . entitled to their freedom from slavery."[57] At trial, she called witnesses, including John Edgar and Henri Bienvenu—among Illinois's wealthiest and most influential merchants. Her verdict does not survive, and it is unclear if she won, but the way her role as a mother informed the case indicates the tactics enslaved women used in pursuit of freedom. In another case from roughly the same period, Sarah, an enslaved woman, claimed her freedom based on her mother's status. At trial, her attorney established that "Winnie mother of the said plaintiff was carried into the new State of Illinois . . . held in slavery during the space of three or four years . . . and that said plaintiff was born after such residence."[58] Basing her claim to emancipation on Winnie's free status, Sarah won her freedom at trial.

Establishing freedom often required proving free lineage. Slaves had to verify their mothers were not "French Negroes" and therefore not legally held in bondage. For instance, in the 1820s in Randolph County, Cynthia won her freedom without resorting to an extended trial. Her owner, Anthony Blay, had carried her from North Carolina to Illinois and held her as a slave for twenty years. Cynthia never signed a servitude contract, and Blay could not produce any legal title to her. When she demanded freedom papers, local clerks investigated if she spoke French. Presumably, they needed to ensure that Cynthia and her mother were not among the legally enslaved "French Negroes." The court confirmed Cynthia's free birth, as well as her Anglophone status, and freed her.[59] Similarly, in St. Clair County, Lydia sued her master Jincy Mitchell for freedom. Lydia became part of her master's estate after his death and brought a motion that she and her daughter Nancy deserved to be free. While the details remain obscure, Lydia established she was not born of a "French Negro," won the suit, and registered her family's freedom at the courthouse.[60]

Motherhood was not the only factor that made women likely to try to win freedom through litigation. Relying on lawsuits required a broad set of relationships with witnesses and attorneys. Women would have had ready access to those networks, as important actors in kinship ties with husbands and children. Moreover, as they served in domestic economies, they could have forged closer ties with their masters and mistresses. This proved useful in the courts. To cite only one case, Aelsey was held as an indentured servant for an unstated number of years, and during the 1830s, she fulfilled her service. Yet she had no manumission papers or expired contracts to register. Instead, she protected her freedom by bringing witnesses to the Gallatin County courthouse in 1835 who swore to her freedom.[61] In another case from the same time and place, Prucey called upon a local white man who testified to her freeborn status.[62] In a variety of ways, black women in diverse circumstances used the courts to their advantage.[63]

As successes in the courts mounted, starting in the 1830s, the state's free black population had a small burst of expansion that continued through the next decades.[64] Some of this growth came from people exiting bondage, but accelerated migration from the Upper South also played a part. During these years, Kentucky, Tennessee, and other states responded to Nat Turner's rebellion by issuing harsh Black Laws. Measures like travel restrictions and legalized persecution became increasingly common, which likely encouraged black men and women to vote with their feet by seeking out free and nominally free states, including Illinois.[65] Once a trickle of black migration began, it grew until the mid-1850s, when Illinois's politicians passed laws to try and halt it. In 1853, the general assembly revised the Black Laws and banned all free black migration, leading to a dramatic falloff in the number of African Americans heading north.

Within these broad contours, family connections and concentrations informed decisions over migration. In one such migration, fifty-eight African Americans whose master had freed them all at his death migrated as a group to Illinois from Montgomery County, Tennessee. They had stayed in Tennessee for roughly a year after being freed and then migrated to Gallatin County, Illinois.[66] In 1836, nine arrived in Gallatin County from Shelby County, Tennessee, and in 1850, forty-seven more relocated en masse from Tennessee to Pope County, Illinois.[67] Although men made up the majority of the free black population, gender ratios remained relatively even because families often relocated intact.[68] These concentrations from specific counties and the families who relocated together shaped the black migration that transformed the landscape of southern Illinois.

Many of these newly arrived freed men and women had used the courts to escape slavery in the South. One such case involved John Jones, who turned to the courts to escape an illegal indenture. Jones was born free in North Carolina to a mixed-race mother. In the 1840s, he moved to Illinois by way of Memphis, and before landing in Chicago, he entered into an indentured servitude contract while he was in Memphis to learn tailoring skills. While he was a servant, his master hoped to coerce him into bondage for years past what the contract specified. Jones turned to the courts and filed for a writ of habeas corpus that would force the master to prove his title to Jones's labor. While these motions often faltered due to an array of technicalities, this one gave Jones an easy victory. His master asserted that Jones had to serve until he reached the age of majority and that, at the time of the trial, Jones was only nine years of age. Standing before the judge as a grown man of nearly thirty, Jones snatched his freedom.[69] Later on, Jones would be an influential black leader in Illinois.

Self-emancipated slaves running north also contributed to the growing black population.[70] As was the case elsewhere, men made up the vast majority of these fugitives, and it seems plausible that a majority of runaways came from neighboring states in the Upper South.[71] In the plantation South, enslaved men routinely enjoyed greater mobility; they ran errands, traveled to markets, and had their master's permission to venture off the plantation. Consequently, an African American man traveling without his master raised less suspicion. Moreover, enslaved men often carried travel passes from their masters and were more likely to have the chance to analyze and then mimic those papers than were women.[72] In several instances, runaway advertisements alerted readers that enslaved men might possess forged papers. For instance, a slaveholder advertised that John and an accomplice absconded from his plantation "with two sets of forged freedom papers." Similarly, in 1830, the Pope County sheriff arrested and imprisoned an African American man who possessed travel papers that, in the sheriff's mind, were "no doubt spurious." In another such case, a man who may have "been on his way to Canada" had "forged freedom papers."[73]

Illinois sheriffs captured hundreds of escaping slaves, and local officials hunted fugitives with fervor. Under Illinois law, local justices of the peace had complete authority and discretion to prosecute runaways. Perhaps not surprisingly, officials in southern counties searched fervently for runaways.[74] As one observer in the 1830s indicated, "This part of the Territory was as much a slave state as any of the States south of the Ohio River."[75] He continued, "Our influential men, and all who held office," including "every Sherriff and every clerk of the county were proslavery men."[76] To cite one instance of many, in 1818, a local sheriff captured a runaway slave in Edwardsville along the Mississippi River. The fugitive then fled his arrest. An inhabitant of the town, George Churchill, recorded that a "mulatto" had "ran away from . . . his master" in Missouri, but local authorities captured him in Illinois. The next morning the "mulatto prisoner . . . cut his cords and . . . made his escape," having "broke the Edwardsville jail." Churchill, the sheriff, and deputy sheriff spent the next two days searching for him but "found him not."[77] In some cases, even the people who sheltered self-emancipated slaves faced reprisals.[78] Into the 1840s, the landscape remained hostile. Local residents hunted runaways and remained vigilant whenever African Americans passed through a town.

Running from slavery was a component of black resistance that formed the bedrock of the state's emancipation process. Roughly forty runaway slaves from within Illinois sought out the fugitive slave networks that could take them to freedom in the state. Masters were well aware of this, and despite slavery's increasingly tenuous legality, they attempted to recover their runaways. In one extraordinary 1829 case, "Paul Vallard" and a "mulatto slave" fled Illinois together and "were suspected to have taken refuge in lower Canada." The master pressed Illinois Governor Ninian Edwards, a former slaveholder himself, to bring diplomatic pressure to bear on the governor general of Canada. Working through the appropriate channels, U.S. Secretary of State Martin Van Buren applied for the return of Vallard and the runaway slave. But it seems that no extradition ever came to pass.[79] As late as 1839, slaveholders in Illinois took out notices in newspapers as far north as Peoria, near Chicago, seeking the return of slaves who had run off from working in the Gallatin County salt marshes.[80]

The runaway slaves captured in Illinois soon became part of the legal emancipation process when they applied for and won manumission orders.[81] To earn freedom papers in this manner, African Americans had to petition the local court, as well as prove that they had been hired out and served faithfully for one year and that no one could claim title to them. Most commonly, this required a sworn statement from the justice of the peace who posted the notice of their capture and oversaw the action. For instance, in 1838, a "negro man named Bill Mitchell" asked "the court for a certificate from the court stating the facts in relation to his claim to be considered a free person." To win this motion, he "produced to the court, the certificate of John Fisher, sheriff of the county," stating the facts of his arrest and labor. After some consideration, "the clerk of the Court certif[ied] the facts in relation to said Bill Mitchell."[82] In another instance, William Robinson, "a man of colour . . . produced to the court the certificate of the sheriff of Johnson County" to establish that "William was legally committed to the custody as a runaway" and "hired out . . . for the space of one year." The certificate also established that "due notice by publication in a public newspaper printed in this state, has been given." William was "henceforth . . . a free person."[83]

Migrants to Illinois, whether free or fugitive, did not find the free state they sought. As African Americans entered freedom and resettled in Illinois, they discovered that in the southern counties, slavery was alive and well. They soon developed the tools required to combat it. Some who arrived in extended family chains elected to found their own settlements.[84] Black freedom villages cropped up across the state: Brooklyn, New Philadelphia, and Rocky Fork along the Mississippi River and Miller Grove near the Ohio River. Settled in 1829, Brooklyn was the first black town in Illinois, and Miller Grove, founded in roughly 1840, was the last. While these towns scarcely housed more than a couple hundred people, their presence in slaveholding counties threatened slavery's survival in Illinois.[85] Located along the border of Missouri and Kentucky, the communities pooled resources, assembled social networks, and acted as guiding lights for runaways escaping neighboring slave states. Freedom villages on Kentucky's and Missouri's periphery helped demarcate the boundaries between slavery and freedom and set out a geography of resistance to slavery in southern Illinois.[86] Black migrants claimed southern Illinois as a free space, north of slavery. The black towns acted as incubators of emancipation, and in time, African Americans would turn to the courts to make Illinois free soil.

Miller Grove, near the banks of the Ohio River, formed when several manumitted families relocated from Tennessee to Illinois.[87] The founders included the Miller family of Bedford County, Tennessee, and an extended African American family network that had formerly belonged to a single slaveholder in nearby Shelbyville County. Together, these families numbered nearly fifty people, and they migrated en masse to Pope County, where their leader, Harrison Miller, identified the Grove as their new home. By the 1850s, its population had grown, perhaps to 150 people.[88] The town was well situated. Since it was 15 miles from the nearest town, residents could distance themselves from the white community and its slaveholders. Yet the town sat adjacent to Hayes Creek, a navigable waterway that let them welcome new settlers and venture to town when necessary. It also let residents reach out to the county seat at Golconda, form partnerships with local white settlers, and integrate selectively into Illinois's social fabric.

Living in the villages supported African Americans as they built a life free from slavery. Many black residents owned land and recorded their ownership in deed books. For instance, in 1860, Harrison Miller owned land valued at $1,500 and a personal estate of an additional $600. His neighbor Robert Sides, a Maryland-born freedman, had similar prosperity with an estate valued over $750. The Hicks family, also residents of Pope County, bought land after emancipation, too. Ephraim Hicks had been born in Virginia around 1810, and in July 1850, along with his family of four, he posted an emancipation bond. In 1860, his son William owned a farm valued at $250. Miller Grove was not unique.[89] In New Philadelphia, "Free Frank" McWorter owned a plot of land, and he effectively used the local courts to protect it from encroachment by local settlers.[90] It seems likely that freed men and women in the villages cleared the land they owned to farm, both for subsistence and to sell surplus for export. Along the Mississippi River, the soil was well suited for grain cultivation, while on the banks of the Ohio, corn and flax would have thrived. It also appears that in Miller Grove, at least, residents ran distilleries and profited from selling alcohol to surrounding towns. At least some of the freed men and women appeared to have made a good living. Most had enough money to post freedom bonds and to pay legal fees. Some of these funds could have also come as freedom dues, paid to indentured servants at the time of their emancipation. But most of it had to be earned over time. In short, some residents of these towns accomplished what few other freed men and women could: they owned land of their own, worked it for profit, and created spaces that would support a more secure life out of emancipation.

Black communities commonly maintained ties to neighboring slave states and welcomed runaway slaves. One runaway notice from the 1840s indicated that a self-emancipated slave was headed toward Golconda, which neighbored Miller Grove.[91] During the 1830s and 1840s, a handful of runaways applied for their freedom and won manumission orders, and some then relocated to freedom villages. Brooklyn in particular was a beacon for Missouri slaves contemplating flight, as settlers there found numerous ways to draw Missouri slaves into Illinois.[92] Its location on the Mississippi River made it Illinois's first station on the so-called Underground Railroad. Led by the town's African Methodist Episcopal minister, the Rev. William Paul Quinn, fugitives hid in churches and cellars until they could be taken to nearby Alton, which connected them with a well-worn migration route to Chicago.[93] Meanwhile, when itinerant ministers came through Illinois, they brought antislavery texts by David Walker and Frederick Douglass and circulated them through Miller Grove.[94]

The residents of these villages had achieved freedom through a variety of routes, and local leaders assembled their legal knowledge into a legal strategy at the local level. Several residents had exited a term of servitude and registered their expired indentures at the courthouse. Some town residents were runaways who petitioned for freedom. Others had sued their masters to escape illegal slavery. These residents would have known how to use the courts, wield evidence to their advantage, enlist white allies, and move through the process of emancipation. And as they traveled in and out of black settlements, their movements began connecting the tiny black enclaves to the wider world of abolitionism. Black towns were beehives of activity as their residents pooled knowledge of antislavery politics and the legal processes of emancipation.

In the close quarters of small, tightly knit black villages, legal information and literacy probably passed through informal networks. Free and enslaved African Americans across the United States commonly relied on gossip, eavesdropping, and idle chatter to spread political information and organize their communities.[95] The legal skills that African Americans possessed do not appear to have hinged on formal literacy. Virtually none of the extant servitude contracts or other legal documents included signatures.[96] Yet illiteracy did not preclude the effective use of courts.[97] The routine exposure African Americans had with the law helped them assemble information about legality in Illinois. It also seems plausible that some members of the black community would have been literate. As information funneled to this small group of leaders, it could have become a basis for broader legal literacy.

Looking at the black inhabitants in St. Clair Country confirms that Brooklyn's residents would have had relationships with people with a diverse set of paths to emancipation. For instance, in 1837, the six members of the Rain family relocated from Missouri and posted emancipation bonds.[98] Those who had been enslaved in Illinois also offered proof of their manumission, as Abraham Padfield did in 1835.[99] More dramatically, one enslaved woman filed a freedom suit and won. While her victory predated Brooklyn's founding, she appears to have remained in St. Clair County and may well have associated with the town's inhabitants.[100] In time, each would have learned something about the law, and leaders in Brooklyn could then knit together the legal knowledge their neighbors possessed.

Brooklyn was by no means unique. Residents of Miller Grove, in Pope County on the Kentucky border, had a range of legal experiences. Miller Grove attracted manumitted slaves from within Illinois, servants whose terms expired, victors in freedom suits, and migrants from the Upper South—all of whom understood at least something about slavery and the law in Illinois. In one instance, a "mulatto slave" and her family applied for freedom papers after being freed by her master in 1846.[101] In another case, a black family that had never been enslaved applied for freedom papers, posted their bonds at the courthouse, and relocated to the Grove.[102] In another instance, Winny and her children relocated to Miller Grove after winning a freedom suit to escape extralegal slavery.[103] In still another 1840s case, Henry Sides "set free from slavery" a thirty-five-year-old man named Thomas who recorded his manumission papers before removing to Miller Grove.[104]

Adept black litigators harnessed local legal knowledge and wielded it to the town's advantage. Moses Lewis of Miller Grove was one, acting as the leader of a small group of amateur black lawyers. Lewis won his freedom in the 1840s and relocated from Tennessee to Miller Grove. He earned part of his living peddling liquor, and though local officials indicted Lewis six times on alcohol-related charges, they never won a conviction. They charged Lewis for "keeping an open tippling house" and "selling and suffering whisky to be sold in his house."[105] After Lewis secured an acquittal on these charges, the local prosecutors indicted him for "selling whisky by a less quantity than one gallon."[106] Within a short time span, authorities brought Lewis up on charges of selling alcohol *and* for selling alcohol in too little quantities. Undeterred, Lewis beat back both sets of charges and continued his commerce.

Lewis's legal acumen—likely drawn from networks in Miller Grove, his own emancipation process, and his frequent battles in court—helped manumitted African Americans use the judiciary to protect their freedom. In three separate instances, freed men relocating from Tennessee to Pope County used Moses Lewis as their agent with the county clerk to post their freedom bond.[107] Recording a migrant's freedom was not a simple process. Clerks required validation of documents: wills or manumission papers had to bear the seals and signatures of other jurisdictions and carry sworn statements of their authenticity. Freed men and women lacking manumission papers had to rely on the testimony of at least two witnesses. Free African Americans could serve in this capacity. Like many of her peers, on two separate instances, a free black woman named Eva Davis testified before the county clerk in Gallatin County and helped document two freedwomen's status.[108] By helping freed men and women navigate the court's registration requirements and acting as witnesses, freed African Americans like Lewis and Davis helped advance the process of emancipation.

The black men and women who founded freedom villages forged a presence in Illinois that outlasted their lifetimes. All that is left of Miller Grove is its cemetery, tucked away inside the Shawnee National Forest. Although many grave markers are in disrepair, some to the point that only their bases remain and the pillars have crumbled, the cemetery testifies to the key role black residents played in ending slavery in Illinois. One of the few graves that remains intact captures the constant conflict, as well as the enduring hope, that undergirded Illinois's transformation into a free state. It reads, "There is hope of a tree that if it be cut down that it will sprout again & that the tender branches thereof will not cease."[109] Miller Grove, Brooklyn, and other free settlements helped to keep the leaves of freedom sprouting.

In a state that grew by the hundreds of thousands annually, black and white antislavery activists represented a fraction of the larger population. But together they were stronger as they pushed for slavery's demise. During the 1830s and 1840s, African Americans drew on their freedom networks of witnesses and attorneys to bring cases before the Illinois Supreme Court. Rather than bringing sweeping claims of freedom and free soil before the court, litigants challenged slaveholders in particular terms in an attempt to make the specific legal requirements for emancipation less burdensome and protracted. In these cases, the court parsed very fine distinctions in Illinois law and clarified the precise legal process certain categories of unfree African Americans had to go through to live in freedom.

One such case took place in 1836 and involved Juliet, an indentured woman who sued over her children's status. In 1809, her master, William Gaston, relocated from Kentucky to Illinois with Juliet. At that time, she was younger than fifteen years, and therefore Gaston held her as a registered servant—not an indentured servant—under the terms of the 1807 Act Concerning Negroes. Because of her age, she did not sign onto a specific term of indenture. Rather, Gaston simply recorded Juliet as a servant until she reached age twenty-eight. While serving this term, she gave birth to three sons who were to be held in servitude until their adulthood. Juliet and her attorney contended that the children did not inherit her condition of servitude because she was a registered servant, not an indentured one. Gaston argued that no such distinction existed in the law and the Act Concerning Negroes treated indentured and registered servants identically.

The state supreme court held in *Bennington Boon v. Juliet, a woman of color* (1836) that the children born to registered servants were "unquestionably free." To sustain their ruling, the court clarified the distinction between registered and indentured servants. It found that "no provision was made affecting the liberty of the children of registered negroes or mulattoes." Consequently, it concluded that they had "little doubt in reference to the children of indentured servants, and their liability to serve out the time prescribed by the Territorial law." The court went on to say that it was "equally clear, that . . . [the law] could in no way alter, abridge, or change the condition of the children of registered servants." According to the court, only "children born in said Territory of a parent of color, owing service or labor by *indenture* according to law" inherited their mother's unfree status.[110] This technical argument that parsed servitude laws succeeded in part because Juliet had support from a lawyer and she faced a court whose membership grew less sympathetic toward slavery. The emancipation process, then, relied on a variety of factors, and the possibility of failure never was far off for African Americans seeking freedom.

And often, residents of black towns helped African Americans working their way through a long emancipation process. One family's freedom struggle illuminates that living in secure freedom required support from the white and black community. In 1841, Elijah Morris, along with his family, relocated to Pope County after gaining his freedom in Tennessee. With his wife and children, he became a modest landholder. This free black family resided outside Golconda, not far from the free black settlement at Miller Grove. They had lived there for a little over a year when "some daring scoundrels entered" Morris's house and stole $600 in cash and kidnapped four of his children: Katherine, Martha, David, and James.[111] The assailants proceeded to "forcibly steal and take" each of them "into the State of Missouri."[112] Later investigations reveal that the gang took the children to Cape Girardeau on the west bank of the Mississippi River before carrying them into the Deep South.[113]

Immediately, Morris turned to the press and a network of white residents who would help his cause. He took out a notice in the Shawneetown *Illinois Republican*, published in neighboring Gallatin County, and pleaded for information identifying the perpetrators. Several months later, he ran a second notice and offered a $300 reward "for such information as will lead to the recovery of said children or to the conviction of the offenders."[114] Seventeen white allies signed his plea for assistance. They came from diverse walks of life, including William Sloan, a Maryland-born resident and judge in Pope County, and John Raum, the county clerk. J. W. McCoy, Thomas McCoy, and N. D. Clark also added their names. These men were all born in southern states and were merchants and store owners in Pope County. Another two signers, John Cosby and James Finney, were southern-born farmers.[115] The press campaign had some effect. The following year, a jury indicted William Vaughn and six members of his gang.[116] Before the trial commenced, Morris pressed Vaughn for information about his children's whereabouts. According to a local history written nearly sixty years after, Vaughn disclosed that the four children had been sold in Mississippi, and Morris by some unknown means managed to locate them.[117] If his children did in fact return to freedom in Illinois, Elijah Morris may still have lived in fear. There is no record the kidnappers were convicted or that anything restrained them from striking again.

Cases like this were not unique, and they pointed to the reality that former slaveholders could kidnap African Americans back into bondage. In 1842, a gang seized Maria Adams, her family, and other African Americans, a dozen or more, all of whom were "free by the law of the land."[118] John Crenshaw delivered members of the Adams family to an agent named Simon Kuykendall for $2,000.[119] The case became a local flashpoint. A grand jury indicted both Crenshaw and Kuykendall for kidnapping.[120] In the meantime, Maria's relatives Charles and Nelson Adams took it upon themselves to recover their family. Crenshaw was "assaulted by a brother of those he had sold," who was presumably trying to gather information about his relatives' whereabouts. The two brothers were not satisfied with the information the kidnapper provided, and the stakes escalated, when "a day or two before Crenshaw's trial his steam mill at Cypress was burnt down." In turn, Crenshaw's defenders struck back against the free black community in Gallatin County, with an ally of Crenshaw storming into the house of an "unoffending old negro" and "whipping him."[121]

In their efforts to establish black freedom, rural communities in Illinois became entangled in fraught political struggles. The Adams and Crenshaw trials, like the Morris case in the neighboring county, had public dimensions: juries were convened, witnesses swore testimony, and lawyers, judges, and even the governor got involved. Crenshaw won an acquittal, even though, according to the editor of the Shawneetown *Illinois Republican*, it was "believed by many" that Crenshaw "connived at this abduction."[122] Meanwhile, Charles and Nelson Adams faced conviction and imprisonment for assault. As time passed and tensions cooled, several prominent citizens began a concerted effort to free the Adams brothers. Benjamin and Ninian Wirt Edwards—children of the former governor who knew Maria from when she had been her father's house servant—wrote the sitting governor urging a pardon.[123] In 1845, on his final day in office, Governor Thomas Ford acquiesced.[124] Even if Charles and Nelson went free, there is no evidence Maria and her children ever did. The Adams case widened the circle of political leaders involved in the contestation over slavery. With local officials like John Raum assisting Elijah Morris and statewide officeholders helping the Adams family, the kidnappings that threatened free African Americans with captivity were poised to ignite a wider political struggle over slavery and freedom in the state. Residents of black freedom villages remained at the vanguard of that struggle as they formed a local antislavery politics that helped to move emancipation forward.

* * *

With antislavery energy coursing out of freedom villages, the arc of abolition ran a different course in Illinois than in northern states along the eastern seaboard. African Americans in Boston, New York, Philadelphia, and Baltimore joined antislavery institutions and forged a politics of abolition that had traction in white reform-minded groups.[125] These African Americans worked with manumission societies and made important contributions to those societies' work.[126] They pioneered tactics that appealed to a broad constituency by chartering antislavery newspapers, authoring pamphlets and petitions, and conducting speaking tours.[127] Additionally, African Americans adeptly used the law to protect their freedom.[128] They frequently turned to courts, managing to enforce the various emancipation statutes on the books in their states. Across the northern United States, free African Americans were coworkers in the politics of abolition. Yet in Illinois, black activism against slavery came out of rural communities. Antislavery societies in Illinois were small and never had the same force as their counterparts in the East. What's more, no gradual emancipation statute that freed all African Americans after a given date existed to help African Americans in their campaigns for emancipation. Instead, residents of Illinois black towns forged a set of resources and networks that supported enslaved men and women in their quests for freedom.

Life in black villages offered African Americans—free, enslaved, and in degrees of unfreedom—an opportunity to build a life apart from the world that slaveholders made. Black migrants who settled in these towns empowered African Americans to express a capacious set of freedom practices:

they served as beacons for runaway slaves from neighboring states as well as those running from within Illinois, they protected freed men and women from kidnapping and reenslavement, they built churches and other civic institutions, and they helped enslaved men and women sue in local Illinois courts for their freedom. These practices insulated African Americans from a world that equated blackness with bondage and freedom with a bundle of political rights, the franchise paramount among them. African Americans in eastern cities waged a robust campaign for full citizenship, and those movements in time helped to transform the nation. Yet the quest for full black citizenship was not the only measure of black freedom politics. Freed men and women in Illinois sought an alternative to slavery but did not necessarily embrace notions of freedom that were commonplace in antebellum America. If, as it has long been argued, human bondage in part defined freedom in the United States, these villages helped to make spaces where African Americans could separate themselves from the contaminated notions of liberty that pervaded the nation.

Notwithstanding their victories, emancipation in Illinois was a contested, fragile process. Racism only grew more virulent over time: emancipation bonds became costlier, and in time, the legislature banned all black migration to the state. Servants and slaves went through various stages of unfreedom before exiting bondage; the threat of kidnapping always loomed. Yet, in black towns, freed men and women managed to buy land and use the courts to protect it and other liberties, and in so doing, they built a life apart from slavery. Through this process of emancipation, African Americans gained a broad exposure to the law and developed a legal literacy that was a potent force in the state's emancipation process. In time, African Americans managed to use this legal literacy in local settings with the assistance of witnesses, attorneys, and a host of legal officials who comprised a freedom network. Black and white migrants who came into the state joined enslaved people in their campaigns against slavery. Although the odds were daunting, they had remarkable success. Yet as John Merry, Elijah Morris, Maria Adams, and a host of other African Americans knew, freedom remained tenuous, emancipation could be reversed, and making Illinois a free state required concerted effort from a broad constituency. By 1840, that constituency had taken rough shape. A robust antislavery movement, however, was still to come.

CHAPTER 6

Freedom Practices, Freedom Politics

In summer 1839, Nance Cromwell faced a dilemma. Born in Maryland around 1810, she was brought to Illinois and converted into a registered servant; she lived near Springfield until she was twenty-eight years old, when she reached the age of majority and her contract expired. Yet her path out of bondage was more turbulent than most. In 1828, Nathan Cromwell sold Nance at public auction to John Howard. She disputed her sale before the Illinois Supreme Court, in *Nance, a Negro girl v. John Howard* (1828), and challenged her sale by attacking the servitude system in the state. Specifically, she argued that contract bondage violated the congressional prohibition on involuntary servitude in Illinois. The justices found for her master and ruled that indentured servitude qualified as voluntary labor. After her defeat, she endured another decade in bondage. Yet even after Nance's term expired, she confronted the prospect of reenslavement. In 1839, Nathan attempted to sell Nance as a "servant or slave" to David Bailey. After the attempted sale, Nathan could not produce a valid indenture, and Nance again disputed her servitude. But without manumission papers or a freedom certificate, she lacked sufficient proof of her free status. In this vulnerable position, Nance elected to seek her freedom by filing suit in the local circuit court. Given her earlier failure before the state's high court, Nance knew the risks attending freedom suits. She also no doubt knew about the countless men and women who were sold into southern cotton fields after turning to the courts. In her second suit, what Nance needed most was a good lawyer—and she found one in Abraham Lincoln.

With Lincoln's aid, Nance won the case in circuit court, but she faced an appeal to the Illinois Supreme Court. As Lincoln argued the case, he could not have known that, roughly twenty years later, he would once again argue about slavery and freedom with one of the justices listening to him:

Stephen A. Douglas. In this exchange at the state supreme court, however, the two men agreed—Nance could not be held in bondage. In 1841, the court ruled in Nance's favor and saved her from another term in servitude. Although she lacked a certificate of freedom, the court held in *David Bailey v. William Cromwell et al.* (1841) that "the presumption of law was, in this state, that every person was free without regard to color." The justices added that the law presumed her freedom and that it was "incumbent upon the plaintiff" to show that "she was bound to service."[1] The case set a new legal basis for black freedom and closed key loopholes that masters had exploited. With this ruling, the court dismantled much of the legal underpinning for slavery in the state and made freedom the normative legal condition for black people in Illinois. Nance's 1828 suit had validated bondage. Her second suit in 1841 helped dismantle it.

A booming migrant population and a burgeoning abolition movement partially explain the dramatic change in Illinois's society and judiciary in the intervening years. In the 1830s, Illinois attracted robust migration from New England, the mid-Atlantic, and Western Europe, which tended to pool in Chicago, and those migrants supported an abolition movement in the state. Unlike northern states along the eastern seaboard, Illinois had not forged an antislavery politics in the wake of U.S. Independence; indeed, it was only during the 1840s and 1850s that the state became fertile ground for abolitionists. While many of those abolitionists hoped to destroy slavery nationally, they also knew that their work began at home: until the mid-1840s, inheritable bondage trapped the small community of "French Negroes," who had descended from indigenous and African slaves brought to the region when it was under French control.

The coalition of nineteenth-century antislavery activists and abolitionists who wanted to make Illinois a free state had to confront France's colonial legacy. To free the lifelong servants and "French Negroes" who had been exempted from emancipation, the state's growing cadre of abolitionists pushed key cases before the state supreme court. Into the 1840s, a few hundred enslaved people remained in the state, mostly clustered in Randolph and Saint Clair Counties, the same territory that Frenchmen and women had colonized at the dawn of the eighteenth century. Slaveholders continued to record men and women in their probate inventories, baptize enslaved infants in the church house, and profit from enslaved labor. Their grasp over their enslaved workers grew increasingly tenuous over time, but masters did not simply relent in the face of growing antislavery forces.

Freeing this small population of slaves took concerted political effort. Abolitionists drew on the legal knowledge and strategies that took shape in the black community at the local level, on new wellsprings of support from Illinois residents, a judiciary increasingly receptive to antislavery jurisprudence, and relentless efforts from African Americans to free the "French Negroes." In time, they won the victories they sought, and Illinois's last group of enslaved African Americans won emancipation.

As jurists and black litigants stamped out exemptions for "French Negroes," slaveholders responded by kidnapping African Americans on the brink of freedom, turning them into captives in neighboring slave states.[2] By the 1840s, the Mississippi River had been both border and bridge between nominally free and slave societies. Year after year, enslavers relied on Illinois's proximity to Missouri and Kentucky to press African Americans into slavery.[3] As midcentury approached, kidnappers grew more sophisticated, aggressive, and arrogant. Facing a new political and legal climate, masters again adapted to keep their power over their slaves at least partly intact. Just as in the eighteenth century, when different conquering empires fostered changing legal landscapes, masters revived forms of black captivity to plunder yet more profit out of enslaved men and women. Servants and slaves continued to live in the state as they had before, and kidnapping represented a major source of enslavement. Just as occurred in the eighteenth century, slavery included captives seized from their native lands and trafficked across the wider Mississippi River Valley, as well as those people born into bondage. This time, however, rather than trafficking captives into Illinois, slaveholders carried them out of the state and into the Deep South.

Facing this latest adaptation, abolitionists did not rest on their laurels. They enlisted a growing cast of people to protect African Americans who were kidnapped and returned to bondage. During the 1840s, juries across southern Illinois indicted kidnappers, and the abolitionist press forged powerful discourses about the traffic in human flesh. These responses to kidnapping birthed a more robust and widespread antislavery movement in the state. During the 1850s, many of Illinois's political leaders bolted from the Democratic Party to join the newly minted Republican Party. Several factors contributed to this political realignment, but chief among them was a desire to combat slavery. As midcentury approached, a free labor ideology flourished, and a growing community of evangelical Christians populated the state.[4, 5] These twin strains of abolitionism had considerable impact but cannot explain why such a broad and diverse community in Illinois, particularly in the state's southern districts, came to embrace antislavery politics, however limited. Kidnapping cases show how communities in southern Illinois that lacked strong antislavery sentiment came to oppose slavery's presence. By fighting to protect free African Americans in circumscribed ways, southern Illinoisans made common cause with the state's abolitionists on this one issue.

Despite being relative latecomers, Illinois's antislavery movement became a powerhouse in the nation at large. Leaders like former representative and then Senator Lyman Trumbull, former state supreme court Justice Gustav Koerner, former representative and then Governor Richard Yates, and former representative and then President Abraham Lincoln all joined the Republican Party and advanced antislavery politics. During the 1850s, Lincoln, by far the most prominent of the state's leaders, articulated a vision of freedom that is more intelligible when seen in the light of antikidnapping campaigns. In his famous debates with Senator Stephen A. Douglas, which built on his earlier work with Nance, Lincoln articulated a defense of self-ownership that became the foundation for abolitionist politics in the 1850s and 1860s. His conception of freedom in part emerged out of Illinois's local history of slavery, black kidnapping, and the dynamic campaigns to end slavery in Illinois. In time, black kidnapping took on national political significance, and the newly formed Republican Party mobilized around protecting free African Americans. Over the course of this at times violent struggle, a new antislavery discourse, a new antislavery activism, and a new antislavery politics came into being. By the eve of the Civil War, it took root among a new antislavery constituency.

* * *

Black kidnapping in the state frequently began as a response to incipient antislavery movements: the ties between Illinois slaveholders and Missouri merchants, first forged in the eighteenth century, enabled slaveholders to sell African Americans downriver rather than free them. In one instance in the 1820s, Tempe, an enslaved woman, complained that her master "has frequently abused and beaten her," which came "for no other cause that she knows of but her present application for freedom."[6] In another case, Pierre Menard, the former Illinois lieutenant governor, transferred his longtime servant Aspasia from his residence in Illinois to his son-in-law in St. Louis in 1827. Once there, Aspasia filed a suit for freedom against her

Figure 9. This 1861 map of southern Illinois depicts the state's proximity to the lower Mississippi River Valley. Cairo, Illinois, is the town at the junction of the Mississippi and Ohio Rivers, and Memphis, Tennessee, looms on the horizon. John Bachman, *Bird's eye view of junction of the Ohio & Mississippi Rivers, showing Cairo and part of the southern states* (New York: A. Rumpf, 1861). Retrieved from the Library of Congress, https://www.loc.gov/item/99447003/. (Accessed June 14, 2017.)

new master, who planned "to carry . . . [her] on board the steam boat America" and sell her "down the river out of the boundaries of this state for the express purpose of preventing . . . [Aspasia] from instituting suit for and obtaining her freedom."[7]

Unlike in other jurisdictions, Illinois had no powerful abolition society to protect African Americans from kidnapping.[8] Beginning in the eighteenth century, eastern states like New York and Pennsylvania had hosted manumission societies dedicated to gradually ending slavery. By the 1830s, those manumission societies had reconfigured themselves to embrace immediate emancipation and begun appealing to a wider audience.[9] During the 1830s, the trend in American abolition was toward immediate emancipation and full citizenship for freed men and women, with many abolitionists following the lead of William Lloyd Garrison and the American Antislavery Society (AAS). Yet in Illinois, the politics of abolition did not have a broad appeal; in fact, many observers lamented that abolition faced such a hostile reception in the state. Writing in 1841, Joshua Leavitt, an influential New York–based editor of the *Emancipator*, called Illinois's place in the battle over slavery "'the seat of war' and that they in N. York and the eastern and middle states are mere powder monkeys."[10] The next year in the *Liberator*, one editorial recognized that "our eastern friends are hardly aware of the fierceness of the contest in this part of the West." Comparing Illinois to the rest of the nation, this author concluded that "the community at large in all Middle and Southern Illinois is as far behind the truth as was Ohio or New York, six, seven, or eight years ago."[11]

This pessimism reflected the early failure to build an abolition movement in Illinois. Before the 1820s, very few free inhabitants in Illinois were working to end slavery. Elijah Lovejoy stood out as one of the few who tried to build a movement. He tried to establish an abolitionist newspaper in Alton, along the banks of the Mississippi north of St. Louis, but the enterprise ended in disaster. Lovejoy was born in New England, the son of a Congregationalist minister, and relocated to St. Louis after attending seminary at Princeton and becoming a Presbyterian minister. His first antislavery newspaper was based in St. Louis, but it faced stiff resistance from the local proslavery community. Hoping to find success elsewhere, Lovejoy moved across the river to Alton, Illinois. His paper, the *Alton Observer*, made him one of the first people in the state trying to push forward a broad-based abolition movement. He became a founding member of the Illinois Anti-Slavery Society and reached out to Edward Beecher, Illinois resident and son of the famed Lyman Beecher, to mobilize the cause. But Lovejoy was not safe in Illinois, and in 1837, a violent proslavery mob surrounded his house and killed him. In the wake of these tragic events, and in a fine example of blaming the victim, many in the state denounced antislavery politics. As a joint committee of the Illinois General Assembly put it, "We highly disapprove of the formation of abolition societies, and the doctrines promulgated by them."[12]

Antislavery activists knew that much of the population of Illinois had migrated from southern regions and were likely to be hostile to abolitionism. The Reverend Albert Hale, an antislavery leader based in Jacksonville, asked, “How many of our population were once slaveholders & are living on the price of blood?” And then there were the “thousands more who never owned slaves” but are “desperately opposed to antislavery movements—because their relatives hold slaves or have held them. . . . We are bordering on the slave states to such an extent as to make the danger of collution [*sic*] no small matter.” Hale concluded that “under all these circumstances, it becomes a matter of immense importance who shall lead the armies of the free in this great moral cause in this state.”[13] In 1841, the *Genius of Liberty*, an Illinois-based antislavery publication, editorialized, saying that “a large minority of the population of this state are from Southern States. Some of them are still slaveholders. Many were formerly slaveholders but sold out their human stock and are now living on the price of blood.” It pressed on that “this state is under the dominion of slavery.”[14] Leaders like the Rev. Hale believed “the truth is that Ill[inois] from its location and the circumstances in which a larger portion of its population were raised and the relations they still sustain must become the great battle field on which the antislavery question is to be settled.”[15]

Hale and the antislavery press overstated slavery’s dominance in Illinois. Still, as late as 1840, slightly more than 300 slaves appeared on the U.S. census—and many more evaded detection.[16] In 1844, an enslaved infant received baptismal sacraments, indicating that inheritable bondage still existed in the French Catholic communities.[17] Prominent residents of the state continued to have sizable slave holdings, with former lieutenant governor Pierre Menard recording twelve slaves in the 1840 census.[18] Further, local courts continued to recognize slavery. In 1838, William Morrison, one of the wealthiest slaveholders in Illinois, died. His probate inventory listed twenty “negroes” with monetary values totaling over $4,000; at least five of the slaves were younger than ten years and held without the legally required indenture.[19] Yet neither the probate judge nor the county clerk objected to the probate inventory including human chattel. Within this legal climate, it is perhaps not surprising that Illinois had a weak antikidnapping law on the books. Passed just after Illinois’s statehood, the state punished perpetrators of kidnappings with up to a $500 fine but no prison time. The law acted as a feeble deterrent, and Illinois’s antikidnapping legislation paled in comparison to the more robust statutes in other states.[20]

In light of these modest punishments for kidnapping and slavery’s continued legality, for the “French Negroes” who lived in the state into the 1840s, the Rev. Hale may have been right that it would take a metaphorical army to end slavery. If so, the state's population explosion was starting to provide some of the needed soldiers. In the two decades from 1840 to 1860, the population grew from 475,000 settlers to 1.7 million.[21] Many of these new residents came from New England and Western Europe, areas generally hostile to slavery. By midcentury, the population in the state's northern districts far outnumbered that of the more proslavery southern reaches.[22] Writing in the 1830s, James Birney, a former Alabama slaveholder turned antislavery organizer in the upper Midwest, asserted that in a "short time," Illinois sentiment would "resort to Gradual Emancipation."[23] By the 1840s, others had shared this opinion, believing that "there is a strong ingredient of New England and New York population diffused over her soil which has not yet forgotten the glorious principles and deeds of the land which gave them birth."[24]

In 1837, a new generation of abolitionist leaders met in Illinois, and they followed the new abolitionist tactics exemplified by William Lloyd Garrison. Rather than pursuing a gradual emancipation that kept African Americans in various states of dependency for decades, American abolitionists increasingly demanded immediate emancipation and full citizenship for blacks. At the root of what one scholar has called a transformation in American abolitionism was a dedication to the equality of all human beings. The 1837 Illinois Anti-Slavery Convention exemplified these trends: its declaration pointed out God's creation of all humankind and declared that slavery "annihilates and destroys the very foundation of all rights, by refusing to acknowledge the slave as a man." All people, it went on to say, including those currently enslaved, were "rational, moral and accountable being[s], made to act forever under the government of God, and responsible to him for the discharge of all his duties to God, and to man." Slavery degraded all humanity by encouraging them to regard slaves "as a mere laboring animal, a mere chattel, an article of merchandize, an item in his master's wealth."[25] They denounced "keeping a human being under a system essentially oppressive, unjust, and ruinous."[26]

The incipient abolition movement, with its societies, papers, and organized networks, soon took root in Chicago. By 1840, Chicago had hosted an urban counterpart to the already powerful and ongoing rural antislavery activities in the southern districts of the state. Chicago formally incorporated itself as a city in 1837, and by 1838, the city's residents had chartered an antislavery society led by evangelical ministers.[27] In 1842, Zebina Eastman established an abolitionist newspaper in Chicago, the *Western Citizen*, to continue Lovejoy's legacy. Born in Massachusetts, Eastman had edited a small paper in Vermont before relocating to Illinois. Arriving in Chicago just as antislavery politics began to take shape, Eastman's paper helped to organize the state's budding antislavery constituencies.[28] He and his colleagues routinely publicized and denounced slavery's continued existence in Illinois. The paper carried notices of the state's lingering slave population, reporting on the census, and pointing out legal exceptions to abolition laws. Authors in the paper pointed to the Illinois Black Codes, concluding that "these [laws] constitute the Slave Code of this state and differ but little from the slave laws of the Southern States."[29] The authors of these articles almost certainly overstated slavery's influence in the state, but they still touched on an underlying truth.

Having established a press and a fledgling antislavery organization, Chicago-based activists fanned out across the state. Ichabod Codding was the Anti-Slavery Society's chief traveling agent. Born in Connecticut, Codding had attended Middlebury College in Vermont before traveling across New England and the mid-Atlantic recruiting followers for the abolition movement. In 1843, he relocated to Illinois and poured his energy into building a movement there, traveling to rural communities to deliver antislavery lectures.[30] "The Executive Committee . . . appointed several agents to go through the State and call the attention of the people to the present wants of the Anti-slavery Cause," one author reported. They worked to build an antislavery infrastructure and raise money from subscribers. "The design now is to make one united effort to pay off the debt incurred by the purchase of the press and to concentrate the patronage of the Friends of Liberty in the support of the Western Citizen."[31] Having formed a liberty association, the *Western Citizen* reported that "our great business now is to awake the people of Illinois, and interest them in this movement." Codding remarked during the 1850s, "We have now labored for the last year and a half. It has been the hardest year and a half's work we have ever done."[32] Nevertheless, newspaperman Eastman and his followers were optimistic as they reflected on the rise of antislavery activism, with one observer concluding that "the Darkness of slavery already begins to melt away before the dawning of liberty."[33]

Extravagant rhetoric aside, the situation in the 1840s suggests some cause for optimism. Local organizations formed across the state, and several rural counties joined in a statewide campaign to oppose slavery. Reflecting on this transformation, one local observer noted that "all that love the poor slave and are interested in his deliverance from bondage . . . have organized a Wesleyan circuit, called the Fox River Circuit, on which we have more than twenty appointments, eleven churches formed, and upwards of one hundred and fifty members, good and true."[34] Over the decade, subscribers to the *Western Citizen* increased to a few thousand.[35] Bearing witness to these key transitions in the state's population and politics, one of the paper's reporters noted that "the truth has produced a silent and gradual but marked change in Illinois during the last five years."[36] But it wasn't easy: "Whoever enters on this work in Ill[inois] needs to be no common man," the Rev. Hale declared in 1838, but still, he sensed that "the field is evidently ripe for harvest" and was convinced that "some person or persons should [swing the] sickle & reap."[37]

With Illinois mobilizing at unprecedented speed, many new communities were now part of a growing regional and national abolition movement that sought immediate emancipation. Across the state, counties hosted liberty conventions and publicized their proceedings.[38] In the mid-1840s, several towns incorporated female antislavery societies, a sign that women had enlisted in the antislavery cause.[39] Word of a major regional antislavery convention began to spread. One out-of-state observer enthusiastically noted "a proposition . . . for a grand North Western Anti-Slavery Convention, for the purpose of more effective organization in Illinois, Iowa, and Wisconsin."[40] In addition to home-grown antislavery societies, national abolition organizations were now establishing Illinois chapters.[41]

Illinois abolitionists poured their energy into the Liberty Party, which was founded in 1840 at a convention in Syracuse, New York, to act as the political arm of the American abolition movement.[42] The creation of a political party to advance the cause of abolition happened only after an acrimonious fight between antislavery activists. Garrison, as onetime leader of the immediate abolitionists, remained strictly opposed to formal party politics and standing for elected office.[43] By 1839, a rival faction of abolitionists led by Gerrit Smith, Joshua Leavitt, James Birney, and William Goodell had begun to urge abolitionists to use political elections as one weapon in the war against slavery.[44] Many antislavery activists in Illinois gravitated toward this position, and the Liberty Party came to have an important presence in the state.

Trying to advance the cause, antislavery politicians ran on the Liberty Party platform as they campaigned for national office. In 1846, Owen

Lovejoy, brother of the slain antislavery editor, ran for the U.S. House of Representatives, conducting one of the Liberty Party's more successful campaigns. In their endorsement of Lovejoy, the editors at the *Western Citizen* noted that "the enemies of Liberty triumphed over one, but the friends of right, and justice, and liberty are coming up [by the] thousands."[45] Lovejoy toured the state lecturing to hundreds of people, receiving a surprisingly warm reception in districts that had been proslavery. One local leader in LaSalle County reported that "six years ago, to my personal knowledge, there were not more than a dozen abolitionists in the county; now we find nearly one fifth of her citizens advocates of the liberty party."[46] The campaign attracted national attention, and John Hale, a leading antislavery senator from New Hampshire, lent his support. Despite valiant efforts, the campaign ended in defeat. Still, Lovejoy won a third of the vote at the polls, indicating that the Liberty Party was gaining support.[47]

Although Eastman, Codding, the younger Lovejoy, and a host of other leading abolitionists worked for the Liberty Party's success, it was still a minor force in state politics, with no hope of toppling Democratic Party control.[48] The state routinely elected Democrats to the statehouse and U.S. Congress, and only the rare official could break their hold on elected offices in the state. While some Whigs made it into the governorship, it was the exception that proved the one-party rule. Surveying the Liberty Party's standing in Illinois, one activist declared that "the probability that we shall be defeated at that time, as we have been before, ought not to discourage or dishearten us." Optimistically, this writer exhorted his readers to "Organize! Organize, then, in your counties."[49]

While many abolitionists joined a national campaign against slavery, they also worked for emancipation in Illinois by using the court system. In a state that grew by the hundreds of thousands annually, black and white antislavery groups represented a fraction of a percent of the larger population. Yet during the 1830s and 1840s, black and white activists joined forces to push for slavery's demise. Surveying a series of cases that found their way before the Illinois Supreme Court, including *Bennington vs. Boone* and Nance's *Bailey v. Cromwell*, one observer noted that "from these decisions of the court, we may understand that we have work yet to do. We must work to carry these cases through to their final decision, to the end of the law: and abolitionists must work in raising the money to prosecute them to the end." The correspondent noted that decades after Illinois nominally banned slavery, "it is not passing strange that the Supreme Court of the State of Illinois should be called upon to decide whether slavery exists in the State of Illinois."[50]

Final legal emancipation in the state required litigating France's colonial legacy in the Mississippi Valley, with both black and white litigators making strategic challenges to free the small population of "French Negroes" living in Illinois. In 1845, the state supreme court handed abolitionists the victory they sought in *Joseph Jarrot, alias Pete, a colored man v. Julia Jarrot* (1845). As one reporter stated, *Jarrot* "involved the right to hold slaves through the old, French settlers—the French slaves as they are called."[51] Joseph Jarrot had descended from an enslaved woman who had resided in Cahokia three generations earlier. In 1818, Jarrot's mother qualified as a "French Negro," and her master registered her in St. Clair County, which meant that she fell under the 1818 constitution's exemptions for slavery. The nature of that legal exemption remained ambiguous. Proslavery lawyers contended that slavery remained inheritable and all children of "French Negroes" could be held as slaves, which for years had been common practice in Illinois.[52] Jarrot's attorney, future U.S. Senator Lyman Trumbull, asserted that only enslaved people who were in the state at the time of ratification had been exempted from emancipation, and since Joseph had been born after statehood, he should be freed.

The supreme court found that Jarrot could not be held in slavery.[53] In the decision, the court explored the nature of slavery and freedom in Illinois. It stressed that the laws exempting "French Negroes" from emancipation also stated that slavery shall not "hereafter be introduced into this State."[54] The court found that children born into bondage qualified as the further introduction of slavery into Illinois and therefore violated that prohibition. Consequently, the ruling held that exemptions for "French Negroes" in the state constitution did not extend to their children. Moreover, they held that slaveholders bringing human chattel into the state for limited periods—even a day—lost legal title to their slaves. In *Jarrot v. Jarrot*, the court extended a version of the so-called Somerset Principle into Illinois. Named after the landmark 1772 British case that freed James Somerset, this free-soil doctrine made freedom the normative condition for all African Americans. The *Jarrot* decision established a precedent that prohibited proslavery lawyers and judges from using Illinois's laws to protect inheritable human bondage.[55] Joseph Jarrot, together with his attorney

Lyman Trumbull, helped to score an important victory for abolition, and it would not be the last.

African Americans won before the high court, and enslaved men and women scored victories in the local courts as well. In circuit courts, a few families of "French Negroes" registered their freedom papers the same year as the *Jarrot* decision. In May 1845, Jean Baptiste, who spoke "both French and English," relied on the testimony of white witnesses to secure his freedom papers. According to testimony, his reputed father was "John, the slave of Adam W. Snyder."[56] At roughly the same time, P. W. Randall "liberated [his] colored woman, Constance, from all further involuntary servitude." Born to a "French Negro" and now fifty years old, she had served in legal bondage for her entire adult life.[57] Constance also registered her children as free people of color.

The *Jarrot* decision gave African Americans a powerful tool to use in local litigation because it both freed the "French Negroes" and made Illinois free soil. In the wake of its ruling, unfree African Americans continually turned to the circuit courts, relying on white attorneys and routinely succeeding. In one case, a slave hunter named Lewis Wynn arrested Joseph Wardman "on suspicion of being a runaway slave." Wardman "failed to produce such certificate of freedom as is required by the laws." Imprisoned while a justice of the peace weighed evidence, Wardman, like Nance before him, came perilously close to being deported into the Deep South. Yet in the wake of the 1845 ruling, Wardman did not have to assemble the cast of witnesses and documents to prove his freedom. Instead, his attorney, Abraham Lincoln, filed a writ of habeus corpus demanding his release. With the *Jarrot* decision in effect, slave catchers had a high burden of proof, and in this case, they could not meet it. Winning the motion, the court set Wardman free.[58] In another 1847 case, a Kentucky slaveholder had trafficked an enslaved woman and her four children into Illinois. When the slaves sued to prevent their return to a slave state, the court found in their favor, and they remained in freedom in Illinois. In this instance, Lincoln argued for the slaveholder. He submitted that the right of transit permitted the family to remain enslaved in Illinois. However, the circuit court judge relied on the *Jarrot* decision and ordered the enslaved family be freed.[59]

Yet as had happened in previous decades, the promise of emancipation remained out of reach for African Americans who were kidnapped and carried into the Deep South. Former masters and other people hostile to black emancipation responded to the political and legal changes in Illinois that made keeping "French Negroes" in bondage increasingly untenable by moving into neighboring states. Although Illinois had passed an anti-kidnapping law in 1819, the law was weak in terms of the fines and punishments it proscribed compared to other states, and continuities remained in black kidnapping practices.[60] Kidnappers more frequently targeted men, presumably because they could command higher prices in southern slave markets.[61] Moreover, African Americans carried into slavery seldom returned to Illinois, and their captors almost never faced consequences. At the turn of the nineteenth century, kidnappers tended to capture African Americans from the southern reaches of Illinois, that is, on the brink of freedom, both legally and geographically. Such cases included children about to leave an indenture or an illegally enslaved person who had turned to the courts. These forms of kidnapping marked the latest adaptation to slavery and harkened back to the forms of Indian captivity that were commonplace in the mid-eighteenth century. Kidnapping could be profitable, but over time it took on key new dimensions and acted as a way for pro- and antislavery communities to organize their politics. Raiding free black communities and trading black captives across long distances became an important part of the state's politics, just as it had been in centuries past, when Indian captivity was a key political force in the region. Statutes and legal doctrines never had the final say on what dimensions slavery would have, no matter if those laws came in the form of the French *Code Noir*, the Northwest Territory Ordinance, or the *Jarrot* decision. If former masters found ways to have their way despite the law, not everybody in Illinois wanted theirs to be the final word on the matter.

Abolitionists mobilized in three crucial ways to try and protect black freedom. First, the state's newspapers launched a press campaign to publicize kidnapping cases, which created a powerful discourse about slavery's constant threat to freedom. Second, local communities formed search and rescue parties to find kidnapped men and women. These liberation campaigns brought a wider swath of the state's population into antislavery circles, as Illinois residents worked to keep African Americans in freedom. In time, the press campaigns and local mobilizations took on political dimensions. Political leaders, from local officials to high statewide elected officials, decried the human traffickers that plagued the state. By denouncing kidnapping and slave trafficking, a diverse constituency popularized antislavery politics in Illinois.

Newspapers published accounts of roaming villains, bloodthirsty bounty men, and the tyranny slaveholders imposed over Illinois, providing a terrifying set of images that embodied activist arguments about slavery's corrupting influence on freedom. In article after article, writers highlighted the ways that white Illinois residents worked with southerners to enable the "monarchy" of "the oppressor's arm" to reach into Illinois and kidnap free black residents. They lamented how time and again the "blood-hound of the slaveholder . . . without process or charge of a crime, save a colored skin" crossed into Illinois, seized free blacks, and dragged them into slave country.[62] Similar accounts appeared in papers around the state, stoking fears about the "bloodhounds" who terrorized local communities. To substantiate this point, the press pointed toward professional traffickers who had targeted at least "forty-four" free blacks "which they would have taken out of this state."[63] Yet another article reported "it is no unusual occurrence for free colored persons in the Free states to be kidnapped and consigned to perpetual slavery."[64]

This discourse most likely overstated the scale of black kidnapping, but it also helped inspire action against kidnappers. When a kidnapping did occur, local communities sometimes mobilized to liberate the kidnapped people before their captors could take them from the state. In one instance, George Calvert, a "notorious kidnapper" and professional bounty hunter who purportedly had "stolen negroes even from Canada," led a group of kidnappers who accosted Lucinda Lea despite the fact she had "obtained her freedom."[65] On her way between her home in Jacksonville and a neighboring farm, she had been "at a house for a short time" when "three men rode by." One of the men "took her hand and hauled her out" of the house, "calling her *his property.*" The house descended into chaos as its inhabitants scrambled to save her and the kidnappers beat them back. They hauled Lea across the state, but her friends "gave notice to the friends of human rights of the affair." Immediately, local residents organized a search party: "four or five individuals were engaged and supplied with horses" and pursued Calvert.[66] Suspecting he would follow familiar routes out of the state, "going to St. Louis by the way of Carlinville and Edwardsville," they managed to catch him, but he was "armed with an eight barreled pistol and two bowie knives." A struggle ensued, and victorious, they arrested the bounty hunter and returned Lea to her home at Jacksonville.

The press in Chicago highlighted other cases as part of their attempt to raise awareness about a slave power that could reach into Illinois to torment

African Americans there. In Ottawa, Illinois, in the north-central section of the state, "a free negro man" and his wife and children were "overtaken by a Missouri man-hunter, who took forcible possession of the woman and children as his property." The slave catcher had the family declared runaways and "lodged in a jail" and "without trial . . . in irons they were put into a stage coach . . . guarded to keep off the abolitionists and were taken away." White residents in Ottawa mobilized to spare this family the fate so many others had faced. "Some legal proceedings were attempted to set the man free" and "the kidnapper was arrested."[67] The reports of these cases often blurred the boundaries between fact and fiction, and it is impossible to know if the family had been kidnapped or lawfully reclaimed as runaways. Yet as a diverse group of whites and blacks attempted to parse out sweeping questions of slavery and freedom, the press brought a wider constituency into the messy and contested history of emancipation.

The attempt to combat former masters and kidnappers included prominent attorneys, some of whom went on to wield greater influence. In the 1840s, Brown and Yates, a Jacksonville firm, took on kidnapping cases. Richard Yates became governor during the Civil War, but before climbing to those heights, he was a courtroom lawyer. In one instance, the firm responded to a request to aid "the negro man Peter" in his suit for freedom. Peter's main attorney, Nathaniel Wickliffe, reached out to the firm because Peter "was emancipated by the will" of his late master but found the will in dispute. Sometime in the 1820s, Peter's master had died, and Peter was passed to his master's wife, Nancy Graff. Graff died intestate, and Peter seems to have used this fact to claim his freedom. Graff's heir disputed this interpretation, wielding a complicated set of wills and probate laws to make his case. Without an explicit provision freeing him, Peter needed all the help he could get; Brown and Yates appear to have undertaken the important work of researching the will and tracing the inheritance laws as they applied to Peter's case. Additionally, Brown and Yates gathered testimony on his behalf. In particular, they collected "the testimony of David Graff," Nancy's son. Peter's attorney was confident that the research Brown and Yates did would "be sufficient for this negro to obtain his freedom."[68]

Kidnapping "French Negroes" in particular could create a political response from the state's leaders. In 1848 in southern Illinois, kidnappers made a "bold attempt . . . to kidnap a man." Grabbing him, they tried to "manacle him" and "dragged him after them," claiming him as a runaway. Residents in southern Illinois knew the captive and rushed to his defense.

They testified that "his mother was a colored women held as a French slave."[69] The local courts indicted the two kidnappers and hoped to bring them to trial.

These cases could bring more than a local response, which happened when three men kidnapped Wade, a "French Negro" living in Cairo, Illinois. By carrying this "French Negro" out of the state just two years after the *Jarrot* decision promised him his freedom, the kidnappers were keeping slavery alive even for people for whom it had been declared dead. Local officials indicted the three captors on kidnapping charges, and the Illinois governor, Augustus French, demanded their extradition from Missouri.

But what should have been a simple extradition case turned into a protracted struggle as the two governors remained deadlocked for the next three years. Governor Austin King of Missouri initially declined to arrest the parties because it "was asserted by some citizens of this state . . . said man Wade was a slave."[70] No doubt Wade's owner rejected the state supreme court's interpretation that children of "French Negroes" were entitled to freedom. King then assured Governor French that he would comply with the order of extradition but only if the facts convinced him of the three men's guilt. He told his fellow governor that he would "be pleased if you can have the facts of this case furnished to me" but that he "must withhold his warrant for arrest" until he had those facts.[71] French insisted that denying extradition would "shield persons from the crime of Kidnapping" and "reduce free men to Slavery."[72] He confessed he did not know "by what title the person charged to have been Kidnapped is claimed to be held by any citizen of Missouri."[73] He then offered the Missouri governor "the most unquestionable evidence that the person charged to have been Kidnapped is not a slave."

Despite this evidence, King shot back that "facts, incontrovertible in their character," show "that those [indicted] men only aided him [Wade's owner] in the exercise of a clear constitutional right to seize and re-possess his slave." Governor King insisted that "no state has the power to make it a felony to do so [re-possess a slave]. It is a positive and unqualified constitutional right."[74] "I feel," he said, that "it is my duty to refuse" the extradition request.[75] Wade's fate is unknown, but it appears that he was deported to the Lower Mississippi Valley and lived in slavery. Wade's three captors never faced justice, leaving them free to strike again.

By the time the case concluded in 1851, black kidnapping had taken on a new significance because Congress had passed the 1850 Fugitive Slave Act.

The law, passed as part of a larger regional compromise, gave slave catchers federal authority to pursue runaways into the North, even creating a new federal bureaucracy of U.S. commissioners whose job was to oversee the extradition of fugitives. Most significantly to abolitionists, African Americans were barred from testifying before the U.S. commissioner in their defense, and masters did not have to provide written proof that the captured person was their slave. Moreover, the federal commissioners earned a $10 fee per head if the runaway was returned to his or her owner, versus the $5 he got from declaring the captured man free. Abolitionists argued the hearings provided a financial incentive for kidnapping because establishing an African American's freedom meant sacrificing half the commission. The statistics confirm this: only a tiny minority of people escaped their apprehension.[76] Given the increasing kidnappings as time pressed on, many of the state's residents feared that the new law would accelerate the traffic in human flesh.[77]

After 1850, many local jurisdictions mobilized against kidnappers, with a few counties issuing their first indictments for kidnapping. It is impossible to determine if these represented the first instances of kidnapping in these jurisdictions or simply the first indictments. Regardless, with new counties taking action, it gave credence to abolitionists' claims that the geography of human trafficking had expanded in the wake of the 1850 act. A growing number of communities involved in such cases may have contributed to an impression that more and more African Americans were hauled into slavery. Counties in the center of the state and farther north began indicting kidnappers.[78] For instance, in 1851, a jury indicted Ephraim Snider for kidnapping a "colored child" named Mathilda from Williamson County, near present-day Carbondale in south-central Illinois. Mathilda's case represented the first recorded kidnapping in this county.[79] In the same year, two counties near the Ohio River, Pulaski County and Massac County, recorded their first two indictments.[80]

New jurisdictions indicted kidnappers to combat real and perceived threats of reenslavement, and Chicago loomed large. The young city housed a sizable cast of abolitionist attorneys, and the city's population was, on the whole, hostile to slaveholders. Moreover, Chicago served as a vital hub of fugitive slave activity, acting as a final stop on the so-called Underground Railroad before African Americans crossed Lake Michigan on their way to Canada.[81] Despite the antislavery climate in Chicago, slave catchers walked the city streets, and both free African Americans and fugitive slaves risked capture. Chicago's fugitive slave courts became a critical venue for adjudicating the contours of black freedom in Illinois. Those trials helped shape an antislavery politics in part because of the urban context in which information traveled faster, communities mobilized in larger numbers, and more prominent political figures weighed in on the debates. The mix of free African Americans, white abolitionists, runaway slaves, and southern bounty hunters in this dense urban space proved to be a crucible for the state's burgeoning antislavery politicians.

In light of the long-running political controversies over kidnapping and the new dynamics surrounding the 1850 Fugitive Slave Act, circumstances were ripe for conflict between pro- and antislavery groups. In 1851, when "Moses Johnson was arrested on suspicion of being a runaway," Chicagoans plunged into the first such trial after enactment of the Fugitive Slave Act. Fugitive slave trials in Boston and New York had proven to be flashpoints, and Johnson's trial was no different.[82] At first, this case looked like many others: Johnson lacked legal counsel, and his deportation seemed certain. His luck turned when the fugitive slave commissioner delayed the trial.[83] While Johnson sat in jail, "rumor of the arrest took wings and a large number of individuals, including many colored persons, gathered about the entrance to" the location where Johnson was kept. "As evening approached, the crowd at the corner of Lake and Clark streets increased, until the sidewalks and a considerable portion of the street were filled."

Abolitionists circulated flyers alerting the city. "Kidnappers!!" the notice exclaimed. "Citizens' vigilance is the price of liberty," they warned.[84] Perhaps afraid that vigilante justice would prevail that evening, "the Mayor and the City Marshal, together with a number of the police as well as volunteers, were present to preserve order." With Chicago's highest ranking officials looking on, the trial assumed outsized proportions.[85] The commissioner dismissed any evidence that Johnson was a runaway—perhaps only Johnson knew the truth. But as a diverse cast of people attempted to determine his status, they relied on the flyers and press to mediate community understanding and confront a perceived slave power in their midst. Antislavery groups had won a key victory over would-be enslavers. It would not be their last.

Both black and white abolitionists thought that the new Fugitive Slave Law was part of a larger assault on black freedom—and not just at the national level. One proof of assault came in 1853, when the state legislature took aim at the Black Codes. The first Black Codes, passed in 1819, had denied African Americans the franchise and other legal rights and mandated them to register proof of their freedom and post a $500 bond at the county courthouse. The emancipation bond was increased in 1847 to $1,000. Failure to comply had dire consequences. In an 1842 case in Chicago, a sheriff seized Edwin Heathcock, a free black man who worked on the Chicago River, and held him for not having free papers. Declared a runaway, in November 1842, he was put up for auction in Chicago, but an abolitionist bought his labor for the minimum bid and spared him a worse fate.[86] The 1853 laws erected yet higher barriers to black equality in the state by barring black migration into the state. Black migrants could remain in Illinois for only ten days; any longer and they were subject to a $50 fine and imprisonment. These restrictions on black mobility denied African Americans rights to move and hire themselves, a broader set of economic rights that the U.S. Supreme Court had ruled were fundamental to citizenship.[87] Together, black and white abolitionists believed that the Fugitive Slave Act and the expanded Black Codes degraded the rights and opportunities free African Americans could exercise in the state.[88]

Local activism joined with larger regional and national movements to combat perceived kidnappers and fight for an end to the Black Codes. Beginning in the 1830s, free African Americans across the nation had organized politically by joining in Colored Citizen Conventions. Roughly fifty conventions met in various states, from Sacramento, California, to Boston, Massachusetts, and from Toronto, Ontario, to Baltimore, Maryland. They debated leaving the United States, organized to combat the Fugitive Slave Law, and put forward a vision of black freedom and full citizenship that sought to shape the politics of emancipation. When Illinois hosted its first black convention in 1853, among its first objectives were the repeal of the Black Laws and the Fugitive Slave Act. Three years later, a second black convention sought to forge a "well directed organized effort for the Repeal of the 'Black Laws' of the State."[89]

The Colored Citizen Convention's expansion into Illinois belonged to a larger reformulation of antislavery politics at the state and national levels. The Whig Party, whose membership tended at times to have at least some modest antislavery sympathies, had long been decaying, with its support eroding in New York, Ohio, Illinois, and Pennsylvania. Meanwhile, antislavery politics was expanding in a variety of forms, including the free soil movement and the Liberty Party. The Republican Party, founded in

Wisconsin in 1856, had connections to all of these trends, and it soon attracted broad support in northern Illinois and across various northern states. The party's founding principle was its free labor ideology: Republicans asserted that self-ownership was a hallmark of the nation and that slavery was an affront to free labor. A key plank of their platform was the idea that all Americans should own their own labor.[90]

Two years after the Republican Party formed, senatorial candidates Stephen A. Douglas and Abraham Lincoln crisscrossed Illinois, putting the ideas at the bedrock of the Republican platform up to public debate. While their seven meetings in 1858 are now famous for elevating Lincoln to national prominence, their exchanges grew out of Illinois's long and particular history of slavery and captivity, as well as the changing degrees of freedom that existed in the state. The flowering of the Republican Party was a product of several forces, including decades of abolitionist agitation, shrewd tactical politics that undercut Whig and Democratic influence, and the maturation of a free labor ideology. Yet there was a deep context of slavery in Illinois and other nominally free states, including New York and Ohio, that helped to inform the thinking of many leaders of the newly minted Republican Party. As is well known, figureheads like Lincoln drew on a supple intellectual tradition and benefited from the kinds of politics that brought the Whig Party into decline. Yet Lincoln also saw close up how challenging it could be to end slavery's intractable, ever-adapting place in society. In fact, Illinois provided a case study and a kind of laboratory for Lincoln's broader thinking about antislavery politics. On this score, Lincoln was not alone. Stephan Douglas's embrace of popular sovereignty also reflected his immersion in Illinois's slavery politics.

Douglas insisted that a politics of popular sovereignty would diffuse sectional conflict over slavery because it would let each locality hold a popular referendum on slavery. By handing the decision to keep or abolish slavery to local communities, Douglas hoped to calm the acrimonious national debate over slavery's expansion. In a reversal of the earlier politics of slavery, Douglas sought to repeal the Missouri Compromise line that banned slavery in much of the West and to allow settlers in Kansas, Nebraska, and elsewhere the right to vote on slavery's fate. The plan, which Douglas championed and pushed through Congress, backfired as violence between pro- and antislavery communities wracked the Kansas territory, just as it did in southern Illinois. Yet Douglas's belief that local communities, not national decrees, would determine slavery's fate stemmed in part from the long history of slavery in rural Illinois that evaded seemingly categorical bans on human bondage.

When Lincoln and Douglas met in Freeport, Illinois, they tangled over popular sovereignty and slavery's expansion into the territories. In extended discussions about free soil and the *Dred Scott* decision—an 1857 U.S. Supreme Court ruling that held that slavery had national protection and that enslaved people could not claim freedom based on living in free states—Lincoln rejected popular sovereignty as an organizing principle for the politics of slavery. He pressed Douglas to spell out the limits of his support for popular sovereignty, asking when, if ever, the national government could ban or protect slavery in a region. In particular, he asked Douglas if he would support local voters who hoped to defy the *Dred Scott* decision and ban slavery in their state. Douglas answered unequivocally with his so-called Freeport Doctrine. "It matters not what way the Supreme Court may hereafter decide as to the abstract question whether slavery may or may not go into a Territory under the Constitution," because "slavery cannot exist a day or an hour anywhere, unless it is supported by local police regulations," and "those police regulations can only be established by the local legislature." Douglas, who had spent decades living, working, and traveling across southern Illinois, knew perfectly well that local arrangements, not national laws, dictated slavery's survival or destruction. After all, two decades after Congress had banned slavery from Illinois, the territorial legislature had erected a system of contract bondage, and local judges and sheriffs continued to sanction inheritable slavery's place in the state. For Douglas, it was clear that if local citizens supported slavery, the "legislation will favor its extension. Hence, no matter what the decision of the Supreme Court may be on that abstract question, still [it is] the right of the people to make a Slave Territory or a Free Territory."[91]

When the two candidates next met, this time in Jonesboro, in the state's southernmost region, it was Lincoln's turn to use Illinois as the template for a national policy. For Lincoln, a crucial part of Illinois's history was its enduring struggle to protect men and women from reenslavement and extra-legal bondage. But even as he inveighed against slavery's survival, he knew that simply banning human bondage would amount to very little. After all, the United States had debated the slavery question for its entire history, a history that, as Lincoln recounted that night, ran from the Constitutional Convention all the way up to contemporary bleeding Kansas. Given that history, Lincoln asked, "What right have we then to hope that the trouble will cease, that the agitation will come to an end [?]" Illinois had seen constant, violent conflicts over emancipation from 1787 to the eve of the Civil War. Caught between local rulings and the state's supreme court, Illinois occupied shifting ground between slavery and freedom, with neither pro- nor antislavery constituencies displaying any signs of retreat. In his exchange with Douglas—perhaps drawing on his own knowledge of slavery in Illinois—Lincoln asked rhetorically, "Do you think that the nature of man will be changed [?]"[92]

By 1858, Republicans like Abraham Lincoln increasingly had felt that slave power controlled the free states. Lincoln needed to look no further than his clients to understand how slavery could infect a free society. His personal experiences defending Nance from reenslavement reveal how he came to defend black freedom, even as he disparaged the idea of black equality. Nance had lived her life in servitude, and in 1827, she was dragged from her home and family near Springfield and sold to another master. In 1839, once her harrowing tenure in bondage expired, she was again clapped into chains and threatened with sale. Like virtually every other free African American, she lived precariously, and her prospects of being sent to the Deep South only grew over time. So long as slavery existed in the nation, northerners like Nance lived under its threat. In court, Lincoln defended Nance's ability to be free in perpetuity: to earn her living and be assured she would not be trafficked out of Springfield. He never thought that she would have full political and social equality. At their debate in Ottawa, Lincoln was at pains to say he was no advocate of "perfect social and political equality" between the races. The only basic right he embraced was "the right to eat the bread, without the leave of anybody else, which his own hand earns."[93] In time he would advance that vision of freedom, with all its limits, for the wider nation.

Lincoln knew all too well that slavery could outlast its abolition and that masters had endless resources to degrade freedom for African Americans. In 1858, he did not hope to create a society free and equal for all, nor did he think the vestiges of slavery would disappear in an instant. Rather, he hoped to empower people to control their own labor, which meant breaking masters' power to own other people. Illinois's uneven movement to freedom taught leaders in the Republican Party, like Lincoln, that emancipation could only be a long, violent, and contested process. Over decades, freedom advanced in opposition to slavery's ever-adapting place in the state. Lincoln knew from his own experiences that dismantling slavery required decades of local activism, a robust set of freedom networks, and command over the migration patterns in the Mississippi River Valley. Even then, the threat of slavery loomed over every free African American in Illinois.

* * *

Illinois's antislavery leaders developed a freedom politics that looked different from the platforms advanced in the northern states. Facing the reality that the Illinois legislature would never pass an abolition law and that slaveholders could circumvent court rulings by kidnapping freed men and women, Illinois's leaders instead tried to make a local politics that would sustain a series of black freedom practices. These included creating chapters of abolition societies in southern Illinois, circulating antislavery newspapers and pamphlets, organizing to rescue kidnapped men and women, drawing on the legal culture that the black freedom villages incubated, and using the local courts to enforce emancipation in rural communities. The key to success, these leaders knew, laid not in passing laws to abolish the institution of slavery but in creating a set of local contexts that could break slaveholders' power over bound workers. African Americans, free and enslaved, did much of the work that brought those local freedom practices into being, and in so doing, they helped to shape the larger politics of slavery and emancipation in the state and the nation.

In light of the reality that several leading Republicans hailed from Illinois, it is possible to see new contexts for key watershed moments in the history of national emancipation. During the Civil War, Lincoln famously embraced a politics of gradual emancipation for loyal slave states like Kentucky and Delaware that would have delayed freedom for a generation or more.[94] The slow movement to emancipation can paint Lincoln as a conservative.[95] Yet instead, his politics of emancipation came from practical, on-the-ground considerations. As he articulated in his 1858 debate with Douglas in Jonesboro, Congress's envisioned immediate emancipation for the Northwest Territory fell far short of its intended outcome. Instead, slavery's abolition required an intervention to force slaveholders' hand. During the great crucible of the U.S. Civil War, universal military emancipation, which was articulated in the now-famous Emancipation Proclamation, forced emancipation on the slaveholding class. The wartime experience provided local context for African Americans to seize their own freedom and rework their societies.[96] Many of these developments undoubtedly came out of the exigencies of the Civil War, emerged from bitter political feuds that played out during the 1860s, originated with Republican leaders who came from other parts of the nation, and belonged to a deep political and intellectual history that the likes of Lincoln embraced during the 1860s.[97] Still, the hallmarks of national emancipation can also be seen in a longer genealogy that stretched across the many forms of slavery, from indigenous bondage to black kidnapping, and the enduring freedom struggle, from Miller Grove to Chicago's south loop, that shaped Illinois's society.

CONCLUSION

North of Slavery, South of Freedom

On September 22, 1872, communities across the United States celebrated the tenth anniversary of the Emancipation Proclamation. In Chicago, John Jones served as the keynote speaker for this celebration. In the 1840s, Jones, a freeborn African American man from North Carolina, had migrated to Chicago. He lived with his wife Mary in the south loop, and their home was a station on the "Underground Railroad" before it headed to Canada. Together, the Jones family protected untold numbers of self-emancipated slaves who charted a course north toward freedom. The couple belonged to prominent abolitionist circles and maintained ties with Frederick Douglass, John Brown, and Wendell Phillips. John Jones had served in official capacities in the Negro Convention Movement, and in 1871, he became the first elected black official in Chicago's history. Having dedicated years of his life to destroying slavery and advancing black equality, John Jones was a fitting speaker for this auspicious celebration.

Standing near where Jean Baptist Point DuSable, a free Haitian Creole man, established the first permanent trading post on the Chicago River, Jones began his remarks declaring, "all nations and branches of the human family have their day to commemorate—some important event that has occurred which formed an epoch in their history." Jones urged his audience to cherish those touchstones and know its history. He proclaimed, "The effort of our enemies has been to prove to the civilized world that we [African Americans] were without history, therefore not entitled to share the respect of the civilized world." He pressed on, "Because, they say, it makes no difference how profound their thinkers may be, or how eloquently their orators may be declaimed, without history behind them they are not entitled to respect." Jones paused and intoned, "My purpose now is to show that we have history."[1]

Figure 10. John Jones. Chicago History Museum, ICHi-062485. Aaron E. Darling, artist.

Although Jones spoke on this occasion about the bloody civil war that led to national emancipation, he also knew that the war years saw a political battle to end slavery in Illinois and protect citizenship rights for the state's black residents. While the central drama of slave emancipation played out in the U.S. South, Illinois's legislature also took steps to stamp out the final

Figure 11. Mary Jones. Chicago History Museum, ICHi62628.

vestiges of human bondage in its borders. Southern emancipation had a smaller northern counterpart, and although much of that story is now forgotten, if Jones is correct about the importance of knowing history, then this tale of northern liberation should be remembered.

In 1864, as the war entered its third gruesome year, activists in Chicago launched a campaign to repeal the state's Black Laws. For nearly a decade,

Jones had led a campaign against the Black Laws, which placed heavy burdens on the state's black residents. These laws restricted black citizenship in countless ways: they forced African Americans to post emancipation bonds, carry freedom papers, and barred their entry into the state. Jones, who had worked with the black convention movement for more than two decades, turned black activists' attention to Illinois's laws. Serving as co-president of the Colored National Convention with Frederick Douglass, he used his position to mount an assault on his home state's restrictive laws.[2] Other leaders of the convention movement had targeted Black Laws in Ohio and Indiana and won their repeal. Jones hoped to build on those victories.

Jones used his growing influence to launch a press campaign against the Illinois Black Laws. During the 1840s and 1850s, he penned a series of articles for Chicago's flagship abolitionist newspaper, the *Western Citizen.* He made the case that the state's Black Laws filled abolitionists with "regret and alarm" because they placed heavy financial burdens on "citizens of the United States . . . on account of the color of their skin."[3] This press campaign attracted some support. In 1856, local activists met at the Illinois State Black Convention in Alton and formed a repeal association to battle against the Black Laws.[4] Yet other issues overshadowed the movement. The 1850 Fugitive Slave Law terrified abolitionists, and fighting for its repeal consumed many in the state. By the 1860s, national emancipation and the Civil War again had eclipsed Jones's nascent campaign against the Black Laws. By the middle of the decade, Jones may have despaired that the Black Laws would never be repealed. But in an instant, a state supreme court ruling transformed the Black Laws into a flashpoint for activists like Jones.

During the war, many African Americans ran afoul of the Black Laws. Free African Americans who came into Illinois to fill labor shortages still had to pay the sometimes substantial freedom bonds. Failure to comply with the Black Laws meant they faced prison and sale at auction to raise money toward those costs. According to local press in 1863, Nelson, an enslaved man in Missouri, entered Illinois with his master and was freed. Although trafficked to Illinois, his entry into the state violated Illinois's Black Laws, which barred black immigration and residency, and he was arrested, imprisoned, and charged for immigrating to Illinois. Nelson was "tried before . . . [a] Justice of the Peace within and for Hancock County Illinois . . . having come into this state and county and remaining therein for ten days with the evident intention of residing in this state." Having been brought up on charges, he was "found guilty by a Jury . . . and fined $50." Recently freed and without money, he could not summon the resources to pay the fine. He was put up for sale at public auction with a group of other men and women who had run afoul of the Black Laws and "the Purchasers will be entitled to the control and services of negroes and mulatto purchased for the period named in the sale."[5]

At auction, his former master purchased Nelson for life. Having been convicted and sold at auction, he was sentenced to "punishment by involuntary servitude" and resumed serving his master.[6] Nelson quickly found an attorney and challenged his sentence. On appeal, his lawyer argued that Illinois's Black Laws sanctioned human bondage and should be invalidated. He further argued that if Nelson could be pressed back into slavery, it would violate the 1787 Northwest Territory Ordinance ban on involuntary servitude. Significantly, Illinois had not rebelled against the Union, and so it was not subject to the Emancipation Proclamation, weakening the case Nelson's attorney could argue. The Illinois Supreme Court found that Nelson's conviction "violate[s] no provision of the State or national Constitutions, or any enactment of Congress."[7] It reached this conclusion on the grounds that Article Six of the Northwest Territory Ordinance banned slavery and servitude except for "punishment of crimes; whereof the party shall have been duly convicted."[8] Nelson, the court contended, had due process during his conviction. With only one dissenting vote, Nelson's fate was sealed. In 1864, masters had found yet another avenue to introduce slavery into Illinois.[9] Judges and juries in the "Land of Lincoln" used criminal law to keep slavery alive.

The ruling inflamed public opinion in Chicago, and Jones's network snapped into action. In November 1864, Jones authored a pamphlet, "Appeal to the People of Illinois to Repeal the Black Laws of This State," which the *Chicago Tribune* and other leading papers reprinted. In it, Jones asserted that "all men are born free and independent," but the Black Code of 1853 that Nelson ran afoul of "denies the colored man equal freedom."[10] He insisted the laws appeared to have "been written in the dark ages" and the state should be ashamed that "they were approved in the nineteenth century by a Christian Legislature." After detailing the legal oppression the Black Laws imposed, Jones pleaded "in the name of the great Republic and all that is dear . . . in this life, erase those nefarious and unnecessary laws and give us your protection. . . . We ask only evenhanded justice."[11] Jones and his followers toured the state urging repeal. As the campaign took off, the Boston *Liberator* reported that "Mr. Jones, of Chicago, a colored man of great energy . . . is among the most active urging in this matter."[12] In January 1865, Jones met with Governor Richard Yates, urging him to rescind the law. At that time, "a petition from fifty thousand citizens of Illinois" was submitted to the "session of the legislature."[13]

Yates knew that slavery was not dead in Illinois, and during the war, he received reports of slaveholders from Missouri trafficking their enslaved workers through the state's southern regions. One such report came from St. Louis late in 1863, which informed Yates there was a "constant shipment of slaves from this state [Missouri] to Kentucky across Illinois chiefly via the O and M. R.R. to Jeffersonville Ind[iana] and thence across to Louisville." Missouri masters sent their slaves to Louisville because they "can be sold for $200 to $300 per head in K[entuck]y."[14] According to the report, "nothing . . . warrant[s] such a prostitution of free soil to slavery." Pressing on, he insisted, "In the eyes of all genuine emancipationists it is important that these transfer of slaves to Kentucky *overland*, should be stopped." The Emancipation Proclamation, which took effect in January 1863, did not apply to Missouri or Kentucky, and therefore there was no clear, unequivocal ban on selling enslaved African Americans in these border states.

This forced migration delayed emancipation in Missouri, and it reenslaved free African Americans in Illinois. As the observer noted, "There is however a feature of this traffic worse than I have suggested, worse than the perpetual enslavement of these poor creatures to whom our sham emancipation ordinance pretends to have proffered a remote freedom, worse than the burdening of Kentucky with a still greater burden of bondage worse than the separation of families." Noting masters' power to reach into Illinois, the observer reported, "There is a system of kidnapping constantly practiced here by slave traders—a kidnapping of both fugitive slaves [and] emancipated *contrabands*—freed by the proclamation." Alarmed by the scale of the traffic, he informed Governor Yates that "this occurs almost daily and the villains evade punishment by reason of the laws which exclude negro evidence and by the sympathies who hold the positions and offices which afford the best opportunities of their detection." He concluded by assuring the governor he had "facts connected with this traffic that would fill you with horror, but a statement of them is needless."[15] The *Liberator* in Boston reported on these kidnappings, stressing that slavery in Kentucky endangered free African Americans in Illinois.[16] As the Civil War raged, northern abolitionists pressed the point that southern slavery threatened northern freedom.

With demands from Jones and others to repeal the Black Laws and with reports of enslavement coming in, Yates took action. When the state legislature convened in February 1865, it ratified the Thirteenth Amendment, which would ban slavery throughout the nation. During the same session, the legislature also repealed the Black Laws. With the legislature approving these revolutionary measures, Yates offered his backing to both bills. Nearly thirty years earlier, as an attorney in private practice, the governor had worked to help a single enslaved man escape bondage. Assuming a new powerful role to attack slavery, Yates pressed ahead on that front. At once, the legislature carved out protections for black freedom in Illinois and dealt a blow to slavery nationally. The long struggle to make Illinois a free state and close down avenues for reenslavement, like the ones that Nelson fell into, and the bloody campaign to destroy southern slavery advanced hand in hand.

Ending slavery in Illinois was a testing ground for the kinds of politics that would result in freedom nationally. Many of the people who worked to make Illinois free soil did not stop in their fight against slavery. In 1841, Abraham Lincoln helped to free Nance Cromwell from bondage in a local case, and during the war, her son William Costley took up arms. He enlisted in the 26th Illinois Volunteers, and after fighting in Missouri and Mississippi, the company went to Virginia, where on April 9, 1865, Costley witnessed Lee's formal surrender at Appomattox Courthouse. He no doubt knew that President Lincoln had helped his mother escape reenslavement. He probably was aware that his home state had just abolished the Black Laws that had once circumscribed his freedom. He may have pieced together that a direct genealogy stretched from him to his mother, Nance, to the polyglot kinds of human bondage that brought the long-term servitude system and category of "French Negroes" into existence. Regardless what Costley thought on that momentous day, it is certain that this road to Appomattox, which Illinois freedom campaigns shaped, is one part of the larger history of slavery and emancipation in the United States.[17]

The long arc of emancipation can make it seem that abolitionism would necessarily triumph. Moreover, the leadership that Lincoln and others exercised suggests they were naturally antislavery.[18] Yet the reinvention of enslavement in the region shatters any notion of freedom's inevitable rise.

Figure 12. William Costley, son of Ben and Nancy Cromwell, age about twenty-one. Boys in Blue, Logan Collection, Abraham Lincoln Presidential Library and Museum, Springfield Ill.

Slaveholders continually adapted their practices, which in turn required a new set of antislavery tactics. This bitter struggle in Illinois reckons with the notion that "the ending of New World slavery lends itself all too easily to notions of an irresistible advance."[19] The multiple empires that brought slaveries to Illinois and the contorted strategies that kept slavery in its many forms alive show that emancipation was neither easy nor even particularly likely. As these developments took decades to play out, the constant threat of reenslavement and black captivity made freedom's final victory seem all the less likely and never a foregone conclusion.

Abraham Lincoln, Stephan Douglas, Lyman Trumbull, Richard Yates, John Jones, and many other national figures confronted slavery in Illinois as part of their evolving antislavery politics. This cast of politicians worked in various ways against slavery's place in the nation. Yet they all studied their freedom politics under the tutelage of local struggles over slavery and freedom. Slavery in French and native North America in time created legal categories that these nineteenth-century abolitionists had to confront. When Lincoln set the nation on a course toward final emancipation, it was not the first time he combated slavery. As Lyman Trumbull pushed through the language of the Thirteenth Amendment, he was adding a chapter to his personal history of freeing slaves. Richard Yates labored to expand black freedom in Illinois, and it was an extension of his earlier work arguing freedom suits at the circuit level. When John Jones pushed to end Illinois's Black Laws, it was an outgrowth of his own personal freedom suit filed decades before. Because masters perpetually reinvented slavery, including during the Civil War, abolitionists routinely innovated in their campaigns to make Illinois free from human bondage. Those local improvisations in time had national significance. The history of many slaveries and local freedom practices in Illinois illuminates how masters reinvented human bondage and the rocky road to abolition that many captive men and women walked. As John Jones reminds us, it is a story we all should know.

NOTES

Archival Abbreviations

ALPLM	Abraham Lincoln Presidential Library and Museum, Springfield, Ill.
ANC	Foreign Copying Project, France Archives Nationales, Colonies, Manuscript Reading Room, Library of Congress, Washington, D.C.
BWM	Papers of Baynton, Wharton, and Morgan
CO, BNA	Colonial Office Records, British National Archives, Kew, England
CHM	Chicago History Museum, Chicago, Ill.
DAB	Diocesan Archives, Belleville, Ill.
DLC	Library of Congress, Washington, D.C.
GRCP	George Rogers Clark Papers, Virginia State Archives, Richmond, Va.
HLO	Huntington Library, San Marino, Calif.
IHLC	Illinois History and Lincoln Collection, University of Illinois, Champaign-Urbana, Ill.
INHS	Indiana Historical Society, Indianapolis, Ind.
IRAD	Illinois Regional Archives Depository, Springfield and Carbondale, Ill.
ISA	Illinois State Archives, Springfield, Ill.
KM	Kaskaskia Manuscripts, Chester, Ill.
LAC, NARA	Legislative Archives Collection, National Archives and Records Administration, Washington, D.C.
MHS	Missouri Historical Society, St. Louis, Mo.
RG59, NARA	State Department Archives, Record Group 59, National Archives and Records Administration, College Park, Md.
RSC, LSM	Records of the Superior Council of New Orleans, Louisiana State Museum, New Orleans, La.
SLCCR	Circuit Court Case Files, Office of the Circuit Clerk, St. Louis, Mo. State Archives–St. Louis, Office of the Secretary of State. http://stlcourtrecords.wustl.edu
TGP	Thomas Gage Papers, William Clements Library, Ann Arbor, Mich.
WHMC	Western Historical Manuscript Collection, State Historical Society of Missouri, Columbia, Mo.

Introduction

1. Thwaits, ed., *The Jesuit Relations*, vol. 70, 230.
2. Ibid., 233.
3. Ibid.

4. Rushforth, *Bonds of Alliance*; Ekberg, *Stealing Indian Women*; Milne, "Bondsmen, Servants, and Slaves."

5. Thwaits, ed., *The Jesuit Relations*, vol. 69, 143.

6. The text of the document can be found in Onuf, *Statehood and Union*, 110.

7. Their indentures are at Deed Book A, pp. 34–35, Office of the County Clerk, Pope County, Ill.

8. On the similarities between slavery and lifelong servitude, see Gorsuch, "To Indent Oneself"; Gorsuch, "Race and Labour Contracts in the Upper Mississippi Valley."

9. *Matthew Chambers v. People of the State of Illinois*, 1843, Case 1465, p. 6, Supreme Court Case Files, ISA.

10. Augustus French to Austin King, July 20, 1849, in Green and Thompson, eds., *Governors' Letter-Books 1840–1853*, 207.

11. Augustus French to Austin King, February 17, 1852, in ibid., 245.

12. The indictment appears at Circuit Court Book B, p. 349, Office of the Circuit Clerk, Alexander County, Ill. On the request, see French to King, July 20, 1849, in Green and Thompson, eds., *Governors' Letter-Books*, 207.

13. Augustus French to Austin King, July 27, 1849, in ibid., 213.

14. Augustus French to Austin King, February 17, 1852, in ibid., 245.

15. *Joseph Jarot, alias Pete, a colored man v. Julia Jarot*, 1845 [no case number in original], p. 12, Supreme Court Case Files, ISA.

16. In this way, it does not meet the definition of an institution as a patterned way of interacting because no one pattern prevailed. For this conception of an institution, see *Blackwell Dictionary of Sociology*, 2nd ed., s.v. "Institution."

17. This focus on the geography of slavery has been a dominant strain of argument for decades. For the broad outlines of this narrative, see Holt, *Children of Fire*, esp. 1–132; Newman, *A New World of Labor*; Morgan, *Slave Counterpoint*; Berlin, *Generations of Captivity*; Blackburn, *The Making of New World Slavery*.

18. In this way, it responds to recent calls to integrate the history of slaveries in North America. See, for instance, the observation that scholars need to "connect more firmly histories of enslaved Indians to histories of enslaved Africans." Goetz, "Indian Slavery," 68. Others have urged scholars to move past a duality between seeing Indian slavery as a form of social capital and African slavery as a form of labor. See Brooks and Martin, eds., *Linking the Histories*, 4–5. On works that integrate the histories of enslaved Indians and people of African descent, see Miles, *The Dawn of Detroit*. Most notably, Miles depicts a "culturally heterogeneous frontier-borderland environment" where "slavery evolved as a palimpsest, with subjects of the population enacting and challenging slavery in different ways, and with new cultural practices of human bondage inscribed on top of old." Miles, *The Dawn of Detroit*, 17.

19. In this flagship work, he defines slavery as the "permanent, violent domination of natally alienated and generally dishonored persons." See Patterson, *Slavery and Social Death*, 13. Endorsements of this interpretation are many, but see the argument for the "remarkable stability and continuity of the *concept* of total subordination, vulnerability, and animalization" in Davis, "Looking at Slavery from Broader Perspectives," 457. As one recent survey of the literature concludes, much of the study of Atlantic slavery accepts Patterson's argument that human bondage almost uniformly uprooted people from their natal ties, subjected them to total violent domination, and condemned them to perpetual dishonor; see Brown, "Social

Death and Political Life in the Study of Slavery." For a broader survey that generally endorses Patterson's approach, see Bodel and Scheidel, eds., *On Human Bondage*. For this conception of an institution, see *Penguin Dictionary of Sociology*, 4th ed., s.v. "Institution."

20. In this way, it takes seriously Joseph Miller's trenchant critique of Patterson's work, which he argues has created a literature that accepts that "slavery—in all times and places—has been a single institution subject to straightforward comparisons." In this estimation, an institutional analysis has minimized or even excluded historical context, all too often leaving those contexts "as decorative background, analytically inert, effectively dismissed as insignificant." Miller, *The Problem of Slavery as History*, 12, 23. For other similar critiques of Patterson, see, for example, Fett, *Reclaimed Africans*, 10; Fuentes, *Dispossessed Lives*, 10, 79; McKinley, *Fractional Freedoms*, 8; Freamon, "Straight No Chaser," 67.

21. In so doing, it joins a growing line of work in Atlantic studies that identifies a "highly compartmentalized nature" of Atlantic history that neglects much of what does not touch the Atlantic basin." Allen, *European Slave Trading in the Indian Ocean*, 5. The result is that scholars have in part neglected forms of slavery that did not directly connect to the Atlantic basin; Alpers, "The African Diaspora in the Northwestern Indian Ocean," 62–81.

22. Lipman, *The Saltwater Frontier*, 9. A similar call comes from Cohen, "Was There an Amerindian Atlantic?" 390. The number of works that adopt this perspective are expanding, and influential titles include Hatfield, *Atlantic Virginia*; Cangany, *Frontier Seaport*; Weaver, *The Red Atlantic*.

23. This move is in line with other studies that critique the Atlantic as a productive framework; Green and Morgan, eds., *The Atlantic World*; Cohen, "Was There an Amerindian Atlantic?" Other notable works include Games, "Beyond the Atlantic"; Gould, "Comparing Atlantic Histories." For more on slavery in economies without plantations, see Shepherd, ed., *Slavery Without Sugar*.

24. The work on Indian slavery is vast and growing rapidly, but landmark works include Resendez, *The Other Slavery*; Kiser, *Borderlands of Slavery*; Newell, *Brethren by Nature*; Rushforth, *Bonds of Alliance*; Snyder, *Slavery in Indian Country*; Barr, *Peace Came in the Form of a Woman*; Miles, *Ties That Bind*; Gallay, *The Indian Slave Trade*; Brooks, *Captives and Cousins*; Ruby and Brown, *Indian Slavery in the Pacific Northwest*; Bossy, "Godin & Co.: Charleston Merchants and the Indian Trade, 1674–1715." For a review of some of this literature, see Bialuschewski and Fisher, "New Directions in the History of Native American Slavery Studies"; Cameron, "Slavery and Freedom in Small-Scale Societies."

25. One recent literature review concludes, "Scholars rightly mark a strong distinction between the kinship slavery practiced by southern Indians and the racialized slavery created by the British in the seventeenth century Atlantic World." Bossy, "The South's Other Slavery," 35. As a recent prize-winning book argues, there was "a contrast between African and Indian slaves that was ultimately rooted in law." Resendez, *The Other Slavery*, 48.

26. On the diversity of slavery during and before the eighteenth century, see Linda Colley, who pushes against any binary construction of slavery in her work *Captives*, 63; Guasco, *Slaves and Englishmen*; Donoghue, "'Out of the Land of Bondage,'" 948; Kolchin, "Variations of Slavery in the Atlantic World," 552; Amussen, *Caribbean Exchanges*, 10–11. New work on indigenous bondage also shows that "a large number of Native Americans were forced into a wide variety of slaveries and unfreedoms in the early modern world." Bialuschewski and Fisher, "New Directions," 2.

27. Scholarship on New France has shown that slavery adapted to local circumstances with "terrific creativity"; Rushforth, *Bonds of Alliance*, 139, 197. Still, the existing work asserts that attempts to force enslaved Indians to work in staple production "largely failed" and that by the mid-eighteenth century, the two forms of slavery evolved in different directions. Rushforth, *Bonds of Alliance*, 13. Rushforth contends it was "impossible to erected a racially defined slave system in New France," which meant "the distinctions between Indian Slavery in the Saint Lawrence Valley and African Slavery in the Caribbean could not have been more clear." Rushforth, *Bonds of Alliance*, 365–66. See also Dan Usner, who calls Indian slavery in the Louisiana plantation economy a largely incidental institution because of demographic collapse, surging imports of Africans, and ease of Indian fugitivity in *Settlers, Indians, and Slaves*, 59.

28. For a recent summation of this trend in the literature, see Goetz, "Indian Slavery." For similar observations about other parts of North Americas, see the claim that "Spaniards adapted Indian slavery to fit the new legal environment, and thus it became the other slavery." Resendez, *The Other Slavery*, 75. Still others observe that Indian and African slavery "evolved and innovated in response to each other" across the Americas. Brooks and Martin, eds., *Linking the Histories*, 4. Scholars of New England are arguing that Indian slavery "shaped the rise of African Slavery in New England in important ways." See Newell, *Brethren by Nature*, 12.

29. The work on the "second slavery" is vast and rapidly growing. Important and representative works in this trend include Tomich, *Through the Prism of Slavery*; Johnson, *River of Dark Dreams*; Baptist, *The Half Has Never Been Told*; Rood, *The Reinvention of Atlantic Slavery*; Ferrer, *Freedom's Mirror*; and Berbel et al., *Slavery and Politics.* A useful overview appears in Kaye, "The Second Slavery."

30. This line of argument is emerging in the current literature. As one scholar notes, the growing trend is to argue that "the American Revolution set in motion a long and bitterly divisive struggle over slavery and race in the new nation." Oakes, "Conflict vs. Racial Consensus in the History of Antislavery Politics," 292. This substantially revises an older literature that asserted that the American Revolution began a process of gradual emancipation in the North that faced little opposition. See especially Litwack, *North of Slavery*. For the broad contours of the newer argument, see Sinha, *The Slave's Cause*, esp. 65–96; Rael, *Eighty-Eight Years*; Berlin, *The Long Emancipation*; Hahn, *The Political Worlds of Slavery and Freedom*, esp. 7–8.

31. For state-based studies, see Gigantino, *The Ragged Road to Abolition*; Gellman, *Emancipating New York*; Melish, *Disowning Slavery*; White, *Somewhat More Independent*; Nash and Soderlund, *Freedom by Degrees.*

32. Studies of the fight for racial equality in the wake of the revolution are numerous, and principles studies include Sinha, *The Slave's Cause*, esp. 130–59; Hodges, *David Ruggles*; Kantrowitz, *More Than Freedom*; Newman, *Freedom's Prophet*; Harris, *In the Shadow of Slavery*; Stauffer, *Black Hearts of Men*; Horton and Horton, *In Hope of Liberty.*

33. Morrissey, *Empire by Collaboration*, 159–61.

34. This builds off of the observation that slavery often acted as a set of coercive "practices that needed to be interpreted." In this sense, "slave status, in effect, could be based on something that looked rather like simple present possession, deflecting inconvenient inquiry into the (perhaps altogether absent) root of the alleged title." Scott, "Social Facts, Legal Fictions, and the Attribution of Slave Status," 11, 17.

35. Tomlins and Mann, eds., *The Many Legalities of Early America*, 2. This insight departs from other influential studies of slavery that assert a "hegemonic function of the law." See Genovese, *Roll Jordan Roll*, 25–49; for other similar evaluations of the hegemonic power of the law, see Patterson, *Slavery and Social Death*, 28–32.

36. On the various forms of bound labor in New World economies going into the early nineteenth century, see Steinfield, *The Invention of Free Labor*, esp. 159–60; Tomlins, *Freedom Bound*, esp. 410–11.

37. For these histories, see Aron, *American Confluence*; Taylor, *Frontiers of Freedom*; Salafia, *Slavery's Borderland*; VanderVeld, *Redemption Songs*; Twitty, *Before* Dred Scott; Kennington, *In the Shadow of* Dred Scott; Arenson, *The Great Heart of the Republic.*

Chapter 1

1. KM 48:7:16:2.

2. A Case of Infanticide, 1748_07_15_1, RSC, LSM.

3. Ibid.

4. Second Interrogation of Marie Jeanne, 1749_06_17_1, RSC, LSM.

5. Attorney General vs. Marie Jeanne, 1749_06_17_1, RSC, LSM.

6. Information about Lisette is pieced together from various statements appearing in A Case of Infanticide, 1748_07_15_1, RSC, LSM.

7. Second Interrogation of Marie Jeanne, 1749_06_17_1, RSC, LSM.

8. Statement of Surgeons Gueydon and Goudeau, 1749_07_1_1, RSC, LSM.

9. Second Interrogation of Marie Jeanne, 1749_06_17_1, RSC, LSM.

10. On this paradigm shift, see Curran, *The Anatomy of Blackness*; Davis, "Constructing Race: A Reflection," 7–18; Davis, *The Problem of Slavery in the Age of Emancipation*, 28–33; Aubert, "'The Blood of France'"; Aubert, "Kinship, Blood, and the Emergence of the Racial Nation"; White, *Wild Frenchmen and Frenchified Indians*; Spear, "Colonial Intimacies"; Delbourgo, "The Newtonian Slave Body."

11. Before the rise of the new sorts of racial thinking that posited immutable differences, French officials in the seventeenth century had believed that they could create "one people and one blood" in New France through the marriages of Frenchmen and Indian women. See quote in Aubert, "The Blood of France," 452. In time, French officials abandoned that policy, concluding that Indians and Frenchmen belonged to different races and that these perceived racial differences could not be changed through "Frenchifying" policies. The literature on this policy is extensive, but generally, see DuVal, "Indian Intermarriage and Métissage in Colonial Louisiana," esp. 284–86; Belmessous, "Assimilation and Racialization in Seventeenth and Eighteenth Century French Colonial Policy"; Jaenen, "The Frenchification and Evangelization of the Amerindians in Seventeenth Century New France"; and Hughes, "Within the Grasp of Company Law."

12. Rushforth, *Bonds of Alliances*, esp. 301, 362–66.

13. The literature on the transformations that plantation revolutions wrought is too substantial to cite in full, but for recent influential work, see Burnard, *Planters, Merchants, and Slaves*; Menard, *Sweet Negotiations*; Berlin, *Many Thousands Gone*, esp. 29–47.

14. A robust literature on Indian slavery is beginning to take shape. On French North America, see Ekberg, *Stealing Indian Women*; Rushforth, *Bonds of Alliance*. On British regions, see Snyder, *Slavery in Indian Country*; Newell, *Brethren by Nature*; Warren, *New England Bound*; Bossy, "The South's Other Slavery." In New Spain, see Resendez, *The Other Slavery.*

For attempts to integrate these histories, see Brooks and Martin, eds., *Linking the Histories*; Goetz, "Indian Slavery."

15. Rushforth, "'A Little Flesh We Offer You.'"

16. This largely departs from a literature that sees slavery as incidental to colonial expansion in the Mississippi Valley. See Furstenberg, "The Significance of the Trans-Appalachian Frontier in Atlantic History"; Faragher, *Sugar Creek*; Hinderaker, *Elusive Empires*; Cayton and Teute, eds., *Contact Points*.

17. This challenges the prevailing idea articulated in Curtin, *The Rise and Fall of the Plantation Complex*, esp. 14–16; and Berlin, *Many Thousands Gone*, esp. 8–9.

18. On the early origins of French settlement in Illinois, see Morrissey, "The Power of the Ecotone"; Morgan, *Land of Big Rivers*; Milne, "Bondsmen, Servants, and Slaves." On this trend more generally, see Smith, *Indian Women and French Men*; Van Kirk, *Many Tender Ties*; Peterson, "The People in Between." On French North America more generally, see Havard and Vidal, *Histoire de l'Amerique Francise*; Royot, *Divided Loyalties in a Doomed Empire*.

19. For a discussion of Rouensa, see White, *Wild Frenchmen and Frenchified Indians*, esp. 33–40, 80–92; Ekberg, *French Roots*, esp. 77–78; on intermarriage patterns generally, see Morrissey, "Kaskaskia Social Network."

20. See, for example, the January 1750 baptism of Rouensa's descendants in Brown and Dean, eds., *The Village of Chartres in Colonial Illinois*, 161.

21. See in particular the conclusion that "Catholicism united [French and Indian] residents in the rituals of baptism, marriage, and Mass." DuVal, "Indian Intermarriage," 284. Another scholar concludes that "religious encounters . . . brought people together in ways that promoted exchange across cultural borders but not in a simple or straightforward fashion." Leavelle, *The Catholic Calumet*, 7.

22. White, *Wild Frenchmen*, esp. 47–54; Aubert, "The Blood of France," 439–78.

23. At times, land came as part of an Indian woman's dowry. For one such dowry, see KM 30:1:23:1.

24. On the nature of slavery and settlement in lower Louisiana, see Usner, *Settlers, Indians, and Slaves*; Hall, *Africans in Colonial Louisiana*.

25. On the West African origins of most slaves in colonial Louisiana, see Peter Caron, "'Of a Nation Which Others Do Not Understand.'"

26. Journal of Diron D'Artaguette, 67–88.

27. Mémoire de Boisbriant concernant le poste des Illinois, Fevrier 9, 1725, ANC, C13A, vol. 8, fol. 447v, DLC.

28. For census data, see Morrissey, *Empire by Collaboration*, 144–45.

29. Leavelle, *The Catholic Calumet*, 65–70.

30. On the *Code Noir* and slavery in French North America, see Aubert, "'To Establish One Law and Definite Rules'"; Ekberg, *French Roots*, 135; Rushforth, *Bonds of Alliance*, 125–28; Curran, *The Anatomy of Blackness*, esp. 56–59.

31. Morrissey, *Empire by Collaboration*, 159–61. In an unpublished manuscript, one historian shows that the local adaptations to slavery openly clashed with the prescriptions of the *Code Noir*. Steinke, "The *Code Noir* in the Illinois Country."

32. On the prevalence of spring and winter wheat, see Ekberg, *French Roots*, 118. No sources preserve the workings of slaves on French grain farms. Still, it seems likely slavery played the same role in this wheat economy as it did elsewhere in North America. Earle, "A

Staple Interpretation of Slavery and Free Labor." For this agricultural thesis, see Irwin, "Exploring the Affinity of Wheat and Slavery in the Virginia Piedmont." For the refutation, see Wright, "Slavery and American Agricultural History." More generally, see Grivno, *Gleanings of Freedom*, esp. 23–63, 92–93. Although there are no records that describe the labor regime in Illinois, other slave labor economies that cultivated cereal grains—such as in Virginia or the piedmont of Maryland—used gang labor during harvest. Ekberg, *French Roots*, esp. 145–57.

33. For the importance of these conditions in making a plantation economy, see Domar, "The Causes of Slavery or Serfdom: A Hypothesis."

34. Ekberg, *French Roots*, 265–73. See also Denny, *Ingenium*, 31–60; Reynolds, *Stronger Than a Hundred Men*; and Kuhlmann, *The Development of the Flour-Milling Industry*.

35. For discussions of the movement around the Upper Mississippi Valley, see Extrait de la Letter Ecrite a M. Salmon, commissaire de la Marine Ordonnateur par M. De La Loere, Ecrivain Principal aux illinois, Novembre 13, 1735, ANC, c13a, vol. 21, fols. 235–235v, DLC.

36. According to one scholar, indigenous slavery in French North America was "driven not by a high demand for slaves, but by the political and cultural imperatives of enslavement" that stemmed from a "regional diplomatic culture" that relied on slavery to organize power. Rushforth, *Bonds of Alliance*, 29.

37. Ibid., 61.

38. DuVal, "Indian Intermarriage," 271 n. 6; Rushforth, *Bonds of Alliances*, esp. 138–39; Morrissey, *Empire by Collaboration*, 32–34. On the point of adoption more generally, see Snyder, *Slavery in Indian Country*, esp. 62–66.

39. Lee, "Rivers of Power," 30. Some estimates place the number of Illinois Indians closer to 7,000, but Lee makes a convincing case for the higher number.

40. Norton, ed., *Illinois Census Returns 1810, 1818*, xxvi.

41. For examples of women whose surnames imply they were Plains Apaches, see Brown and Dean, eds., *The Village of Chartres in Colonial Illinois*, 20, 51, 134. For slaves called Pawnee, see ibid., 24, 28. Fox slaves appear at ibid., 78.

42. Rushforth, *Bonds of Alliance*, 136–37, 182–83.

43. Morrissey, *Empire by Collaboration*, 157.

44. For one instance of many, see Brown and Dean, eds., *The Village of Chartres in Colonial Illinois*, 14. Importantly, Turpin, a slaveholder and aspiring planter, was also married to an Illinois Indian woman. For more on this trend, see DuVal, "Indian Intermarriage," 282.

45. Brown and Dean, eds., *The Village of Chartres in Colonial Illinois*, 14.

46. This is merely impressionistic and comes from entries in the church records. See, for example, Brown and Dean, eds., *The Village of Chartres in Colonial Illinois*, 325.

47. One Indian slave sale appears at KM 48:12:20:1.

48. Norton, ed., *Illinois Census Returns 1810, 1818*, xxiii.

49. Brown and Dean, eds., *The Village of Chartres in Colonial Illinois*, 75 (godfather) and 46, 180 (owning Indian slaves).

50. Janvier 26–Mars 25, 1736, Relátion de la parties Chicachias comme Francais, ANC c13a, vol. 21, fol. 22, DLC.

51. Brown and Dean, eds., *The Village of Chartres in Colonial Illinois*, 36, 46, 53.

52. Thwaits, ed., *The Jesuit Relations*, vol. 70, 231.

53. Brown and Dean, eds., *The Village of Chartres in Colonial Illinois*, 28. "Pawnee" was often an open signifier for all Indian slaves, and we cannot assume a national or racial origin of this enslaved woman. On this point see Miles, *Dawn of Detroit*, 40–1.

54. Boisbriant a Perier et Salmon, Octobre 5, 1731, ANC c13a, vol. 13, fol. 12, DLC.

55. Ibid., fol. 9v.

56. Ibid., fols. 17v–18.

57. He also noted the importance of the fur trade, remarking that "the commerce in pelts in considerable." See Instruction sommaire pour achever un solide etablissement dans la Louisiane dirige par le Sr Drouot de Valdeterre [1722?], ANC, c13a, vol. 6, fols. 362v–363.

58. Mémoire de Boisbraint concernant le poste des Illinois, Fevrier 9, 1725, ANC, c13a, vol. 8, fol. 447v, DLC.

59. Ibid., fol. 448v.

60. Ibid.

61. Boisbriant a le compte de Maurepas, Mars 29, 1731, ANC c13a, vol. 13, fols. 49–49v, DLC.

62. For instance, one French settler fathered at least two children with "a Fox Woman belonging to Chauvin." See Brown and Dean, eds., *The Village of Chartres in Colonial Illinois*, 78. In another prominent case, the French commander of the garrison at Fort de Chartres held enslaved Fox Indians. See Rushforth, "Slavery, Fox Wars, and the Limits of Alliance," 74. Edmunds and Peyser, *The Fox Wars*; Ekberg, *Stealing Indian Women*, 23.

63. Mouvements des sauvages de la Louisianne depuis la prise du fort des Natches par Mr de Perier sul la fin de Janvier 1731, ANC, c13a, vol. 13, fol. 85, DLC.

64. Boisbrian a Mrs. Perier et Salmon La Louisianne, Octobre 5, 1731, ANC, c13a, vol. 13, fols. 17–17v, DLC.

65. Mouvements des sauvages de la Louisianne, ANC, c13a, vol. 13, fol. 85, DLC.

66. Mémoire sur les marriages des Sauvagesses avec les francois, Louisianne 1738, ANC c13a, vol. 23, fol. 242v, DLC.

67. Rushforth, *Bonds of Alliances*, 193–252. Unlike the Yamassee War in the Carolinas, the Fox Wars did not appear to trigger a large-scale abandonment of Indian slavery. On the Carolinas, see Gallay, *The Indian Slave Trade*, 315–44.

68. See the statistics in Ekberg, *French Roots*, 152. For specific instances, see Registry of Baptisms, 1759–1815, Parish of the Immaculate Conception of Notre Dame, pp. 22, 32, DAB.

69. Bienville a Vaudreuil, Octobre 6, 1744, ANC, c13a, vol. 28, fol. 247, DLC.

70. Bienville [a Vaudreuil?], Fevrier 4, 1743, ANC, c13a, vol. 28, fol. 32v, DLC.

71. Bienville a Vaudreuil, Octobre 6, 1744, ANC, c13a, vol. 28, fol. 245v, DLC.

72. Extrait sur les Islinois et la post de S. Demis, Boisbriant a M. de Bienville Aoust 27, 1734, ANC, c13a, vol. 18, fol. 188v.

73. La Louisianne Islinois a Mrs Perrier et Salmon, [n.d., 1731], ANC, c13a, vol. 13, fol. 28, DLC.

74. M le Cher de L'Auboey, Mars 20, 1733, ANC, c13a, vol. 17, fol. 226, DLC.

75. M salmon a [Unknown], Mai 20, 1733, ANC, c13a, vol. 17, fol. 147v, DLC.

76. M le Cher de L'Auboey, ANC, c13a, vol. 17, fol. 226, DLC.

77. La Louisianne Islinois, a Mrs Perrier et Salmon, [n.d.] 1731, ANC, c13a, vol. 13, fols. 29v–30, DLC.

78. Ibid., fol. 30.

79. A M. de Vaudreuil, Avril 1751, ANC, c13a, vol. 35, fol. 80v, DLC.

80. A M. de Vaudreuil et Michel, May 21, 1751, ANC, c13a, vol. 35, fols. 21–21v, DLC.

81. A M. de Vaudreuil, May 2, 1751, ANC, c13a, vol. 35, fol. 91, DLC. For a second statement of the need for garrisons and safe passage of convoys from the Illinois Country, see

Vaudreuil to Maurepas, May 2, 1751, and May 28, 1751, letter book vol. 2, Vaudreuil Papers (French Colonial Manuscripts), HLO.

82. These calculations come from Norton, ed., *Illinois Census Returns 1810, 1818,* xxi, xxvii. Importantly, the 1752 census records land values at 6,658 livres. Norton identified errors in the original census tabulations and accordingly revised the number upward. For a detailed breakdown of the population and its holdings, see Hinderaker, *Elusive Empires*, 98–99.

83. Morrissey, *Empire by Collaboration*, 145–47.

84. On this planter, see Vidal, "Antoine Bienvenu, Illinois Planter and Mississippi Trader." There are no extant business records or correspondence from Bienvenu's estate. Norton, ed., *Illinois Census Returns 1810, 1818*, xxi.

85. Presente Etate de la Louisiane, [n.d.] 1749, ANC, c13a, vol. 33, fol. 167v, DLC.

86. Ibid.

87. Mémoire Sur Administration, [n.d.] 1749, ANC, c13a, vol. 33, fol. 152v, DLC.

88. Bienville a Vaudreuil, Mai 8, 1747, ANC, c13a, vol. 31, fol. 73, DLC.

89. A M. Michel, Janvier 22, 1750, ANC, c13a, vol. 34, fol. 300, DLC.

90. Joint a la Lettre de m. Michel a Bordeaux du May 21, 1748 a l'Alphabet de la marine, ANC, c13a, vol. 32, fol. 248v, DLC.

91. Bienville [a Vaudreuil?], Fevrier 4, 1743, ANC, c13a, vol. 28, fol. 35v, DLC.

92. Bienville a M. d'Auberville, Juin 11, 1748, ANC, c13a, vol. 32, fol. 192v, DLC.

93. Sur les Equipements et le Retard des Voyageurs aux Illinois, Avril 8, 1751. ANC, c13a, vol. 36, fol. 81, DLC.

94. M. Michel a Macarty a la Nouvelle Orleans, Mai 27, 1751, ANC, c13a, vol. 35, fol. 362, DLC.

95. Sur les Equipements et le Retard des Voyageurs aux Illinois, Avril 8, 1751. ANC, c13a, vol. 36, fol. 81v, DLC.

96. M. Michel, La Situation de la Colonie Louisianne, Juilliet 23, 1752, ANC, c13a, vol. 36, fols. 270–270v, DLC. Another statement on the region's importance can be found at Vaudreuil to Maurepas, April 30, 1746, Box 2, Vaudreuil Papers (French Colonial Manuscripts), HLO.

97. Sur les Equipements et le Retard des Voyageurs aux Illinois, Avril 8, 1751. ANC, c13a, vol. 36, fol. 81v, DLC.

98. M. Michel, La Situation de la Colonie Louisianne, Juilliet 23, 1752, ANC, c13a, vol. 36, fols. 270–270v, DLC.

99. Ibid., fol. 271.

100. M. de Bienville a [unknown], Avril 26, 1738, ANC, c13a, vol. 23, fol. 52, DLC.

101. Mémoire sur la Louisiane, Decembre 27, 1756, ANC c13a, vol. 38, fol. 207, DLC.

102. "Mémoir of La Galissoniere," 22. Other mentions of the convoys arriving in New Orleans with provisions include Vaudreuil to Marupas, November 20, 1746, Letter Book vol. 1, Vaudreuil Papers (French Colonial Manuscripts), HLO.

103. Copie de la letter ecrit a M de Macarty, Juin 1, 1756, Joint a la letter de m De Kerlerec, ANC, c13a, vol. 39, fol. 71, DLC.

104. Ibid., fols. 71–71v.

105. Etat des nations sauvages, [n.d.], ANC, c13a, vol. 40, fol. 135, DLC.

106. Bienville a Vaudreuil, Mai 24, 1748, ANC, c13a, vol. 32, fols. 63v–64, DLC.

107. Rushforth, *Bonds of Alliance*, 13. Rushforth contends it was "impossible to erected a racially defined slave system in New France," which meant "the distinctions between Indian

Slavery in the Saint Lawrence Valley and African Slavery in the Caribbean could not have been more clear." Rushforth, *Bonds of Alliance*, 365–66. See also Usner, who calls Indian slavery in the Louisiana plantation economy a largely incidental institution because of demographic collapse, surging imports of Africans, and ease of Indian fugitivity. Usner, *Settlers, Indians, and Slaves*, 59.

Chapter 2

1. On the history of slavery in Pennsylvania, see Berlin, *Many Thousands*, 55–56; Nash and Soderland, *Freedom by Degrees*, 3–41.

2. The cargo of slaves in Philadelphia came from the firm Bean and Cuthbert. See Invoice of Goods, September 14, 1766, Kent et al., *Baynton, Wharton, and Morgan.*

3. On the history of slavery in Jamaica, generally see Burnard, *Mastery, Tyranny, Desire.*

4. [John] Baynton to [James] Rumsey, March 1, 1768, in Alvord and Carter, eds., *Trade and Politics*, 181.

5. George Morgan to Alexander Williamson, November 1768, Kent et al., *Baynton, Wharton, and Morgan Papers.*

6. Morgan to Baynton and Wharton, December 2, 1767, in Alvord and Carter, eds., *Trade and Politics*, 126.

7. Morgan to Baynton and Wharton, July 20, 1768, in ibid., 360.

8. Calloway, *The Scratch of a Pen*, 131. On the nature of Britain's dominance in the West, see also Furstenberg, "The Significance of the Trans-Appalachian Frontier in Atlantic History"; Hammond, "Slavery, Sovereignty, and Empires"; Hammond, "Slavery, Settlement, and Empire"; Wigmore, "Before the Railroad"; Crouch, "The Black City."

9. This dynamic of local knowledge trumping imperial control played out across the British Empire in this period. Edleson, *The New Map of Empire*, esp. 10–11, 166–67.

10. There are no complete census data for the British period of occupation. Consequently, it is safe to infer that as the number of towns grew and as new settlers arrived, in addition to natural growth, the enslaved population increased by several hundred—perhaps reaching a thousand—and the free population likely grew similarly.

11. Pitman, *The Present State of the European Settlements*, 84.

12. On the population of Illinois in this period, see Ekberg, *French Roots*, 152–60.

13. On the firm's founding, Dewar, "George Morgan's American Life," esp. xii–xvii.

14. To cite only one example, General Gage allowed them to travel under the cover of the "Kings Boats" to offer them "a safe convoy." Thomas Gage to Messers Baynton, Wharton, and Morgan, New York, July 23, 1766, in TGP.

15. Reason for establishing a British Colony at the *Illinois* with some Proposals for carrying the same into immediate Execution, July 10, 1766, CO 5/67, p. 188, BNA.

16. Lyman's Reasons for Settlement Along the Mississippi, in Alvord and Carter, eds., *The New Regime*, 271–72. See n. 1 for the documentary editors' observation that Lord Dartmouth endorsed this position during his first presidency of the Board of Trade.

17. Lord Hillsborough to Thomas Gage, July 31, 1770, TGP.

18. Kren, "The 'Grand Illinois Venture,'" 74–75.

19. One scholar notes that "their goal was to block the British occupation of the Illinois and Wabash country and to maintain it as a de facto French-Algonquian island in the midst of the British empire." White, *The Middle Ground*, 297.

20. See also Dowd, *War Under Heaven*; Rushforth, *Bonds of Alliance*, 369–45; Cagney, *Frontier Seaport*, 112–17.

21. For the earliest settlers in St. Louis, see Gitlin, *The Bourgeois Frontier*, esp. 13–18; Hyde, *Empires, Nations, and Families*, esp. 29–37; Foley and Rice, *The First Choteaus*; Ekberg and Person, *St. Louis Rising*.

22. George Croghan to Whitehall, December 12, 1765, CO 5/66, p. 169, BNA.

23. George Morgan to Messers Walker, Stepple, and Skelhorn, March 2, 1764, in Kent et al., *Baynton, Wharton, and Morgan Papers*.

24. Thomas Sterling to General Gage, October 18, 1765, in Alvord and Carter, eds., *The New Regime*, 108–9.

25. Ibid., 109.

26. Jennings Journal, April 6, 1766, in Alvord and Carter, eds., *The New Regime*, 177.

27. [Thomas] Sterling to [Thomas] Gage, December 15, 1767, in Alvord and Carter, eds., *The New Regime*, 125.

28. Lord Hillsborough to Thomas Gage, January 2, 1771, TGP.

29. [Antonio d'] Ulloa to [Thomas] Gage, August 29, 1768, in Alvord and Carter, eds., *Trade and Politics*, 386.

30. Spear, *Race, Sex, and Social Order*, 100–29, and on the nature of turmoil in the city more generally, see Johnson, *Slavery's Metropolis*, 28–38.

31. "Butricke to Barnsley, February 12, 1769," in Alvord and Carter, eds., *Trade and Politics*, 498.

32. KM 68:4:19:1. The damage to the document prevents any clear re-creation of the signatures.

33. This marriage contact appears in KM 70:1:29:2. For other examples, see KM 68:5:14:1, 68:5:15:1.

34. For probate on Beauvais, see KM 73:5:4:2. For an example of families who had members on both sides of the river buying goods, see the Beauvais entries in the Account of the Negro Sales at Kaskaskia, in Kent et al., *Baynton, Wharton, and Morgan Papers*.

35. KM 73:5:4:2 and the Census of 1752 in Vaudreuil Papers (French Colonial Manuscripts). The probate record shows Jean Baptiste owned thirty-one slaves, up from twenty-four in 1752, while the closest enumeration for his brother is fifteen, on the 1752 census.

36. On provision grounds generally, see Berlin and Morgan, eds., *Cultivation and Culture*; Hilliard, *Masters, Slaves, and Exchange*.

37. Morgan to Baynton and Wharton, December 6, 1767, in Alvord and Carter, eds., *Trade and Politics*, 128.

38. For instance, he carried "Negro Magnets" to sell into the slave quarter; see, Bought of James & Drinker, Philadelphia, July 9, 1768, in Kent et al., *Baynton, Wharton, and Morgan Papers*.

39. Registry of Baptisms, Parish of the Immaculate Conception of Notre Dame, 1759–1815, pp. 70, 110, DAB.

40. Brown and Dean, eds., *The Village of Chartres in Colonial Illinois*, 296.

41. Ibid., 62 [July 1763], 71 [February 1765].

42. Parish Records of St. Joseph's Parish, 1761–1798, entry on September 27, 1771 [no page in original], Prairie du Rocher Collection, CHM.

43. The lack of complete family information and irregular racial identifiers make unpacking the contours of this racial intermixing impossible. For one instance, see ibid., 38.

44. Registry of Baptisms, 1759–1815, Immaculate Conception, 32, DAB.

45. The Louisiana governor halted all slave imports to Illinois in 1747. See Maurepas to Vaudreuil and Le Normant, October 9, 1747, in Pease, ed., *Illinois on the Eve of the Seven Years' War*, 36.

46. Morgan to Baynton and Wharton, December 6, 1767, in Alvord and Carter, eds., *Trade and Politics*, 125–26.

47. George Morgan to John Fitzpatrick, July 27, 1770, in Kent et al., *Baynton, Wharton, and Morgan Papers*.

48. [George] Morgan to John Finney, May 3, 1768, in Alvord and Carter, eds., *Trade and Politics*, 274.

49. Lieutenant Governor Durnford to the Earl of Hillsborough regarding the state of fortifications, French settlers, and trade with American Indians, February 3, 1770, CO 5/587, p. 107, BNA.

50. Ibid.

51. Contract between Antoin Morreau and Mr. Bently, March 22, 1776, Box 1, Folder 7, Kaskaskia Collection, CHM.

52. Lieutenant Governor Durnford to the Earl of Hillsborough regarding the state of fortifications, French settlers, and trade with American Indians, February 3, 1770, CO 5/587, p. 107, BNA.

53. For the Blue Water doctrine, see Gould, *The Persistence of Empire*, esp. 35–71; see also Armitage, *The Ideological Origins of the British Empire*, 1–23; and the observation that the Board of Trade envisioned the American empire as a "coastal, commercial empire in 1763" and one that prized "maritime commerce" as the glue of empire in Edleson, *The New Map of Empire*, 54, 332. On the British state's growth generally in this period, see Brewer, *The Sinews of Power*, esp. 59–60, 65–69.

54. On postwar military policy, see Anderson, *Crucible of War*, esp. 720–24.

55. Thomas Gage to Colonel Thomas Reid, New York, August 10, 1767, TGP.

56. Ibid.

57. Ibid.

58. John Wilkins to Thomas Gage, May 30, 1770, TGP.

59. Thomas Gage to Lord Hillsborough, November 10, 1770, TGP.

60. Lord Hillsborough to Thomas Gage, July 31, 1770, TGP.

61. Lord Hillsborough to Thomas Gage, December 4, 1771, TGP.

62. Thomas Gage to John Reed, July 22, 1767, TGP. For more on the debates in London over the extension of civil jurisdiction into Illinois, see Edleson, *The New Map of Empire*, 312–13.

63. Between 1770 and 1773, the extant record preserves the names of plaintiffs and defendants in thirty-five actions. Five cases dealt with the same matter, so for purposes of tabulation, they have been excluded. In the remaining thirty-five cases, the parties had names indicating the same national origin in twelve cases and different national origins in eighteen cases.

64. Court Record in Alvord and Carter, eds., *Trade and Politics*, 458–59.

65. Court Record in ibid., 457.

66. "Butricke to Barnsley, February 12, 1769," in ibid., 497.

67. Thomas Gage to Officers in Illinois, May 17, 1768, TGP.

68. George Morgan to Samuel Wharton, January 13, 1772, in Kent et al., *Baynton, Wharton, and Morgan Papers.* For an account of this episode and the lawsuits pending, see Dunn, *Choosing Sides on the Frontier*, 19–22.

69. George Morgan to Samuel Wharton, September 1, 1774, in Kent et al., *Baynton, Wharton, and Morgan Papers.*

Chapter 3

1. To the Senate and House of Representatives in Congress Assembled, January 23, 1801, Sen. 6a, G2, LAC, NARA.

2. For a contemporary politician offering Menard this title, see Nathaniel Pope to Henry Eddy, August 7, 1834, Box 1, Folder 13, Henry Eddy Papers, ALPLM. For more on Therese Chouteau and her family, see Hyde, *Empire, Nations, Family*, esp. 30–57.

3. Onuf, *Statehood and Union*, 110. See Fehrenbacher, *The Slaveholding Republic*, esp. 15–48.

4. To the Senate and House of Representatives in Congress Assembled, January 23, 1801, LAC, NARA.

5. On these changes generally, see Saunt, *West of Revolution*; DuVal, *Independence Lost*, esp. 270–91; Calloway, *American Revolution in Indian Country*, esp. 26–65.

6. Patrick Henry, Written Instructions to George Rogers Clark, January 2, 1778, Box 614, Folder 2, GRCP. For more on Clark, see Griffin, *American Leviathan*, esp. 142–47. See also Saunt, *West of the Revolution*, 149.

7. George Rogers Clark to Captain James O'Hara, July 15, 1778, Box 1, Folder 13, Kaskaskia Collection, CHM.

8. Entire passage comes from Diario General by the Secretary of Barnado de Galvez, Box 1, Folder 13, Kaskaskia Collection, CHM.

9. Previous quotes from ibid. For treatment of Clark's voyage, see Griffith, *American Leviathan*, 141–45.

10. Address to the Citizens of Kaskaskia on the Arrival of John Todd in Illinois After the Conquest by George Rogers Clark, transcript letter, Kaskaskia Collection, miscellaneous papers, CHM.

11. John Todd Record Book, p. 3, Rare Book Vault, CHM.

12. Reda, "From Subjects to Citizens," 173.

13. Address to the Citizens of Kaskaskia on the Arrival of John Todd in Illinois After the Conquest by George Rogers Clark, Kaskaskia Collection, miscellaneous papers, CHM. For more on Clark in Illinois, see Clark, *The Conquest of Illinois*, 65.

14. The entire slave code quoted in the following paragraph is from Proclamation by Clark, in *George Rogers Clark Papers*, 94–96. On this code, see Miles, *Dawn of Detroit*, 82–83.

15. All quotations from this paragraph are from ibid.

16. The trial appears KM 79:6:10:1, 79:6:10:2. The trial is transcribed in *CISHL, II*, 14–21. Evidence of Manuel and Moreau's arrival appears at Clerk's Record, December 1778, in *Cahokia Records 1778–1790*, 13–21.

17. For a discussion of enslaved testimony in trial proceedings, see Finch, *Rethinking Slave Rebellion in Cuba*, 10–18.

18. Quotations taken from the translation offered in ibid., 15.

19. Although it is possible that the deaths resulted from an epidemic, a doctor testified that the cause of death of at least one victim was poisoning. While not air tight, the evidence

suggests that murders were committed. It remains possible that Manuel and Moreau were innocent and the enslaved community conspired in their execution.

20. Clerk's Record, *Cahokia Records 1778–1790*, 12.

21. Poisonings occurred in slave societies around the New World. See Paton, "Witchcraft, Poison, Law." In the U.S. South, see Forret, *Slave Against Slave*, 64–66. See the observation that slaves used "herbal medicinal practices" and pharmacopeia, which could "serve as a prophylactic to radical degradation, stanching the living death of bondage." Holt, *Children of Fire*, 78.

22. George Rogers Clark to unknown, Kaskaskia, December 17, 1778, Box 614, Folder 11, *GRCP*. On Clark's dealings with the French more generally, see Marvin, "A Thousand Prejudices."

23. No official documents record the violent repression that masters meted out. However, in the trial testimony, slaves discuss punishments on at least two occasions. See *Cahokia Records 1778–1790*, 5–6.

24. John Todd's Record Book 1778–1779, p. 19, CHM.

25. Ibid., p. 18. Heavy dark lines appear over the death warrant, perhaps indicating the extant document was a draft copy of the warrant. For another entry with these lines that is unambiguously a draft, see p. 15.

26. KM 81:8:14:1.

27. Ibid. For another case concerning a dispute over the ownership of a slave, see KM 81:12:22:1.

28. For instances, see KM 81:5:5:1; John Todd's Record Book, pp. 11, 19, CHM.

29. "Resolutions for a cession of the lands on the north-west side of the Ohio to the United States," Doc. No. 36 in *Journal of the House of Delegates*, 2.

30. On the erection of the "empire of liberty," see Hinderaker, *Elusive Empires*, esp. 185–86. See also Onuf, *Jefferson's Empire*, esp. 147–89.

31. KM 85:6:17:1.

32. For demography generally in this period, see Clayton, *The Illinois Fact Book*, 36–38.

33. Onuf, *Statehood and Union*, 110.

34. See, for example, the claim that "slavery was definitively excluded in states lying north of the Ohio River," in Drescher, *Abolition*, 138. This claim is endorsed by another scholar, who notes the ordinance excluded slavery from the region; Rael, *Eighty-Eight Years*, 117. Another historian notes that "the American Revolution had the effect of committing the Northern states to eventual emancipation"; Davis, *Inhuman Bondage*, 152. Another scholar referred to the Northwest Territory Ordinance as an "emphatic ordainment of freedom"; Fehrenbacher, *The Slaveholding Republic*, 255.

35. St. Clair's Journal, 1788–1789, Box 1, Folder 31, Northwest Territory Collection, INHS.

36. Arthur St. Clair to Thomas Jefferson, May 1, 1790, vol. 47, item 912, RG 59, NARA State Department Papers, RG 59, NARA.

37. Throughout this period, the registries continued to be written in French. It is difficult to make sense of the nomenclature used for slaves. As a general rule, Indian slaves were identified as "panis," and slaves of African descent usually had the label "esclave." However, the term "negre" could be used as a general marker for an enslaved person and was not interchangeable with "noir," which more clearly indicated a person's place in a racial hierarchy. While not a perfect metric, using the distinction between "panis" and "esclave" is the best guide in these sources, and it seems to hint that the population of Indian slaves declined.

38. Registry of Burials, 1721–1834, Parish of the Immaculate Conception, p. 158, DAB.

39. Registry of Baptisms, 1759–1815, Parish of the Immaculate Conception, p. 232, DAB.

40. Between 1776 and 1787, fourteen burials of infant slaves are indicated in the Registry of Burials, 1721–1834, Parish of the Immaculate Conception, pp. 100–25, DAB.

41. John Todd's Record Book, p. 40, CHM.

42. On this "new phase of conflicts," see Calloway, *American Revolution in Indian Country*, 280. On the most important of these Indian Wars in this region, see Calloway, *The Victory with No Name*.

43. Calloway, *American Revolution in Indian Country*, 272–91; Griffith, *American Leviathan*, esp. 183–240; White, *The Middle Ground*, 315–66; and DuVal, *Independence Lost*, xxi–xxiv.

44. John Todd's Record Book, p. 40, CHM.

45. David Duncan to Josiah Harmar, May 28, 1785, Box 2, Josiah Harmar Papers, William L. Clements Library, Ann Arbor, Mich.

46. Israel Shreeve Diary, 154, William L. Clements Library, Ann Arbor, Mich.

47. Ibid., 154–55.

48. Ibid., 156.

49. Ibid.

50. Ibid., 85.

51. Ibid., 141–42.

52. This observation about the earliest stages of western expansion is confirmed in Deyle, *Carry Me Back*, 38. He concluded that before the War of 1812, "the majority of Chesapeake slaves forced west went with migrating planters."

53. A Slave Sale in 1786, Slaves and Slavery Collection, Folder 1, MHS.

54. Charleville to Boldoc, Folder 405, St. Genevieve Archives, WHMC.

55. A Slave Sale in 1786, Slaves and Slavery Collection, Folder 1, MHS.

56. On this point generally, see Kennington, "Law, Geography and Mobility."

57. Jean Cons to John Edgar, Folder 406, St. Genevieve Archives, WHMC.

58. *Betsy, a woman of color v. Phillip Rocheblave*, July term, 1826, Case 77, p. 1, SLCCR.

59. Antoine Louvien dit Amour to Antoine LaChance, 1798, Folder 411, St. Genevieve Archives, WHMC.

60. For the various activities listed above, see clearing land in Journal of the Voyage, August 7, 1796, Menard Family Papers, CHM; plough work, common labor, and loading warehouses are recorded at Broullard C, Voyage to New Madrid 1792–1794, pp. 31, 34, 37, 41, CHM; building structures are noted in Journal of the Voyage, August 28, 1796, CHM; milling appears in Journal of the Voyage, August 19, 1796, CHM; and animal husbandry is noted in Charles Gratiot to Barthelemi Tardiveau, October 16, 1790, Box 1, Folder 6, Pierre Menard Papers, ALPLM.

61. Unknown to Pierre Menard, Box 2, Folder 20, Pierre Menard Papers, ALPLM.

62. Record of Auction of the Charleville Estate, November 7, 1782, pp. 13–17, ISA.

63. McMurtie, "Negotiations for the Illinois Salt Springs."

64. Thomas Jefferson to Miami and Delaware Indians, January 8, 1803, Thomas Jefferson Papers, Series 1, General Correspondence, DLC.

65. On calls for diffusion in this period generally, see Deyle, *Carry Me Back*, 26.

66. Finkelman, "Evading the Ordinance."

67. Report of the Committee on the Petition of Sundry Inhabitants of the Counties of St. Clair and Randolph, U.S. 4th Congress, 1795–1797, Evans Series 31395, p. 6.

68. Ibid.

69. Ibid.

70. Report on the Petition of 1805, in Dunn, ed., *Slavery Papers and Petitions*, 53.

71. Memorial of Randolph and St. Clair Counties, January 17, 1806, in Dunn, ed., *Slavery Papers and Petitions*, 59.

72. Legislative Resolutions of 1807, in Dunn, ed., *Slavery Papers and Petitions*, 66.

73. Ibid.

74. The Petition of 1796, in Dunn, ed., *Slavery Papers and Petitions*, 6.

75. Ibid.

76. Legislative Resolution of 1807, in Dunn, ed., *Slavery Papers and Petitions*, 66.

77. Report on the Proceeding, in Dunn, ed., *Slavery Papers and Petitions*, 29.

78. Report on the Proceeding, in Dunn, ed., *Slavery Papers and Petitions*, 79.

79. Ibid.

80. The quotes appear in The Memorial of the French Inhabitants of the Illinois, July 8, 1788, Box 1, Folder 4, Pierre Menard Papers, ALPLM.

81. The Petition of 1796, in Dunn, ed., *Slavery Papers and Petitions*, 6.

82. On this point of cross-cultural collaborations, see Gitlin, *The Bourgeois Frontier.*

83. For instance, the Bienvienu family appears in these records. Other family names from the 1760s also appear. For those earlier families, see Invoice of Goods, September 14, 1766, in Kent et al., *Baynton, Wharton, and Morgan Papers.*

84. Importantly, this was part of a trend whereby the territorial legislature passed laws modeled on southern statues. Examples of these legal similarities include An Act Concerning Appeals from the Judgment of Justices of the Peace, which was modeled on the Kentucky Code, KM 810:1:26:2; An Act to Prevent Unlawful Gaming, modeled on the Virginia Code, KM 810:3:9:1; and An Act to Suppress Dueling, also adopted from the Virginia Code, KM 810:4:7:1.

85. An Act Concerning the Introduction of Negroes and Mulattoes into This Territory, Illinois Territorial Papers, IHLC.

86. Ibid.

87. Report of a Committee of the Legislature of the Territory of Indian and a Petition of Sundry Inhabitants of that Territory to the said Legislature upon the Subject of Slavery within the said Territory, [n.d.], 10th Congress, H.R. 10A, f. 10.3, LHA, NARA.

88. Petition dated 1808, beginning, "We the People of the Illinois Country," Box 9, Folder 83, Pierre Menard Papers, ALPLM.

89. Robert Morrison to Joseph Morrison, December 31, 1805, Robert Morrison Letters, ALPLM.

Chapter 4

1. Dunky, a colored woman v. Andrew Hay, July term, 1831, Case 12, p. 1, SLCCR. Her contract appears at Registry of Negroes 1809–1863, p. 13, Office of the County Clerk, Randolph County, Ill.

2. For more on the indenture system, see Foner, *The Fiery Trial*, 3–32; Simeone, *Democracy and Slavery in Frontier Illinois.*

3. On the similarity between servitude and slavery in Illinois, see Gorsuch, "To Indent Oneself"; Gorsuch, "Race and Labour Contracts in the Upper Mississippi Valley"; Kennington, *In the Shadow of* Dred Scott, 98–99.

4. On the idea that servitude acted as de facto slavery, see Finkelman, "Evading the Ordinance"; Finkelman, "Slavery and the Northwest Ordinance."

5. In the first decades of the nineteenth century, Illinois developed a system of human bondage that created distinctions between types of bound labor that can be difficult to parse. Inheritable bondage survived in the state. Slaves carried into the state frequently entered lifelong servitude contracts, although just as often, masters held their slaves without going to the trouble of signing them to an indenture. Meanwhile, children of servants frequently won their freedom when they reached adulthood, and a sizable minority of servants labored under short, compensated labor contract. At times, such as in court, these distinctions mattered immensely. Yet at other times, including in daily work routines, the divisions between servant and slave had little importance. I will refer to workers by their formal legal category whenever possible. Throughout, I use the most specific language possible, but frequently, bound workers were simply identified as "negroes" and their specific legal category is not clear.

6. *Edwardsville Spectator*, October 29, 1825. On the population totals in 1830, see *Abstract of the Returns of the Fifth Census*, 38.

7. Birbeck, *Notes on a Journey in America*, 94. In this passage, Birbeck was writing specifically about Vincennes, but it is an observation that holds true for the wider Illinois and Indiana territory. On Birbeck's observations, see Schroeder, "Dreams of a Prairie Republic."

8. Gillespie, *Recollections of Early Illinois and Her Noted Men*, 16.

9. Federal census data are unreliable for these three decades. The 1818 census records 751 slaves in Illinois, but this number is certainly incorrect, as the returns for Madison, Randolph, and St. Clair Counties are lost or incomplete. St. Clair and Randolph Counties were some of the largest slaveholding counties. Additionally, counties with large slaveholding populations, like Pope County, simply reported the aggregate size of the African American population without specifying what proportion was slave or free. The 1820 census reports 668 slaves in Illinois, but this does not capture the slaves who were hired from Kentucky into the salines in Gallatin County—hundreds of people annually by the 1820s—or the slaves from Missouri hired into Illinois's mining districts. The 1830 census that records 747 slaves in Illinois suffered from similar shortcomings. Consequently, adjusting the census data for this period, the population appears to have grown slightly between 1818 and 1830—due to in-migration from slaveholders arriving from Virginia and Kentucky—but it largely held constant at or below 1,000. On the missing census data and the material that informs these calculations, see Norton, ed., *Illinois Census Returns 1810, 1818*, introduction, and Norton, ed., *Illinois Census Returns 1820.*

10. For the census data of Randolph County in 1820, see Norton, ed., *Illinois Census Returns 1820*, 237–49. The census reports 342 African American and 3,191 free white inhabitants. It does not distinguish between free and enslaved African Americans, so the exact percentage of slaves in the county is ambiguous. In Gallatin County, the 1818 census records 321 slaves and 3,348 free inhabitants, meaning slaves amounted to 8.3 percent of the population. For these census returns, see Norton, ed., *Illinois Census Returns 1810, 1818*, 102.

11. For these comparative data, see Warren, *New England Bound*, 10–11; Nash and Soderland, *Freedom by Degrees*, 7; White, *Somewhat More Independent*, 16–17; Grivno, *Gleanings of Freedom*, esp. 11–12; and Johnson, *Ante-Bellum North Carolina*, 53–58.

12. For a comparative analysis of gradual emancipation, see Engerman, *Slavery, Emancipation and Freedom*, esp. 35–50, and Hahn, *The Political Worlds of Slavery and Freedom*, 1–53.

13. Melish, *Disowning Slavery*, 11–49.

14. Gigantino, *The Ragged Road to Abolition*; Gellman, *Emancipating New York*; White, *Somewhat More Independent*; Van Cleve, *A Slaveholders' Union*; Nash and Soderlund, *Freedom by Degrees.*

15. Gigantino, *The Ragged Road to Abolition*, 96.

16. Dorsey, *Hirelings*; Grivno, *Gleanings of Freedom*; Whitman, *The Price of Freedom.*

17. Taylor, *Frontier of Freedom*; Middleton, *The Black Laws*; Steinfield, *The Invention of Free Labor*, esp. 160; Tomlins, *Freedom Bound*, esp. 410–11.

18. Salafia, *Slavery's Borderland*, 43–69, 96–106; Weiner, *Race and Rights*, 38–40.

19. Meyer, *Making the Heartland Quilt*, 136–68; Simeone, *Frontier Democracy*, 33. For a more detailed breakdown of the southern origins of Illinois migrants, see Buck, *Illinois in 1818*, 98–100.

20. Indentures in Randolph County are drawn largely from the Registry of Negroes 1809–1863, Office of the County Clerk, Randolph County, Ill. Indentures are also recorded in Deed Record G-H-I-J, Deed Record J, Deed Record K, Deed Record L, Deed Record M, and Deed Record O in Office of the County Clerk, Randolph County, Ill. From these sources, I have identified 224 indentures from Randolph County, 160 of which identify the servant as a recent arrival. Idiosyncrasies in the sources from other counties prevent any comprehensive statistics about the introduction of slaves from other states. It seems that in several counties—such as St. Clair County—clerks stopped recording these data. Moreover, in counties where this information appears to have been recorded—such as Randolph County—several people whom I can independently verify were trafficked from slave states were not recorded as migrants. Consequently, any statistics are merely impressionistic.

21. An Act Concerning the Introduction of Negroes and Mulattoes into This Territory, Illinois (Territory) Legislature Laws, Statues, etc., 1807–1818, Illinois (Territory) Legislature Collection, Box 1, IHLC. On the indenture system more generally, see Gorsuch, "To Indent Oneself," 137–39; Faragher, *Sugar Creek*, 45–50.

22. This is a dynamic that played out across the Atlantic world, whereby masters had to change the status of their slaves as they crossed into new jurisdictions. See Scott, "Slavery and the Law in Atlantic Perspective."

23. In total, I have examined 622 servitude contracts. It must be stressed that several counties do not have extant records, so the 622 contracts underrepresent the total number of indentured servants. Hardin County, between Pope and Gallatin Counties, for example, had a fire in 1884 and has no prefire records. Similarly, a 1937 flood destroyed one of the registries of servants and slaves for Gallatin County. Out of the 622 servitude contracts I have consulted, 354 are for adults and contain information about the term of service. Eighty-seven of these contracts—or 24 percent—held the indentures in bondage until past the age of seventy, making manumission an unlikely occurrence. To calculate these statistics, I have consulted all extant servitude contracts from Illinois in this period, drawing on the following counties: Edwards, Gallatin, Hardin, Madison, Monroe, Pope, Randolph, St. Clair, and Union. These indentures are recorded in the registries of African Americans as well as the deed books listed in the public records section of the bibliography. For indentures with ninety-year terms, see, for instance, Jean Pearce's indenture at Registry of Negroes 1809–1863, p. 11, Office of the

County Clerk, Randolph County, Ill. See also Esther's indentureship to Joshua Vaughn and Ketty's indentureship to Jacob Baker, St. Clair Record of Indentures, 1807–1832, pp. 11–12, ISA.

24. Pope County Deed Record A, p. 35, Office of the County Clerk, Pope County, Ill. One scholar has rightly called those who worked their entire lives without compensation "slaves in all but name." Faragher, *Sugar Creek*, 48.

25. Indenture contracts that offered the servant payment at the expiration of the term were rare. More common were terms of indenture that gave African Americans reasonable hope of leaving bondage during their natural lives. Out of the 622 extant contracts I have consulted, 354 are for adults and are complete enough to contain both information about terms of service and freedom dues. Twenty-four contracts—or 6 percent—provided freedom dues that African Americans would likely live long enough to collect. And 126 contracts—or 36 percent—would emancipate the worker before age sixty. These contracts were signed between 1805 and 1835, with the vast majority dated between 1807 and 1818. To calculate these statistics, I have consulted all extant servitude contracts from Illinois in this period, covering the following counties: Edwards, Gallatin, Hardin, Madison, Monroe, Pope, Randolph, St. Clair, and Union.

26. St. Clair Record of Indentures, 1807–1832, p. 56, ISA.

27. Two such examples are in ibid., pp. 57–58, ISA.

28. Indenture of William to Nathaniel Anderson, March 31, 1813, and indenture of Ned to Nathaniel Anderson, March 31, 1813, Folder 1, Box 1, Gallatin County Legal Documents, ALPLM.

29. *Bob and Lydia v. Jincy Mitchel*, 1810, Case 1754, St. Clair Circuit Court Records, ISA. It must be noted that this case was exceptional for its period. No similar cases survive from the first decade of the nineteenth century. In time, this legal tactic would become more common, as discussed in Chapter 5.

30. Cahokia Record Book B, p. 339, Raymond Hammes Collection, ISA. The large sum paid for these workers, including a child age fourteen, indicates Morrison purchased a slave to be held for life, not a servant to be freed in roughly fifteen years.

31. Deed Record L, p. 115, Office of the County Clerk, Randolph County, Ill.

32. Cahokia Record Book B, p. 603, Raymond Hammes Collection, ISA.

33. Deed Record M, p. 168, Office of the County Clerk, Randolph County, Ill. The record suggests these workers were servants or term slaves.

34. William Morrison to [Eliza] Morrison, August 27, 1815, William Morrison Letter, ALPLM.

35. Ibid.

36. For examples, see the entry for Charles Edmund, March 24, 1823, and Eduard, May 4, 1830, Registry of Baptisms 1815–1851, Parish of the Immaculate Conception of Notre Dame, pp. 51, 113, DAB. In total, between 1800 and 1845, 194 baptism entries for African American children are recorded in the parishes in Cahokia and Kaskaskia. Out of those entries, 159 appear to be for children born into slavery, inheriting their parents' status. Thirty-five entries are for children born free, who again inherit their parents' status. Roughly one-quarter of cases, or 54 cases out of 194 instances, do not give a clear indication of the child's condition of servitude. In these instances, the entry simply records the child as a "negro" without stating if the infant is free or enslaved. This leaves room for estimation about how widespread enslaving children at birth remained in this period. The overwhelming trend in the evidence is that

children inherited their parents' condition of servitude. Consequently, the ambiguous cases have been reassigned based on the parents' condition of servitude.

37. Registry of Baptisms, 1815–1851, Parish of the Immaculate Conception, p. 64, DAB. For her census entry confirming LaChapelle owned no slaves, see Taylor ed., *Census of Randolph County*, 4.

38. For their census holdings, see ibid., 5. Their baptism entry is at Registry of Baptisms, 1815–1851, Immaculate Conception, p. 68, DAB.

39. June 16, 1806, Registry of Burials 1784–1819, Holy Family Parish Cahokia, [no page number], DAB. This conception of the relationship between race and the enslavement of indigenous persons "recognizes race as a site of dialogic exchange and contestation" that is "artificially and arbitrarily contrived to produce and maintain relations of power and subordination." Higginbotham, "African-American Women's History and the Metalanguage of Race," 252–53. This builds on the observation that race "is always mediated by the social context within which the two come in contact." Fields, "Ideology and Race in America," 153.

40. No original copy of this newspaper survives. See its republication in Reynolds, *The Pioneer History of Illinois*, 366 n. 2.

41. Receipt dated January 1812, Blotter 1811–1813, Folder 13, Box 2, Pierre Menard Papers, IHLC.

42. *Kaskaskia Illinois Intelligencer*, June 1, 1820.

43. *Edwardsville Spectator*, May 31, 1823; *Kaskaskia Republican Advocate*, July 31, 1823.

44. *Kaskaskia Illinois Intelligencer*, June 24, 1818. These advertisements contrast with contemporaneous advertisements for indentured servants. The notices for servants delineated the servant's limited condition of servitude and indicated the years left to serve—both vital pieces of information for potential buyers. The advertisements cited above make no reference to indentured servitude, simply indicating that humans were for sale in Illinois's labor market. Examples include *Kaskaskia Republican*, February 8, 1824, and *Kaskaskia Republican Advocate*, March 16, 1824.

45. Deed Record O, pp. 410–11, Office of the County Clerk, Randolph County, Ill.

46. Bill of Sale of a Negro Boy Slave, May 16, 1822, Folder 3, St. Clair County Indentures, ISA.

47. Pope County Deed Record A, p. 75, Office of the County Clerk, Pope County, Ill.

48. Probate Court Book, 1822–1836, inscribed on front cover, Office of the Circuit Clerk, Johnson County, Ill. For other sales, see the case of Annica, a negro woman, Deed Record C, p. 335, and Sidney Breese to Alexander Fields, Deed Record 4, p. 66, Office of the County Clerk, Union County, Ill.

49. *Edwardsville Spectator*, May 10, 1825. For the sale of an indentured woman as property, see *Kaskaskia Republican*, August 14, 1826.

50. Inventory of Goods and Chattels of Pierre Pettet, alias Lasond, March 3, 1820, Bin 66, Office of the Circuit Clerk, Randolph County, Ill.

51. Registry of Negroes 1809–1863, p. 205, Office of the County Clerk, Randolph County, Ill.

52. *Maria Whiten, a free woman of color v. Garland Rucker*, November Term, 1829, Case 14, p. 18, SLCCR. This quote appears incorrectly in an earlier article of mine. The incorrect passage is in Heerman, "In a State of Slavery," 134.

53. Clark, "The Ohio Country in the Political Economy of Nation Building." On this change more generally, see Clark, *The Grain Trade in the Old Northwest*; Bouge, *From Prairie to Corn Belt*.

54. For instance, an enslaved woman named Julia was hired to spread flax in Randolph County. See *Julia, a woman of color v. Samuel T. McKenney*, March term, 1831, Case 66, pp. 3–4, SLCCR.

55. For example, see entry for a "negre" for one day of common labor in Bryan and Morrison Cahokia Ledger D, 1807–1825, p. 60, CHM.

56. Bryan and Morrison Cahokia Ledger D, 1807–1825, p. 206, CHM.

57. Ibid., p. 215.

58. Ibid., pp. 211, 213.

59. Ninian Edwards to A. G. S. Wright, August 19, 1825, in Fergus, ed., *The Edwards Papers*, 244.

60. *Edwardsville Spectator*, May 31, 1823.

61. *Kaskaskia Illinois Intelligencer*, June 1, 1822.

62. Bryan and Morrison Ledger C, p. 358, Chester Public Library, Chester, Ill.

63. Pierre Menard acct. to Bryan and Morrison, Box 9, Folder 84, Pierre Menard Papers, ALPLM.

64. Bryan and Morrison Day Book, Cahokia, March 18, 1811–July 3, 1813, p. 82, Pierre Menard Papers, ALPLM. Beauvais was one of Illinois's many slaveholders who baptized enslaved infants during the 1820s, suggesting that the worker on Morrison's voyage had been born into slavery in Illinois. For instance, see Registry of Baptisms 1815–1851, Parish of the Immaculate Conception of Notre Dame, pp. 12. 19, 50, DAB.

65. Recettes et Depenses pour le compte de ma soicete, Menard Family Papers, Business Records 1794–1843.

66. See entries on August 8, 1818, Pierre Menard Blotter, May 1817–1819, Folder 15, Box 2, Pierre Menard Papers, IHLC.

67. [Entry not dated], Ned the Negro, Ferry Book, September 1, 1833–September 1, 1836, Folder 24, Box 2, Pierre Menard Papers, IHLC. Inferred from context, the entry likely appeared in early February 1833.

68. For a detailed account of a downriver voyage, see "The Daily Journal of a Trip Down the Mississippi," [1805–1806], ALPLM.

69. On steam travel, see Johnson, *River of Dark Dreams*, 73–96; Buchannan, *Black Life on the Mississippi*, esp. 24–27; Gudmestad, *Steamboats and the Rise of the Cotton Kingdom.*

70. On the making of salt, see Blackmore, "African Americans and Race Relations in Gallatin County," esp. 10–46; Cornelius, "John Hart Crenshaw and Hickory Hill," James Cornelius Papers, IHLC; Metzger, "The Gallatin County Saline."

71. Cornelius, "John Hart Crenshaw and Hickory Hill," 16, James Cornelius Papers, IHLC. On slavery in the salines, see Bahde, " 'I Would Not Have a White Upon the Premises.' "

72. *Kaskaskia Illinois Journal*, January 24, 1835.

73. Cornelius, "John Hart Crenshaw and Hickory Hill," 15–16.

74. Blackmore, "African Americans and Race Relations," 17.

75. Blackmore, "African Americans and Race Relations," 17. See also Cornelius, "John Hart Crenshaw and Hickory Hill," 15, James Cornelius Papers, IHLC.

76. Benjamin Talbott to Governor Edwards, May 17, 1812, in Carter, ed., *Territorial Papers of the United States*, 225.

77. Norton, ed., *Illinois Census Returns 1810, 1818*, 20.

78. Phillis indenture to John Posey, August 22, 1819, Folder 5, Box 1, Gallatin County Legal Documents, ALPLM.

79. Ibid.

80. *Milly, a free woman of color v. Rose Mathais*, August term, 1819, Case 20, p. 1, SLCCR.

81. *Jack, a man of color v. Absalom Link*, November term, 1837, Case 38, p. 1, SLCCR.

82. *Vincent, a man of color v. James Duncan*, November term, 1829, Case 110, p. 19, SLCCR.

83. "Disobedient," ibid., p. 8; "collect his money," ibid., p. 12; "settle his business," ibid., p. 20.

84. One newspaper report noted that "the question of slavery is not yet decided; a majority however, are said to be opposed to it." *Illinois Intelligencer*, August 19, 1818.

85. The entire paragraph comes from M Lyon to John Messigner, July 31, 1818, Folder 3, Box 1, John Messinger Papers, ALPLM.

86. *Kaskaskia Illinois Intelligencer*, August 26, 1818.

87. Verlie, ed., *Illinois Constitutions*, 38–39. After a concession from slaveholders, the 1818 constitution did reform the indenture system. Specifically, it forbade any further indentures "unless such person shall enter into such indenture while in a state of perfect freedom and on condition of a bona-fide consideration received or to be received for their service." With this tiny reform, Illinois masters exited the convention with their power over slaves largely intact. For the reform to the indenture system, see Davis, *Frontier Illinois*, 165.

88. 33 *Annals of Cong.* 305 (1818).

89. Ibid., 307.

90. Ibid., 308.

91. For more on this episode, Hammond, "'Uncontrollable Necessity,'" esp., 150–51. As Hammond notes, the 1818 constitution made Illinois a "proto-slave state wrapped in free state garb." Ibid., 150. See also Hammond, *Slavery, Freedom and Expansion*, esp. 96–124.

92. For census data reporting these four men's slaveholdings in 1820, see Norton, ed., *Illinois Census Returns 1820*, 238 (Schadrach Bond), 248 (Pierre Menard), 153 (Jesse Thomas). For Ninian Edwards on the 1818 census, see Norton, ed., *Illinois Census Returns 1810, 1818*, 130. Most of these early leaders lived in Randolph County, which does not have extant census returns for 1818, the year of their election. As a consequence, in most cases, I have relied on the 1820 census. However, the 1820 census does not distinguish between free and enslaved African Americans in Randolph County. However, both Bond and Menard owned slaves in this period, and much of that evidence appears in this chapter.

93. Weiner, *Race and Rights*, esp. 60–61, 71–73, and LaRoche, *Free Black Communities and the Underground Railroad*, 44–45.

94. Hall, *Dividing the Union*.

95. Onuf, *Jefferson's Empire*, 147–89; Mason, "The Maine and Missouri Compromise." Some observers noted that Congress had placed restrictions on Illinois's state constitution through the Northwest Territory Ordinance, thus violating the principles protected in the Missouri crisis. As one newspaper account noted, "It is incontrovertibly true, that, if Congress has exceeded her constitutional limits, in imposing restrictions upon Illinois, that this illegitimate exercise of excessive power, never did, neither can it create an obligation." *Kaskaskia Republican Advocate*, January 8, 1824.

96. Guasco, "The Deadly Influence of Negro Capitalists," 9–10.

97. Guasco, *Confronting Slavery*, 97–103.

98. For the petitions that were important to these campaigns, see Petition to Thomas Mather, Folder 1, Thomas Mather Papers, CHM. For more on their organization, see James Simeone, *Democracy and Slavery in Frontier Illinois*, 16–38.

99. There are three extant petitions in the Thomas Mather Papers, Folder 1, CHM. The documents are badly torn and prevent any complete analysis, but there are 101 signatures. Of the legible signatures, twenty-two names appear on an 1825 census of Randolph County. Of those names, a majority of the signatories owned at least one servant or slave.

100. Reynolds, *My Own Times*, 155.

101. Election results in this and the following paragraph are taken from Pease, ed., *Illinois Election Returns*, 27–29, 207–16; Smith, *A History of Southern Illinois*, 150–54. It should be also noted that some large slaveholders may have opposed the amendment because it would have attracted national attention and perhaps jeopardized that status quo that had worked well for them.

102. Guasco, "The Deadly Influence of Negro Capitalists," 8–11.

103. Simeone, *Democracy and Slavery*, esp. 68–72.

104. Niveah S[haw] to William S[haw], [n.p.], November 30, 1824, Folder 1, Shaw Family Papers, ALPLM.

105. Last Will of Benjamin Farmer, Probate Record B, pp. 88–89, Office of the Circuit Clerk, Sangamon County, IRAD, Springfield.

106. On Ninian Edwards's biography, see Bakalis, "Ninian Edwards and Territorial Politics in Illinois"; Robert Howard, *The Illinois Governors*, 33–43; Simeone, *Frontier Democracy*, 68–96.

107. *Kaskaskia Republican Advocate*, August 7, 1823.

108. Pro-Slavery Views of Governor Edwards, [n.d.], Folder 3, Box 1, Ninian Edwards Papers, IHLC. Original manuscript copy in Ninian Edwards Papers, Box 2, Folder 10, CHM.

109. Ibid., p. 3.

110. Ibid., p. 6.

111. Ibid., p. 8.

112. Ibid. The Latin maxim translates as "that which is brought forth follows the womb." Black, *Black's Law Dictionary*, 1278.

113. *Kaskaskia Republican Advocate*, June 12, 1823.

114. *Kaskaskia Republican Advocate*, September 25, 1823. A similar declaration appears in the *Kaskaskia Republican Advocate*, January 4, 1823.

115. *Kaskaskia Republican Advocate*, January 20, 1824.

116. *Amy, a woman of color v. Ettienne Penconneau*, 1820, Case 2798, St. Clair Circuit Court Records, ISA.

117. To the Honourable Judge of the First Judicial Circuit of the State of Illinois, [n.d.], Nance Legens Costly Collection, ALPLM. Cox also claimed the sale was voluntary in Sangamon County Deed Record, Vols. A and B, pp. 148–49, IRAD, Springfield, and [Petition?] of Thomas Cox, June 16, 1826, Sangamon County Circuit Court Case Files, Folder 88, Box 2, IRAD, Springfield. For Cox's initial purchase of Nance and Dice, see Schedule of Property Delivered to Nathan Cromwell, Nance Legens Costly Collection, ALPLM.

118. To the Honourable Judge of the First Judicial Circuit of the State of Illinois, [n.d.], Nance Legens Costly Collection, ALPLM.

119. Affidavit of Jane Cox, [n.d.], Nance Legens Costly Collection, ALPLM.

120. Ibid.

121. *Nance, a Negro Girl v. Nathan Cromwell*, October term, 1827, [no case number], Sangamon County Circuit Court, Nance Legens Costly Collection, ALPLM. In Illinois, African Americans had to rely on a legal fiction for their suits. By filing a writ in civil court, they would prompt the question of their enslaved status and their standing.

122. Ibid.

123. *Nance, a girl of color v. John Howard*, 1828, [no case number], Supreme Court Case Files, ISA.

124. Ibid.

125. Ibid.

126. *Phoebe, a girl of color v. William Jay*, 1828, [no case number in original], majority opinion, Supreme Court Case Files, ISA.

127. Ibid.

128. Ibid.

129. Ibid.

130. Ibid.

131. The New York State Supreme Court ruled on this matter in *Link v. Beuner* (1805) and *Fish v. Fisher* (1800). My gratitude to Sarah Gronningsater for pointing out these citations.

132. On the observation the 1830s were a "turning point," see Gigantino, *Ragged Road to Abolition*, 194. On the reaffirmation of gradual emancipation, see ibid., 150.

Chapter 5

1. Keita Cha-Jua, *America's First Black Town*; LaRoche, *Free Black Communities and the Underground Railroad.*

2. In this sense, black towns were not simply "maroon communities," as some scholars have argued. For treatment of the towns as maroon communities, see Slaughter, *Bloody Dawn*, 49; Sinha, "Coming of Age"; Hahn, *Political Worlds of Slavery and Freedom*, 1–53; Hahn, *A Nation Without Borders*, 75.

3. In these disputes, the sets of values, assumptions, customs, and practices that undergirded the law were brought to bear on the legal institutions and court procedures that sustained local governance. On the distinction between governance and the law, see Edwards, *The People and Their Peace*, esp. 3–4, 27–29. On enslaved people's knowledge of the law in St. Louis, see Kennington, *In the Shadow of* Dred Scott, esp. 51–55, 191–94; Twitty, *Before* Dred Scott, esp. 71–83.

4. Notably, Abraham Lincoln took a slaveholder as a client. On this episode, see Foner, *The Fiery Trial*, 48–50. See also Steiner, *An Honest Calling*, esp. 103–9.

5. *John Merry, a free man of color v. Clayton Tiffon and Louis Menard*, November term, 1826, Case 18, p. 1, SLCCR.

6. Ibid., p. 16.

7. Ibid.

8. Ibid.

9. Ibid., pp. 1–2.

10. Ibid, p. 2.

11. Ibid., p. 3.

12. Ibid., p. 3.

13. Ibid., p. 4.

14. Ibid., p. 16. For more on Merry's case, see Lea Vandervelde, *Redemption Song*, 78–90; Twitty, *Before* Dred Scott, 93–94.

15. For instance, 70 percent of people in Gallatin County relied on witnesses.

16. Tregellis, ed., *River Roads to Freedom*, 1–14.

17. Instances of these are numerous. For example, see Alexis (1832), Amos (1832), Rebecca (n.d.), Nancy (1833), George Crain (1839), Maria (1844), and Catherine Ram (1839) in Randolph County Circuit Court Book A, pp. 13, 30, 35, 137, 305, 363, and Randolph County Circuit Court Book B, p. 264, Office of the Circuit Clerk, Randolph County, Ill.

18. For the Adams indenture and freedom papers, see Schmook, ed., *Gallatin County, Illinois Slave Register*, 61. Other instances from this period are numerous, but they include Registry of Negroes 1809–1863, p. 203, Office of the County Clerk, Randolph County, Ill.; Rebecca Schmook, ed., *Gallatin County, Illinois Slave Register*, 35–36. For another instance of term slavery, see *John, a man of color v. William Campbell*, July term, 1831, Case 15, SLCCR. For a collection of apprenticeships, see New Salem Ill., 1827–1838, ALPLM.

19. See Elizabeth, John Morrison, and Elizabeth Jones, Edwards County Servitude and Emancipation Register, pp. 6, 21, ISA. See also the emancipation of an "old negro" in Registry of Negroes 1809–1863, p. 200, Office of the County Clerk, Randolph County, Ill.

20. Randolph County Deed Book N, p. 223, Office of the County Clerk, Randolph County, Ill.

21. Randolph County Deed Book O, p. 436, Office of the County Clerk, Randolph County, Ill.

22. Linder, *Reminiscences*, 52–54. See also Elizabeth Eddy Carroll to C. M. [McIlvaine?], n.d., Elizabeth Caroll (Eddy) Papers, CHM.

23. Cases of Eddy acting as a witness appear in Schmook, ed., *Gallatin County, Illinois Slave Register*, 48, 55, 64, 66.

24. J. H. C. Ellis to Post Master, December 26, 1843, Box 1, Henry Eddy Papers, ALPLM.

25. Ibid.

26. Solomon Wills to Henry Eddy, August 25, 1829, Box 1, Henry Eddy Papers, ALPLM. The judgments for these cases are nonextant.

27. For the initial inquiry, see Robert G. Green to Henry Eddy, May 14, 1828, Box 1, Henry Eddy Papers, ALPLM. The quotation comes from Green's reply, Robert G. Green to Henry Eddy, August 6, 1828, Box 1, Henry Eddy Papers, ALPLM.

28. Solomon Wills to Henry Eddy, August 25, 1829, Box 1, Henry Eddy Papers, ALPLM. On the motivations of lawyers taking these cases in St. Louis, see Kennington, *In the Shadow of* Dred Scott, esp. 71–78.

29. For Illinois census data in 1840, see *Compendium of the Enumeration of the Inhabitants and Statistics of the United States*, 84–87; on growth trends, see Table 1, Population of the United States Decennially from 1790 to 1850, *The Seventh Census of the United States*, ix–x.

30. On Chicago's ascent, see Cronon, *Nature's Metropolis*, esp. 104–7. On the rise of an abolitionist class in Chicago, see Campbell, *Fighting Slavery in Chicago*, esp. 22–26.

31. Hansen and Nygard, "Stephen A. Douglas, the Know-Nothings, and the Democratic Party in Illinois, 1854–1858"; Huston, "The Illinois Political Realignment of 1844–1860."

32. Meyer, *Making the Heartland Quilt*, 171–73.

33. Ibid., 253–56.

34. Faragher, *Sugar Creek*, 48.

35. Ibid.

36. See, for instance, John Raunch's experiences in ibid., 70–71. No sizable body of servitude contracts for white laborers survives. For a collection of these indentures, see Bin 317, Office of the County Clerk, Pope County, Ill.

37. See, for instance, William Caldwell, "a poor child of color" indentured to James Whitesides, June 3, 1834, and the unraced (and therefore presumed white) James Modglin indentured to the same owner, May 7, 1855, Bin 317, Office of the County Clerk, Pope County, Ill.

38. Thirteen extant contacts for white and black children in Sangamon County, dated between 1832 and 1841, are housed in Sangamon Co, IL Indentures of Apprenticeship, 1834–1854, ALPLM.

39. Entry on January 30, 1823, Kaskaskia Poor Book 1811–1827, Folder 22, Box 2, Kaskaskia Collection, CHM.

40. St. Clair County Record of Emancipations, 1822–1832, p. 8, ISA. No explanation is given as to why the clerk suspected fraud.

41. Fowkes, ed., *Historical Encyclopedia of Illinois*, 442.

42. "Kidnapping," *Shawneetown Democrat*, October, 8, 1842.

43. Schmook, ed., *Gallatin County, Illinois Slavery Register*, 50–52.

44. Ibid., 64.

45. Ibid., 29.

46. Ibid., 43.

47. Gallatin County maintained its records in a way that enables this reconstruction. Other counties, such as Randolph, tended not to include this information systematically. Consequently, statewide data are impossible to assemble. Nevertheless, in Gallatin County, 310 extant case files show that 214 cases relied on witnesses to certify a man or woman's freedom. Ninety-six cases merely recorded documents without the assistance of white witnesses.

48. *Pelagie, a woman of color v. Francois Valois*, February term, 1822, Case 12, p. 1, SLCCR.

49. There is no evidence of African Americans in Illinois writs of *de homine replegiando*, which were commonly filed in New York and Pennsylvania.

50. The fragmentary nature of the record forestalls any comprehensive statistical analysis.

51. Census data in Illinois did not record slaves' gender, but the extant servitude contracts and emancipation bonds reveal that men outnumbered women in the bound population. Of the indentured population where identity can be determined, men composed 53 percent of the workforce. Similarly, the free papers registered at courthouses indicate that men made up 53 percent of the population. The extant servitude contracts show 327 men statewide compared to 288 women. These contracts are compiled from the servitude registries noted in the public records section of the bibliography. The emancipation bonds record that 652 men and 570 women lived in the state. These bonds are compiled from the records cited in the public records section of the bibliography.

52. Of the existing suits, women filed four, while men filed three.

53. Of the suits before the high court that began as suits for freedom, women filed four and men filed three.

54. This is makes sense in light of enslaved and free black women's experiences elsewhere in the United States, where they vigilantly used the courts. See, for example, Myers, *Forging Freedom*, esp. 68–70. In other parts of the South, see Edwards, "Enslaved Women and the Law." See also the case of Amy Johnson in the Natchez District in Welch, *Calling to Account*.

55. Myers, *Forging Freedom*, 49–52.

56. *Mary, a woman of color v. Francis Menard*, November term, 1827, Case 7, p. 1, SLCCR.

57. Ibid., pp. 1–2.

58. *Sarah, a free girl v. Michael Hatton* April term, 1821, Case 191, p. 5, SLCCR.

59. Registry of Negroes 1809–1863, p. 218, Office of the County Clerk, Randolph County, Ill.

60. St. Clair County Servitude Register, 1805–1832, p. 73, ISA.

61. Schmook, ed., *Gallatin County, Illinois Slave Register*, 64.

62. Ibid., 65.

63. This mirrors a trend in other parts of the nation. Notably, in Charleston, women maintained the "variety of alliances" that could make the courts a useful tool in their campaigns for freedom. See Myers, *Forging Freedom*, 4. These experiences in Illinois are largely in line with women's experiences in slave systems, and for a useful overview, consult Campbell, Miers, and Miller, "Women in Western Systems of Slavery."

64. The state's free black population reached 8,000 people in 1860, up from just 1,000 people in 1820. See a summary to 1850 in Table 1, Population of the United States Decennially from 1790 to 1850, *The Seventh Census of the United States*, ix–x. For the 1860 data, see The Colored Population and Its Proportions—1860 in *The Population of the United States in 1860*, xiii.

65. On the broad reaction to the Turner rebellion, see Ford, *Deliver Us from Evil*, 269–98.

66. Schmook, ed., *Gallatin County, Illinois Slave Register*, 34–35.

67. Pope County Deed Book E, pp. 46–53, Office of the County Clerk, Golconda, Ill.

68. The emancipation bonds record 652 men and 570 women, making men 53 percent of the population, according to this one metric.

69. For more on John Jones's biography, see Gliozzo, "John Jones"; Junger, " 'God and Man Helped Those Who Helped Themselves.' " For his freedom suit, see John Jones (alias Broomfield), January 16, 1838, Madison County Emancipation Register, p. 38, ISA.

70. Data from 412 advertisements compiled from thirty-three newspapers listed in the bibliography.

71. Seventy-eight percent of extant runaway notices came from Missouri, Kentucky, and Tennessee.

72. Franklin and Schweninger, *Runaway Slaves*, esp. 210–13.

73. *Shawneetown Illinois Gazette*, March 13, 1830.

74. Haines, *A Practical Treatise*, 36–39.

75. Flower, *The History of the English Settlement in Edwards County*, p. 134, CHM.

76. Ibid., p. 137. This is the manuscript draft of Flower and Birbeck's *History of the English Settlement in Edwards County.*

77. Diary of George Churchill, May 22, May 24, 1818, George Churchill Papers, ALPLM. Damage to the diary obscures any further information about this runaway, who appears to have received another entry on May 26.

78. *Matthew Chambers v. People of the State of Illinois*, 1843, Case 1465, Supreme Court Case Files, ISA.

79. Martin Van Buren to Ninian Edwards, September 9, 1828, Folder 8, Box 2, Ninian Edwards Papers, CHM.

80. See, for instance, *Peoria Register*, October 5, 1839. See also *Springfield Sangamo Journal*, February 9, 1832.

81. Some examples include the entry on December 23, 1841, Edwards County Slave Register, 1815–1860, p. 14, ISA; Union County Deed Book 3, p. 440, Office of the County Clerk,

Union County, Ill.; Record Book D, p. 196, Office of the Circuit Clerk, Union County, Ill.; Musgrave and Allen, eds., *Gallatin County, Illinois, Slave and Emancipation Records*, 79; Schmook, ed., *Gallatin County, Illinois Slave Register*, 63. In total, no more than twenty runaways won their freedom in this manner.

82. Circuit Court Book Record No. 5, April 1836–May 1843, p. 185, Johnson County, Ill.

83. Ibid., p. 354.

84. Across the North, black migrants adopted a similar strategy, and in time, over seventy-five black towns dotted the U.S. North. For the study of one such town in Michigan, see Cox, *A Stronger Kinship*.

85. Brooklyn's 1829 founding is well established, and some scholars assert it was the first black town in America. Rocky Fork was home to free African Americans as early as 1816 but was probably not formally established until 1830. New Philadelphia was settled in 1836 and Miller Grove in 1840. Their sizes are impossible to determine, but during this period they ranged from roughly fifty inhabitants to perhaps as many as two hundred. For a discussion of these towns, see Keita Cha-Jua, *America's First Black Town*; LaRoche, *Free Black Communities and the Underground Railroad.*

86. LaRoche, *Free Black Communities and the Underground Railroad*, ix. On this point more generally, see the claim that "the location of the law as essential to the operation of the law. Liberty, in other words, was determined by geography." Hunter, "Geographies of Liberty," 43.

87. Deed Book E, p. 53, Office of the County Clerk, Pope County, Ill.

88. Firm census data do not exist. The Pope County courthouse has evidence of 273 free African Americans posting emancipation bonds after 1840. It is not known how many of those people relocated to the Grove.

89. Holdings for Harrison Miller, Robert Sides, and William Hicks are from the 1860 U.S. Census, s.v. Pope County, Ill., Township 12S, Range 5E.

90. LaRoche, *Free Black Communities and the Underground Railroad*, 114–15.

91. *Shawneetown Illinois Republican*, November 26, 1842.

92. Keita Jua-Cha, *America's First Black Town*, 33. For a similar evaluation in other locations, see Hahn, *The Political Worlds of Slavery and Freedom*, 31.

93. Hahn, *The Political Worlds of Slavery and Freedom*, 40. See also LaRoche, *Free Black Communities and the Underground Railroad*, 23.

94. LaRoche, *Free Black Communities and the Underground Railroad*, 48–52.

95. Williams, *Self Taught*, esp. 7–29. See also Kaye, *Joining Places*, esp. 178–81; Kennington, *In the Shadow of* Dred Scott, esp. 43–47.

96. In Gallatin County between 1815 and 1840, thirty-four servitude contracts contain signatures of African Americans. All of the servants signed with a mark rather than their name, which implies their illiteracy. In neighboring Pope County between 1817 and 1840, nineteen servitude contracts or emancipation bonds contain African American signatures. All nineteen signatures are made with a mark. Idiosyncrasies in the ways in which these documents are recorded at the courthouse made these statistics unreliable and impressionistic, but they strongly suggest a widespread illiteracy.

97. Some masters relied on servitude contracts or other legal instruments to keep African Americans in bondage, despite their inability to sign their name. See, for instance, William Wilson using a mark on a servitude contract, Deed Book A, p. 34, Office of the County Clerk, Pope County, Ill.

98. St. Clair County Emancipation Book, 1822–1832, p. 16, ISA.

99. St. Clair County Emancipation Book, 1822–1832, p. 12, ISA.

100. St. Clair County Negro Book, 1805–1832, p. 73, ISA.

101. Emancipation of Lucy, "mulatto slave," and her children, December 1846, Bin 317, Office of the County Clerk, Pope County, Ill.

102. Pope County Deed Book D, p. 32, Office of the County Clerk, Pope County, Ill.

103. Pope County Deed Book C, pp. 339–44, Office of the County Clerk, Pope County, Ill.

104. The 1849 case is at Deed Book D, p. 435, Office of the County Clerk, Pope County, Ill. For other instances, see Emancipation bonds for Dolly Sides and Mary, December 1847; Sally Fryer, April 1, 1848; and John Averett, July 31, 1850, Bin 317, Office of the County Clerk, Pope County, Ill.

105. For his criminal indictments for selling alcohol without a permit, see *People v. Moses Lewis*, 1850-CC-044; *People v. Moses Lewis*, 1852-CC-32; *People v. Moses Lewis*, 1852-CC-35; and *People v. Moses Lewis*, 1853-CC-76, Office of the Circuit Clerk, Pope County, Ill.

106. For selling too little of quantities, see *People v. Moses Lewis*, 1856-CC-26; *People v. Moses Lewis*, 1856-CC-68; and *People v. Moses Lewis*, 1864-CC-016, Office of the Circuit Clerk, Pope County, Ill.

107. These bonds appear at Pope County Deed Book D, p. 394; Pope County Deed Book E, p. 447; and Emancipation Bond, July 31, 1850, Bin 317, Office of the County Clerk, Ill.

108. Schmook, ed., *Gallatin County, Illinois Slave Register*, 46. This case comes from neighboring Gallatin County and is suggestive of the kinds of legal processes residents in Pope County would have gone through.

109. Author's transcription from the Shawnee National Forest.

110. *Bennington Boon v. Juliet, a woman of color*, 1836, Case 406, pp. 9–11, Supreme Court Case Files, ISA.

111. *Shawneetown Illinois Republican*, October 8, 1842.

112. *People v. Peyton Gordon, William G. W. Fitch, Caleb Slankard, Joshua Hanly, John Simpkins, and Joseph Lynn*, 1844-CC-065, Office of the Circuit Clerk, Pope County, Ill.

113. Ibid.

114. *Shawneetown Illinois Republican*, February 11, 1843.

115. This information comes from the 1850 U.S. Census, s.v. Pope County, Ill.

116. *The People v. Peyton H. Gordon, Joshua Hanly, Caleb Slankard*, 1844-CC-102, and *People v. Peyton Gordon, William G. W. Fitch, Caleb Slankard, Joshua Hanly, John Simpkins, and Joseph Lynn*, 1844-CC-106, Office of the Circuit Clerk, Pope County, Ill.

117. Page, *History of Massac County*, 169.

118. "Negrophobia," *Shawneetown Illinois Republican*, April 9, 1842.

119. A. Cronk saw the Negroes Delivered, [n.d.], Box 2, Henry Eddy Papers, ALPLM. Another press account of this case appears in *Springfield Sangamo Journal*, April 22, 1842.

120. Order Book M, pp. 8–9, Office of the Circuit Clerk, Gallatin County, Ill.

121. "Negrophobia," *Shawneetown Illinois Republican*, April 8, 1842.

122. Ibid.

123. To His Excellency the Governor, [n.d.], Charles Adams Executive Clemency Files (1846), ISA.

124. Henry Eddy to Thomas Ford, December 8, 1846, Charles Adams Executive Clemency Files (1846), ISA.

125. For instances of this, see Kantrowitz, *More Than Freedom*; Harris, *In the Shadow of Slavery*; Newman, *Freedom's Prophet.*

126. Sinha, *The Slave's Cause*, esp. 66–85, 130–59.

127. Newman, *The Transformation of American Abolitionism*, esp. 60–106, 131–51.

128. See, for instance, Jones, "Time, Space, and Jurisdiction in Atlantic World Slavery"; Gronningsater, " 'On Behalf of His Race and the Lemmon Slaves.' "

Chapter 6

1. *David Bailey v. William Cromwell et al.*, 1841, [no case number], Supreme Court Case Files, ISA; Adams, "Lincoln's First Freed Slave."

2. This happened in other parts of the United States as well. See, for instance, Van Cleve, *A Slaveholder's Union*, esp. 59–101. See also Gellman, *Emancipating New York*, esp. 204–19.

3. The existing historical consensus about an explosion of kidnapping after 1850 due to the passage of the Fugitive Slave Act distorts the lived reality of African Americans in Illinois. For instances of this trend, see the claim that black communities "faced hardships, persecution, and physical insecurity, all of which grew after 1850 as the Fugitive Slave Act increased the risk in the Northern of being kidnapped into slavery." Kolchin, *American Slavery*, 84. This idea is further endorsed by Wilentz, who writes, "After 1850, goaded by panic among northern blacks," many believed that "even the freeborn [were] more vulnerable than ever to being kidnapped into slavery." Wilentz, *The Rise of American Democracy*, 649.

4. On the evangelical antislavery movement, see Campbell, *Fighting Slavery in Chicago*; Sewell, *Ballots for Freedom*, 24–42; Howe, *What Hath God Wrought*, 285–328, 425–28. As one recent historiographic evaluation concludes, "Until recently, the standard narratives of abolitionism—both celebratory and critical—have emphasized the evangelical impulses of white middle-class and elite male reformers." McCarthy and Stauffer, eds., *Prophets of Protest*, xx. See also Evans, "Abolitionism in the Illinois Churches, 1830–1865."

5. Many scholars have followed Foner, *Free Soil, Free Labor, Free Men*. For other expositions of the rise of antislavery politics in Illinois, see Gienapp, *The Origins of the Republican Party*; Sewell, *Ballots for Freedom*, 45–47; and Wilentz, *The Rise of American Democracy*, 602–33, esp. 627–30.

6. *Tempe, a black woman v. Risdon Price*, April term, 1821, Case 181, p. 27, SLCCR.

7. *Aspasia a woman of color* v. *Francois Choteau*, July term, 1827, Case 24, p. 7, SLCCR.

8. For how abolition societies in other states protected African Americans from kidnapping, see Gellman, *Emancipating New York*, 66–68; Van Cleeve, *A Slaveholder's Union*, 79–81, 86–90. As one scholar noted, "Garrisoning found little support anywhere from Alton to Chicago." Robertson, *Hearts Beating for Liberty*, 45. Another has observed that for a long time, "abolitionism could not have been weaker or more unpopular in Illinois." See Foner, *The Fiery Trial*, 26.

9. On this trend generally, see Newman, *The Transformation of American Abolitionism*, 131–52.

10. The Rev. Albert Hale to the Rev. Asa Turner, January 26, 1838, Albert Hale Papers, ALPLM.

11. *Boston Liberator*, July 7, 1843.

12. Basler, ed., *Collected Works of Abraham Lincoln*, 75. For more on Lovejoy, see Sinha, *The Slave's Cause*, 237–38; Brooks, *Liberty Power*, 21.

13. Hale to Turner, January 26, 1838, Albert Hale Papers, ALPLM.

14. Slave Code of Illinois, *Lowell, Genius of Liberty*, July 24, 1841.

15. Hale to Turner, January 26, 1838, Albert Hale Papers, ALPLM. To confirm the slow rise of abolition in Illinois, see Foner, *A Fiery Trial*, 19–25.

16. The summary of the enslaved population is tabulated in Table 1, Population of the United States Decennially from 1790 to 1850, *The Seventh Census of the United States*, ix–x.

17. Registry of Baptisms 1826–1849, Holy Family Parish, Cahokia, p. 192, DAB.

18. U.S. Census, 1840, s.v. Pierre Menard.

19. Inventory of Personal Property Belonging to the Estate of William Morrison, March 26, 1838, Folder 4, Box 1, William V. Morrison Papers, ALPLM. For another example, see Inventory of the Goods and Chattels Belonging to Pierre Lasonde, March 5, 1820, Probate Records, Bin 67, Office of the Circuit Clerk, Randolph County, Ill.

20. For the antikidnapping laws, see Middleton, ed., *The Black Laws of the Old Northwest*, 309. On comparative perspective, see Finkelman, "Slavery, the 'More Perfect Union' and the Prairie State"; Miller, *Lincoln and His World*, 263.

21. Census figures in *Compendium of Enumeration of the Inhabitants and Statistics of the United States*, 84–87, and "Population of the United States" in Introduction, *The Population of the United States in 1860*, iv; Klein, *A Population History of the United States*, 78–79.

22. Meyer, *Making the Heartland Quilt*, 169–95.

23. Birney to Unknown, July 19, 1832, Folder 21, Box 1, James Birney Papers, Clements Library.

24. *Chicago Western Citizen*, July 12, 1843.

25. *Proceedings of the Illinois Anti-Slavery Convention Held at Upper Alton*, 15.

26. Ibid., 19.

27. Cronon, *Nature's Metropolis*, esp. 23–55. For contemporary accounts on Chicago's and the state's explosive growth, see "Slave Hunt in Chicago," *Chicago Western Citizen*, July 20, 1852.

28. Campbell, *Fighting Slavery in Chicago*, 28–29.

29. *Chicago Western Citizen*, November 11, 1842.

30. Ichabod Codding Family Papers, 1807–1935, ALPLM.

31. *Chicago Western Citizen*, January 13, 1843.

32. Ibid., March 19, 1852.

33. Ibid.

34. Ibid., March 21, 1844.

35. Johnson, *The Liberty Party*, 198.

36. *Chicago Western Citizen*, July 12, 1843.

37. Hale to Turner, January 26, 1838, Albert Hale Papers, ALPLM. The document is badly damaged, and the two words "swing the" are unclear and are the author's best possible transcription.

38. "State Anti-Slavery Society," *Chicago Western Citizen*, June 10, 1846. For other meetings, see Eglin Convention, February 16, 1847; Meeting at Sparta, March 21, 1848; Liberty Meetings, May 2, 1848; "Colored Person Meeting," September 16, 1848; Convention at Chicago, March 18, 1851, all in the *Chicago Western Citizen*.

39. In the estimation of one scholar, "Illinois boasted the most widespread advocacy of the party among female antislavery societies." Robertson, *Hearts Beating for Liberty*, esp. 45–51, quotation on p. 45.

40. *Chicago Western Citizen*, May 25, 1843.

41. Davis, *Frontier Illinois*, 294–301.

42. For a summary of the Liberty Party's founding, see Sinha, *The Slave's Cause*, 261–65. See also Johnson, *The Liberty Party*.

43. On Garrison's politics, see McDaniel, *The Problem of Democracy*.

44. For more on this cohort of activists who were animated "by intense moral animus against slavery" and their resulting "antislavery political agenda," see Brooks, *Liberty Power*, esp. 32–39. Quotation appears on p. 2.

45. *Chicago Western Citizen*, May 6, 1846.

46. Ibid., January 25, 1844.

47. For a discussion of Lovejoy's bid, see Brooks, *Liberty Power*, 20–22; Johnson, *The Liberty Party 1840–1848*, 199. See also his conclusion: "the Liberty Party in Illinois at the end of 1847 was the fastest growing and among the most united in the country." On the rise of antislavery politics more generally, see Guasco, *Confronting Slavery*.

48. Davis, *Frontier Illinois*, 227–31; Davis, "The People in Miniature"; Simeone, *Democracy and Slavery in Frontier Illinois*, 210–12.

49. *Chicago Western Citizen*, February 1, 1844.

50. Ibid., February 22, 1844.

51. Ibid.

52. See a discussion of the 1818 constitution in Chapter 4 and "Pro-slavery Views of Governor Edwards," Edwards Papers, n.d., CHM.

53. The chief justice had the "sincere pleasure . . . to break the fetters of the slave and declare the captive free." *Joseph Jarrot, alias Pete, a colored man v. Julia Jarrot*, 1845, [no case number in original], p. 12, Supreme Court Case Files, ISA.

54. Ibid.

55. On the Somerset Principle, see Brown, *Moral Capital*, 96–98; Finkelman, *An Imperfect Union*, 150–53; Paley, "Imperial Politics and English Law"; Van Cleve, "'Somerset's Case' and Its Antecedents in Imperial Perspective."

56. St. Clair County Emancipations, Vault, Folder 5, ISA.

57. Ibid.

58. Petition for Writ of Habeas Corpus, June 1845, Office of the Circuit Clerk, Menard County, Ill.

59. Foner, *The Fiery Trial*, 48–50.

60. Finkelman, "Slavery, the 'More Perfect Union' and the Prairie State."

61. Of instances that give a clear indication of the gender of the person kidnapped, men composed fifty-six cases and women composed twenty-five; twenty-seven were children.

62. *Chicago Western Citizen*, August 22, 1844.

63. Ibid., February 20, 1845.

64. Ibid., April 6, 1843.

65. Ibid., October 12, 1843.

66. Ibid.

67. "A Negro Rescued from a Kidnapper," *Lowell Genius of Liberty*, November 6, 1841.

68. Nathaniel Wickliffe to Brown and Yates, November 17, 1849, Nathaniel Wickliffe Papers, Filson Historical Society, Louisville, Ky.

69. "More Kidnapping," *Chicago Western Citizen*, June 20, 1848.

70. Austin King to Augustus French, June 30, 1849, in Green and Thompson, eds., *Governors' Letter-Books 1840–1853*, 207.

71. Ibid., 207–8.

72. Augustus French to Austin King, February 17, 1852, in ibid., 245.

73. Ibid.

74. Augustus French to Austin King, July 27, 1849, in ibid., 212.

75. Ibid., 213.

76. On the Fugitive Slave Act of 1850, see Sinha, *The Slave's Cause*, 502–4; Fehrenbacher, *The Slaveholding Republic*; 231–53; Kantrowitz, *More Than Freedom*, 175–264; Slaughter, *Bloody Dawn*, 43–58.

77. Owing to the fragmentary nature of the archive, it is impossible to find firm data on kidnapping. In total, I have uncovered specific evidence for 118 instances of kidnapping. For the purposes of this tabulation, a kidnapping is any instance where a person is captured and detained, whether or not he is taken out of the state. Evidence of these cases comes from three main groups of sources. It relies most heavily on criminal indictments reported as part of the court's docket book. These docket books are housed in Alexander, Gallatin, Johnson, Pope, Randolph, and Williamson Counties and are listed in the public records section of the bibliography. However, these records do not always give details about the cases. Consequently, it is possible that more than one person was kidnapped in any given entry. Second, it draws on suits for freedom in St. Louis that make mention of kidnap victims being trafficked out of Illinois. Third, it draws on press accounts that publicized kidnappers' activities. These accounts at times made passing references to an unspecific "family" or "group" that was kidnapped, making specific tabulation impossible. For the purposes of the above total, I have not included instances where the press referred to a general phenomenon or vaguely alluded to earlier cases. Only specific press accounts are included. In sum, the extant records undercount the number of kidnapped African Americans in Illinois. Moreover, there are counties with missing records, meaning there were certainly kidnappings that have left no extant record. For example, Hardin County, Illinois, was adjacent to Pope and Gallatin Counties, which recorded several criminal indictments each, but Hardin County has no extant records from this period due to an 1884 fire. In total, I have looked for evidence of kidnapping practices in 104 suits for freedom filed in the St. Louis Circuit Court between 1820 and 1848, in thirty-three newspapers published both in Illinois and in other major U.S. cities, and in fifteen county courthouses, all of which are listed in the bibliography.

78. In addition to those listed in the rest of this paragraph, see Circuit Court Book B, p. 488, and Circuit Court Book C, p. 51, Office of the Circuit Clerk, Alexander County, Ill.; Order Book M, p. 39, Office of the Circuit Clerk, Gallatin, County, Ill.

79. *People v. Ephraim Snider*, CR-040-1851, Records of the Circuit Clerk, Williamson County Historical Society, Marion, Ill.

80. For instance, see October 7, 1851, *People v. Marchus Burtin and William Brien*, Order Book, 1844–1853, p. 496, Office of the Circuit Clerk, Pulaski County, Ill.; see also *People v. Henry Edwards and Asa Bungardner*, 1857-CF-008, and *People v. Jacob Gates and Benjamin Davis*, 1859-CF-015, Office of the Circuit Clerk, Massac County, Ill.; and Circuit Court Book C, p. 239, Office of the Circuit Clerk, Alexander County, Ill.

81. For instance, the *Liberator* reported, "In company with four other fugitive slaves, Turner left this city on Sunday evening, on the Chicago branch of the Underground Railroad

for Canada—the land of freedom." Reprinted from the *Chicago Tribune* and *Chicago Journal*, "The Missouri Slave-Catchers," *Boston Liberator*, September 22, 1854.

82. See Sinha, *The Slave's Cause*, 515–20.

3. "Fugitive Slave Excitement in Chicago, Ill.," *Boston Liberator*, June 13, 1851.

84. *Chicago Western Citizen*, June 10, 1851.

85. "Fugitive Slave Excitement in Chicago, Ill.," *Boston Liberator*, June 13, 1851.

86. On this episode, see Horton and Horton, *Slavery and the Making of America*, 136.

87. On these mobility rights and the "Passenger Cases," see Jones, *All Bound Up Together*, 95–98.

88. Weiner, *Race and Rights*, esp. 200–8.

89. Foner and Walker, eds., *The Proceedings of the Black State Conventions*, 55. For more on this movement in Chicago, see Weiner, *Race and Rights*, 206–8.

90. For the notion of party decay, see Gienapp, *The Origins of the Republican Party*; Burton, *The Age of Lincoln*, esp. 104–33. More generally, see Oakes, *Freedom National.*

91. Sparks, ed., *The Lincoln-Douglas Debates*, 43.

92. Ibid., 58.

93. Ibid., 31.

94. Levine, *The Fall of the House of Dixie*, esp. 107–41.

95. Oakes, *The Scorpion Sting*, esp. 18–23.

96. Hahn, *Political Worlds of Slavery and Freedom*, 55–114. See also Downs, *After Appomattox.*

97. Oakes, *Freedom National*, esp. 1–48.

Conclusion

1. Entry dated September 22, 1872, John Jones Scrap Book, Folder 1, CHM.

2. Weiner, *Race and Rights*, 221–25.

3. On the press campaign, see Gliozzo, "John Jones."

4. Ibid.

5. "Barbarism in Illinois," *Boston Liberator*, March 27, 1863.

6. *Nelson, a mulatto v. People of Illinois*, 1864, January term, Case 3531, p. 1, Supreme Court Case Files, ISA.

7. Ibid., 2.

8. Ibid.

9. The dissenting justice did so without filing a written opinion. However, he discussed his views on the case in a private letter: C[roydon] Beckwith to J Grimshaw Esq., January 10, 1865, Croydon Beckwith Collection, ALPLM.

10. John Jones, "The Black Laws of Illinois and a Few Reasons Why They Should be Repealed," p. 2, John Jones Manuscripts, Folder 2, CHM.

11. Ibid., pp. 13–14.

12. "Black Laws of Illinois," *Boston Liberator*, December 9, 1864.

13. Ibid.

14. Lucien Eaton to Hon. Richard Yates, St. Louis, October 16, 1863, Logan Reavis Papers, Folder 1, CHM.

15. Ibid.

16. "Kidnapping in Southern Indiana," *Boston Liberator*, March 27, 1863. My thanks to Dr. Adam Rothman for this reference.

17. Varon, *Appomattox*, 94.

18. Foner, *The Fiery Trial*, chap. 1. Lincoln referred to himself as "naturally" antislavery.

19. Blackburn, *The American Crucible*, 277. See also the observation that "a chronology of abolition gives the impression of a constantly forward-moving steamroller, but, when looked at closely, each case has its own logic." Klein, "The Emancipation of Slaves in the Indian Ocean," 213.

BIBLIOGRAPHY

Unpublished Manuscript Collections

Abraham Lincoln Presidential Library and Museum, Springfield, Ill.

Albert Hale Papers, 1838
Bryan and Morrison Ledger B
Corydon Beckwith Letter
Daily Journal of a Trip Down the Mississippi [1805–6]
Elijah Iles Papers
Enos Family Papers, 1796–1868
Gallatin County Legal Documents, 1813–46
George Churchill, Madison County Anti-Slavery Party Papers, 1816–71
Henry Eddy Papers, 1817–75
Henry Hitchcock, Galesburg Abolition Papers
Icabod Codding Family Papers, 1807–1935
James and John Dunlap Papers, 1818–53
Jaral Jackson, Bill of Sale
Jesse B. Thomas Papers, 1785–1866
Jo-Davis County, Certificates of Freedom
John Messinger Papers
John Reynolds Papers, 1814–37
Lucinda Casteen Letter
Lyman Trumbull Papers, 1841–70
Madison County Illinois, Circuit Court Docket
Menard County Records, 1828–36
Menard Family Papers, 1829–44
Nance Legins Costley Legal Papers, 1825–27
Napoleon Bond Collection
Nathanial Pope Papers, 1819–24, 1835
New Salem Collection
Ninian Edwards Day Books, 1811–15
Ninian Edwards Papers, 1800–35
Niveah Shaw Papers, 1822–42
Robert Morrison, Kaskaskia Letters, 1805, 1819
Russell Family Papers
Sangamon County Indentures of Apprenticeship, 1834–54

Schadrach Bond Account Book, 1818–19
Sidney Breeze Papers, 1731–1896
Shaw Family Papers
St. Clair County Indentures, 1815
Thaddeus Hurlbut Papers
William Morrison Letter, 1815
William V. Morrison Papers, 1836

British National Archives, Kew, England
Colonial Office Records, Class 5

Chester Public Library, Chester, Ill.
Bryan and Morrison Ledger C

Chicago History Museum, Chicago, Ill.
Bryan and Morrison Ledger D
Elias Kent Kane Papers
Elizabeth Carroll (Eddy) Papers
Fort Chartres Collection
French America Collection
George Flower Manuscript, *The History of the English Settlement in Edwards County*
George Rogers Clark Papers
John Jones Papers
John Todd's Record Book, Rare Book Vault
Joseph Conway Papers, 1815
Joseph Gallagher Papers, 1837
Joseph Street Papers
Kaskaskia Collection
Logan Reevis Collection
Menard Family Papers
Ninian Edwards Papers
Prarie du Rocher Collection
Samuel Cochran Papers, 1820
Samuel Hunter Papers
Schadrach Bond Family Bible
Thomas Mather Papers

Diocesan Archives, Belleville, Ill.
Registry of Baptisms, 1692–1733, Parish of the Immaculate Conception of Notre Dame
Registry of Baptisms, 1741–61, Holy Family Parish
Registry of Baptisms, 1759–1815, Parish of the Immaculate Conception of Notre Dame
Registry of Baptisms, 1812–49, Holy Family Parish
Registry of Baptisms, 1815–50, Parish of the Immaculate Conception of Notre Dame
Registry of Burials, 1721–1834, Parish of the Immaculate Conception of Notre Dame
Registry of Burials, 1834–63, Parish of the Immaculate Conception of Notre Dame
Registry of Marriages, 1724–1834, Parish of the Immaculate Conception of Notre Dame
Registry of Marriages, 1834–89, Parish of the Immaculate Conception of Notre Dame

Filson Historical Society, Louisville, Ky.
Nathaniel Wickliffe Papers

Huntington Library, San Marino, Calif.
Vaudreuil Papers (French Colonial Manuscripts)
Illinois History and Lincoln Collection, University of Illinois, Champaign-Urbana, Ill.
Bryan and Morrison Records, 1800–57
George Morgan Papers, 1766–1826
Illinois (Territory) Legislature Collection
Illinois Territorial Papers
James Cornelius Papers
Ninian Edwards Papers, 1799–1880
Pierre Menard Papers, 1741–1910
Illinois Regional Archives Depository, Carbondale, Ill.
Gallatin County Circuit Court Case Files, 1814–1920
Randolph County Circuit Court Records, 1815–51
St. Clair County Circuit Court Dockets
Territorial French Court Papers
Illinois Regional Archives Depository, Springfield, Ill.
Sangamon County Circuit Court Files, 1825–1901
Sangamon County Deed Record Books
Sangamon County Probate Case Files, 1821–1906
Sangamon County Probate Index Files, 1821–1910
Illinois State Archives, Springfield, Ill.
Auction of Charleville Estate, 1784
Edwards County Slave Register, 1815–60
Executive Clemency Files
Governor's Correspondence, Record Groups 101.001–101.009
Madison County Servitude and Emancipation Records, 1830–60
Nick Perrin Collection
Pope County Servitude Record, 1816–19
Randolph County Servitude and Emancipation Records, 1809–63
Raymond C. Hammes Collection
St. Clair County Circuit Court Records
St. Clair County Emancipation Records, 1812–43
St. Clair County Legal Documents
St. Clair County Servitude Records, 1805–32
St. Clair County Servitude Records, 1846–63
St. Clair County Indentures, Vault, 1800–60
St. Clair County, Registre of Insinuations
Supreme Court Case Files
Union County Emancipation Records, 1835–44
Indiana Historical Society, Indianapolis, Ind.
Northwest Territory Collection
Library of Congress, Washington, D.C.
Foreign Copying Project, France
Thomas Jefferson Papers, Series 1
Louisiana State Museum, New Orleans, La.
Records of the Superior Council of New Orleans

Missouri Historical Society, St. Louis, Mo.
- Kaskaskia, Illinois Collection
- Morrison Family Papers
- Slaves and Slavery Collection
- St. Anne Parish Register
- St. Genevieve Archives, 1761–1854

National Archives and Records Administration, Washington, D.C./College Park, Md.
- Legislative Archive Collection
- U.S. State Department Papers, R.G. 59

Newberry Library, Chicago, Ill.
- Edward Ayers Collection
- Everett D. Graff Collection
- Rudy Lamont Ruggles Collection

Western Historical Manuscript Collection, State Historical Society of Missouri, Columbia, Mo.
- St. Genevieve Archives, 1756–1930
- St. Genevieve Parish Records, 1764–93, Western Historical Manuscript Collection
- The State Historical Society of Missouri, Columbia, Mo.

William Clements Library, Ann Arbor, Mich.
- African American History Collection
- Anthony Wayne Papers
- James Birney Papers
- Josiah Harmar Papers
- Schoff Revolutionary War Collection
- Thomas Gage Papers

Government Documents

Abstract of the Returns of the Fifth Census. Doc. No. 263. Washington, D.C.: Duff Green, 1832.

Annals of Congress

Compendium of the Enumeration of the Inhabitants and Statistics of the United States. Washington, D.C.: Thomas Allen, 1841.

Journal of the House of Delegates of the Commonwealth of Virginia. Richmond: Virginia General Assembly, 1835.

The Population of the United States in 1860. Washington, D.C.: Government Printing Office, 1864.

Report of the Committee on the Petition of Sundry Inhabitants of the Counties of St. Clair and Randolph. U.S. 4th Congress, 1795–97. Evans Series 31395.

The Seventh Census of the United States. Washington, D.C.: Robert Armstrong, Public Printer, 1853.

Illinois State Public Records

These records are largely housed in courthouse storage facilities. They are idiosyncratic in several ways, making uniform citations impossible. In each case, I have identified the repository and the most obvious identifying information for the entry, which in some cases is page numbers, in others is dates, and in still others is marking on the outside of boxes that store them.

ALEXANDER COUNTY COURTHOUSE, CAIRO, ILL.

Office of the County Clerk
    Deed Record C
Office of the Circuit Clerk
    Circuit Court Record Books B, C

GALLATIN COUNTY COURTHOUSE, SHAWNEETOWN, ILL.

Office of the County Clerk
    Deed Books A, B
    Slave Register 1815–39
Office of the Circuit Clerk
    Order Books M, N

IBERVILLE PARISH COURTHOUSE, PLAQUEMINE, LA.

Office of the Circuit Clerk
    Fourth Judicial Circuit

JOHNSON COUNTY COURTHOUSE, VIENNA, ILL.

Office of the Circuit Clerk
    Circuit Court Books A, B, C
    Circuit Court Book No. 5
    Criminal Court Case Files 1813–23, 1824–38, 1844–50
    Common Law Case Files 1838–40
    Probate Court Book 1822–36
Office of the County Clerk
    Deed Books A, B

MASSAC COUNTY COURTHOUSE, METROPOLIS, ILL.

Office of the County Clerk
    Registry of Negroes (contained at the end of "Marriage Record beginning in 1843")
Office of the Circuit Clerk
    Criminal Court Records 1850–60

MENARD COUNTY COURTHOUSE, PETERSBURG, ILL.

Accessed through Lincoln Legal Papers. See Published Manuscript Collections

MONROE COUNTY COURTHOUSE, WATERLOO, ILL.

Office of the County Clerk
    Deed Books A, B

PULASKI COUNTY COURTHOUSE, MOUND CITY, ILL.

Office of the Circuit Clerk
    Order Book 1844–53

POPE COUNTY COURTHOUSE, GOLCONDA, ILL.

Office of the County Clerk
    Deed Books A, B, C, D, E

Probate Inventories 1830–60
Registry of Indentures Bin 317
Registry of Emancipations Bin 320
Office of the Circuit Clerk
Criminal Court Case Files 1820–60

RANDOLPH COUNTY COURTHOUSE, CHESTER, ILL.

Office of the County Clerk
Deed Book 1795–99
Randolph County Emancipation Records 1807–53
Record Books G-H-I-J, J, K, L, M, N, O, P, Q, R, S, T
Registry of Negroes 1809–63 (differs from the item in the Illinois State Archives)
Registry of Negroes, Marks, and Brands 1800–49
Office of the Circuit Clerk
Probate Inventories 1820–1825
Randolph County Circuit Court Books A, B, C, D

SANGAMON COUNTY, SPRINGFIELD, ILL.

Held in Illinois Regional Archives Depository, Springfield. See Unpublished Manuscript Collections

SHELBY COUNTY, MEMPHIS, TENN., SHELBY COUNTY HISTORICAL SOCIETY

Office of the Circuit Clerk
Circuit Court Minute Book 1828–36
Circuit Court Minute Book 1840–42

ST. CLAIR COUNTY, BELLEVILLE, ILL.

Held in Illinois State Archives in Unpublished Manuscript Collections.

UNION COUNTY COURTHOUSE, JONESBORO, ILL.

Office of the Circuit Clerk
Circuit Court Books A, B, C, D
Office of the County Clerk
Record Book C-3, Deed Record 4

WILLIAMSON COUNTY, MARION, ILL., WILLIAMSON COUNTY HISTORICAL SOCIETY

Office of the Circuit Clerk
Criminal Court Case files 1850–54

Newspapers

Advocate (Belleville, Ill.)
Alton Telegraph and Democratic Review (Alton, Ill.)
Cairo City Times (Cairo, Ill.)
Cairo Delta (Cairo, Ill.)
Cairo Sun (Cairo, Ill.)
Edwardsville Spectator (Edwardsville, Ill.)

Galena Advertiser (Galena, Ill.)
Galena Miner's Journal (Galena, Ill.)
Galenian (Galena, Ill.)
Genius of Liberty (Lowell, Ill.)
Genius of Universal Emancipation (Alton, Ill.)
Illinois Gazette (Shawneetown, Ill.)
Illinois Intelligencer (Vandalia, Ill.)
Illinois Journal (Shawneetown, Ill.)
Illinois Patriot (Jacksonville, Ill.)
Illinois Republican (Shawneetown, Ill.)
Illinois State Gazette (Jacksonville, Ill.)
Kaskaskia Republican (Kaskaskia, Ill.)
Liberator (Boston, Mass.)
Peoria Register (Peoria, Ill.)
Randolph County Record (Sparta, Ill.)
Republican Advocate (Kaskaskia, Ill.)
Sangamo Journal (Springfield, Ill.)
Shawneetown Democrat (Shawneetown, Ill.)
Sparta Register (Sparta, Ill.)
St. Clair Gazette (Belleville, Ill.)
Voice and Journal (Shawneetown, Ill.)
Western Citizen (Chicago, Ill.)
Western Intelligencer (Kaskaskia, Ill.)
Western Voice (Shawneetown, Ill.)

Published Manuscripts

Alvord, Clarence W., ed. *Cahokia Records: 1778–1790*. Collections of the Illinois State Historical Library. Vol. II. Springfield: Illinois State Historical Library, 1907.

Alvord, Clarence W., ed. *George Rogers Clark Papers: 1771–1781*. Collections of the Illinois State Historical Library. Vol. VIII. Springfield: Illinois State Historical Library, 1912.

Alvord, Clarence W., and Clarence E. Carter, eds. *The New Regime: 1765–1767*. Collections of the Illinois State Historical Library. Vol. XI. Springfield: Illinois State Historical Library, 1915.

Alvord, Clarence W., and Clarence E. Carter, eds. *Trade and Politics: 1765–1767*. Collections of the Illinois State Historical Library. Vol. XVI. Springfield: Illinois State Historical Library, 1915.

Bachman, John. *A Bird's Eye View of the Ohio and Mississippi Rivers*. New York: A. Rumpf, 1861.

Basler, Roy P., ed. *Collected Works of Abraham Lincoln*. Vol. 1. New Brunswick, N.J.: Rutgers University Press, 1953.

Benner, Martha L., and Cullom Davis et al., eds. *The Law Practice of Abraham Lincoln: Complete Documentary Edition*. 2nd ed. Springfield: Illinois Historic Preservation Agency, 2009. http://www.lawpracticeofabrahamlincoln.org.

Birbeck, Morris. *Notes on a Journey in America from the Coast of Virginia to the Territory of Illinois*. London: Stevens and Co., 1818.

Birbeck, Morris, and George Flower. *History of the English Settlement in Edwards County, Illinois, Founded in 1817 and 1818.* Chicago: Fergus Printing Company, 1887.

Blackstone, William. *Commentaries on the Laws of England.* Philadelphia: J. B. Lippincott Co., 1893.

Brown, Margaret Kimball, and Laurie Cena Dean, eds. *The Village of Chartres in Colonial Illinois.* New Orleans: Polyanthos, 1977.

Carter, Clarence E., ed. *The Territorial Papers of the United States.* Vol. 2. Washington, D.C.: Government Printing Office, 1934.

Circuit Court Case Files. Office of the Circuit Clerk–St. Louis. Missouri State Archives–St. Louis Office of the Secretary of State. http://stlcourtrecords.wustl.edu.

Clark, George Rogers. *The Conquest of Illinois.* Ed. Milo Milton Quaife and Rand Burnette. Carbondale: Southern Illinois University Press, 2001.

Dean, Laurie Cena, and Margaret Kimball Brown, eds. *Kaskaskia Manuscripts, 1714–1816: Calendar of Civil Documents in Colonial Illinois.* Chester, Ill.: Randolph County Archives, 1981. 14 reels.

Dunn, Jacob Piatt, ed. *Slavery Papers and Petitions.* Indianapolis, Ind.: Bowen-Merrill, 1894.

Fergus, Charles, ed. *The Edwards Papers: Being a Portion of the Collection of the Letters, Papers, and Manuscripts of Ninian Edwards.* Chicago: Fergus Printing Company, 1884.

Foner, Philip S., and George E. Walker, eds. *The Proceedings of the Black State Conventions, 1840–1865.* Vol. 2. Philadelphia: Temple University Press, 1979.

George Rogers Clark Manuscripts. Lyman Copeland Draper Collection. State Historical Society of Wisconsin. Department of Photographic Reproduction, University of Chicago, 1977. Reels 22–36.

George Rogers Clark Papers. Richmond: Virginia State Library and Archives, 1991. 12 reels.

Gillespie, Joseph. *Recollections of Early Illinois and Her Noted Men.* Chicago: Fergus Printing Co., 1880.

Greene, Edvarts Boutell, and Charles Manfred Thompson, eds. *Governors' Letter-Books 1840–1853.* Springfield: Illinois State Historical Society, 1911.

Haines, Elijah M. *A Practical Treatise on the Powers and Duties of Justices of the Peace in the State of Illinois.* Chicago: Keen and Lee, 1855.

Hutchins, Thomas. *A New Map of the Western Parts of Virginia, Pennsylvania, Maryland, and North Carolina.* London, 1778.

Kent, Donald H., Martha L. Simonetti, and George R. Beyer, eds. *Baynton, Wharton, and Morgan, Papers in the Pennsylvania State Archives.* Harrisburg: Pennsylvania Historical and Museum Commission, 1967. 10 reels.

Linder, Usher F. *Reminiscences: Early Bench and Bar of Illinois.* Chicago: Chicago Legal News Company, 1879.

Mereness, Newton, ed. *Journal of Diron D'Artaguette, 1722–23.* In *Travels in the American Colonies.* New York: Macmillan, 1916.

Middleton, Stephen, ed. *The Black Laws of the Old Northwest: A Documentary History.* New York: Praeger, 1993.

Musgrave, Jon, ed., and John W. Allen, trans. *Gallatin County, Illinois, Slave and Emancipation Records 1839–1849.* Marion: IllinoisHistory.com, 2004.

Norton, Margaret Cross, ed. *Illinois Census Returns 1810, 1818.* Collections of the Illinois State Historical Library. Vol. XXIV. Springfield: Illinois State Historical Library, 1935.

Norton, Margaret Cross, ed. *Illinois Census Returns 1820*. Collections of the Illinois State Historical Library. Vol. XXV. Springfield: Trustees of the Illinois State Historical Library, 1935.

Page, O. J. *History of Massac County, Illinois; with Life Portraits and Sketches*. Metropolis, Ill: O. J. Page, 1900.

Pease, Theodore Calvin, ed. *Anglo-French Boundary Disputes in the West, 1749–1763*. Springfield: Illinois State Historical Library, 1936.

Pease, Theodore Calvin, ed. *Illinois on the Eve of the Seven Years' War*. Collections of the Illinois State Historical Library. Vol. 29. Springfield: Trustees of the State Historical Library, 1940.

Pease, Theodore Calvin, ed. *Illinois Election Returns, 1818–1848*. Springfield: Illinois State Historic Library, 1923.

Pitman, Phillip. *The Present State of the European Settlements on the Missisippi with a Geographical Description of That River*. London: J. Nourse & Co., 1770.

Proceedings of the Illinois Anti-Slavery Convention Held at Upper Alton. Alton: Parks and Breath, 1838.

Reynolds, John. *My Own Times: Embracing Also the History of My Life*. Belleville, Ill.: B. H. Perryman and H. L. Davison, 1855.

Reynolds, John. *The Pioneer History of Illinois: Containing the Discovery, in 1673, and the History of the Country to the Year 1818, When the State Government Was Organized*. Chicago: Fergus Printing Company, 1887.

Schmook, Rebecca, ed. *Gallatin, County, Illinois Slave Register 1815–1839*. Equality, IL: Saline County Genealogical Society, 1994.

Sparks, Edwin, ed. *The Lincoln-Douglas Debates*. Danville, N.Y.: F. A. Owen Publishing, 1918.

Taylor, Harlin, ed. *Census of Randolph County, Illinois, 1825*. Decatur, Ill.: Vio-Lin Enterprises, 1972.

Thwaits, Ruben Gold, ed. *The Jesuit Relations and Allied Documents*. Cleveland, Ohio: Burrow Brothers Company, 1899.

Tregellis, Helen Cox, ed. *River Roads to Freedom: Fugitive Slave Notices and Sheriff Notices Found in Illinois Sources*. Bowie, Md.: Heritage Books, 1998.

Verlie, Emile Joseph, ed. *Illinois Constitutions*. Collections of the Illinois State Historical Library. Vol. XIII. Springfield: Illinois State Preservation Agency, 1919.

Secondary Sources

Adams, Carl. "Lincoln's First Freed Slave: A Review of Bailey v. Cromwell, 1841." *Journal of the Illinois State Historical Society* 101 no. 3–4 (Fall–Winter 2008): 235–59.

Allen, Richard B. *European Slave Trading in the Indian Ocean, 1500–1850*. Athens: Ohio University Press, 2014.

Alpers, Edward A. "The African Diaspora in the Northwestern Indian Ocean: Reconsideration of an Old Problem, New Directions for Research." *Comparative Studies of South Asia, Africa and the Middle East* 17 no. 2 (1997): 62–81.

Amussen, Susan Dwyer. *Caribbean Exchanges: Slavery and the Transformation of English Society, 1640–1700*. Chapel Hill: University of North Carolina Press, 2007.

Anderson, Fred. *Crucible of War: The Seven Years' War and the Fate of Empire in British North America 1754–1766*. New York: Vintage, 2000.

Arenson, Adam. *The Great Heart of the Republic: St. Louis and the Cultural Civil War.* Cambridge, Mass.: Harvard University Press, 2011.

Armitage, David. *The Ideological Origins of the British Empire.* New York: Cambridge University Press, 2000.

Aron, Steven. *American Confluence: The Missouri Frontier from Borderland to Border State.* Bloomington: Indiana University Press, 2006.

Aubert, Guillaume. "'The Blood of France': Race and Purity of Blood in the French Atlantic World." *William and Mary Quarterly* 61 no. 3 (July 2004): 439–78.

Aubert, Guillaume. "Kinship, Blood, and the Emergence of the Racial Nation in the French Atlantic World, 1600–1789." In *Blood and Kinship: Matter for Metaphor from Ancient Rome to the Present,* ed. Christopher J. Johnson et al. New York: Berghahn Books, 2013.

Aubert, Guillaume. "'To Establish One Law and Definite Rules': Race, Religion, and the Transatlantic Origins of the Louisiana Code Noir." In *Louisiana: Crossroads of the Atlantic World,* ed. Cecil Vidal. Philadelphia: University of Pennsylvania Press, 2014.

Bahde, Thomas. "'I Would Not Have a White Upon the Premises': The Ohio Valley Salt Industry and Slave Hiring in Illinois, 1780–1825." *Ohio Valley History* 15 no. 2 (Summer 2015): 49–69.

Bakalis, Michael John. "Ninian Edwards and Territorial Politics in Illinois." PhD diss., Northwestern University, 1966.

Baptist, Edward. *The Half Has Never Been Told: Slavery and the Making of American Capitalism.* New York: Basic Books, 2014.

Barr, Juliana. *Peace Came in the Form of a Woman: Indians and Spaniards in the Texas Borderlands.* Chapel Hill: University of North Carolina Press, 2007.

Belmessous, Saliha. "Assimilation and Racialization in Seventeenth and Eighteenth Century French Colonial Policy." *American Historical Review* 110 no. 2 (April 2005): 322–49.

Berbel, Márcia Regina, Rafel de Bivar Marquese, and Tâmis Parron. *Slavery and Politics: Brazil and Cuba, 1790–1850.* Albuquerque: University of New Mexico, 2016.

Berlin, Ira. *Generations of Captivity: A History of African American Slaves.* Cambridge, Mass.: Harvard University Press, 2003.

Berlin, Ira. *The Long Emancipation: The Demise of Slavery in the United States.* Cambridge, Mass.: Harvard University Press, 2015.

Berlin, Ira. *Many Thousands Gone: The First Two Centuries of Slavery in North America.* Cambridge, Mass.: Harvard University Press, 1998.

Berlin, Ira, and Philip D. Morgan, eds. *Cultivation and Culture: Labor and the Shaping of Slave Life in the Americas.* Charlottesville: University of Virginia Press, 1992.

Bialuschewski, Arne, and Linford D. Fisher. "New Directions in the History of Native American Slavery Studies." *Ethnohistory* 64 no. 1 (January 2017): 1–17.

Black, Henry Campbell. *Black's Law Dictionary.* Rev. 4th ed. St. Paul, Minn.: West, 1968.

Blackburn, Robin. *The American Crucible: Slavery, Freedom, Human Rights.* London: Verso, 2011.

Blackburn, Robin. *The Making of New World Slavery: From Baroque to the Modern, 1492–1800.* London: Verso, 1998.

Blackmore, Yvonne Jacqueline. "African Americans and Race Relations in Gallatin County, Illinois from the Eighteenth Century to 1870." PhD diss., Northern Illinois University, 1996.

Bodel, John, and Walter Scheidel, eds. *On Human Bondage: After* Slavery and Social Death. New York: Wiley Blackwell, 2016.

Bossy, Denise I. "Godin & Co.: Charleston Merchants and the Indian Trade, 1674–1715." *South Carolina Historical Magazine* 114 no. 2 (April 2013): 96–131.

Bossy, Denise I. "The South's Other Slavery: Recent Research on Indian Slavery." *Native South* 9 (2016): 27–53.

Bouge, Allan G. *From Prairie to Corn Belt: Farming on the Illinois and Iowa Prairies in the Nineteenth Century*. Chicago: University of Chicago Press, 1963.

Brewer, John. *The Sinews of Power: War, Money and the English State, 1688–1783*. New York: Routledge, 1995.

Brooks, Corey M. *Liberty Power: Antislavery Third Parties and the Transformation of American Politics*. Chicago: University of Chicago Press, 2016.

Brooks, James F. *Captives and Cousins: Slavery, Kinship, and Community in the Southwest Borderlands*. Chapel Hill: University of North Carolina Press, 2002.

Brooks, James F., and Bonnie Martin, eds. *Linking the Histories: North America and Its Borderlands*. Santa Fe, N.M.: School for Advanced Research Press, 2015.

Brown, Christopher Leslie. *Moral Capital: Foundations of British Abolitionism*. Chapel Hill: University of North Carolina Press, 2006.

Brown, Vincent. "Social Death and Political Life in the Study of Slavery." *American Historical Review* 114 no. 5 (December 2009): 1231–49.

Buchannan, Thomas. *Black Life on the Mississippi: Slaves, Free Blacks, and the Western Steamboat World*. Chapel Hill: University of North Carolina Press, 2004.

Buck, Salon J. *Illinois in 1818*. Urbana: University of Illinois Press, 1967.

Burton, Orville Vernon. *The Age of Lincoln*. New York: Hill and Wang, 2007.

Burnard, Trevor. *Mastery, Tyranny, Desire: Thomas Thistlewood and His Slaves in the Anglo-Jamaica World*. Chapel Hill: University of North Carolina Press, 2004.

Burnard, Trevor. *Planters, Merchants, and Slaves: Plantation Societies in British America 1650–1820*. Chicago: University of Chicago Press, 2015.

Calloway, Colin. *American Revolution in Indian Country*. New York: Cambridge University Press, 1995.

Calloway, Colin. *The Scratch of a Pen: 1763 and the Transformation of North America*. New York: Oxford University Press, 2006.

Calloway, Colin. *The Victory with No Name: The Native American Defeat of the First American Army*. New York: Oxford University Press, 2016.

Cameron, Catherine M. "Slavery and Freedom in Small-Scale Societies." In *On Human Bondage: After* Slavery and Social Death, ed. John Bodel and Walter Scheidel, 210–25. New York: Wiley and Blackwell, 2016.

Campbell, Gwyn, Suzanne Miers, and Joseph C. Miller. "Women in Western Systems of Slavery." *Slavery and Abolition* 26 no. 2 (August 2005): 161–79.

Campbell, Tom. *Fighting Slavery in Chicago: Abolitionists, the Law of Slavery and Lincoln*. Chicago: Ampersand Music, 2009.

Cangany, Kathleen. *Frontier Seaport: Detroit's Transformation into an Atlantic Entrepôt*. Chicago: University of Chicago Press, 2014.

Caron, Peter. "'Of a Nation Which Others Do Not Understand': Bambara Slaves and African Ethnicity in Colonial Louisiana, 1718–60." *Slavery and Abolition* 18 (1997): 98–121.

Carpenter, Richard V. "The Illinois Constitutional Convention of 1818." *Illinois State Historical Society Journal* 6 no. 3 (October 1894): 328–54.

Cayton, Andrew, and Fredrika Teute, eds. *Contact Points: American Frontiers from the Mohawk Valley to the Mississippi, 1750–1830.* Chapel Hill: University of North Carolina Press, 1998.

Clark, Christopher. "The Ohio Country in the Political Economy of Nation Building." In *The Center of a Great Empire: The Ohio Country in the Early American Republic,* ed. Andrew R. L. Cayton and Stuart D. Hobbs. Athens: Ohio University Press, 2005.

Clark, John G. *The Grain Trade in the Old Northwest.* Urbana: University of Illinois Press, 1966.

Clayton, John. *The Illinois Fact Book and Historical Almanac 1673–1968.* Carbondale: Southern Illinois University Press, 1970.

Cohen, Paul. "Was There an Amerindian Atlantic? Reflections on the Limits of a Historiographical Concept." *History of European Ideas* 34 (2008): 388–410.

Colley, Linda. *Captives: Britain, Empire, and the World, 1600–1850.* New York: Random House, 2002.

Conway, Chris. *The British Isles and the War of American Independence.* New York: Oxford University Press, 2000.

Cox, Anna-Lisa. *A Stronger Kinship: One Town's Extraordinary Story of Hope and Faith.* New York: Little, Brown, 2006.

Craig, Michelle. "Grounds for Debate? The Place of the Caribbean Provisions Trade in Philadelphia's Prerevolutionary Economy." *Pennsylvania Magazine of History and Biography* 138 no. 2 (April 2004): 149–77.

Cronon, William. *Nature's Metropolis: Chicago and the Great West.* New York: W. W. Norton & Co., 1992.

Crouch, Christian Ayne. "The Black City: African and Indian Exchanges in Pontiac's Upper Country." *Early American Studies* 14 (Spring 2016): 284–318.

Curtin, Philip D. *The Rise and Fall of the Plantation Complex.* 2nd ed. New York: Cambridge University Press, 1998.

Curran, Andrew S. *The Anatomy of Blackness: Science and Slavery in an Age of Enlightenment.* Baltimore: Johns Hopkins University Press, 2011.

Davis, David Brion. "Constructing Race: A Reflection." *William and Mary Quarterly* 54 no. 1 (January 1997): 7–18.

Davis, David Brion. *Inhuman Bondage: The Rise and Fall of New World Slavery.* New York: Oxford University Press, 2006.

Davis, David Brion. "Looking at Slavery from Broader Perspectives." *American Historical Review* 105 no. 2 (April 2000): 452–66.

Davis, David Brion. *The Problem of Slavery in the Age of Emancipation.* New York: Vintage, 2014.

Davis, James Edward. *Frontier Illinois.* Bloomington: Indiana University Press, 2000.

Davis, Rodney O. "The People in Miniature: The Illinois General Assembly, 1818–1848." *Illinois Historical Journal* 81 (1988): 95–108.

Delbourgo, James. "The Newtonian Slave Body: Racial Enlightenment in the Atlantic World." *Atlantic Studies* 9 no. 2 (June 2012): 185–207.

Denny, Mark. *Ingenium: Five Machines That Changed the World.* Baltimore: Johns Hopkins University Press, 2007.

Dewar, David Paton. "George Morgan's American Life 1743–1810." PhD diss., University of Kansas, 2005.

Deyle, Steven. *Carry Me Back: The Domestic Slave Trade in American Life.* New York: Oxford University Press, 2005.

Domar, Evsey D. "The Causes of Slavery or Serfdom: A Hypothesis." *Journal of Economic History* 30 no. 1 (March 1970): 18–32.

Donoghue, John. "'Out of the Land of Bondage': The English Revolution and the Atlantic Origins of Abolition." *American Historical Review* 115 no. 4 (October 2010): 943–74.

Dorsey, Jennifer Hull. *Hirelings: African American Workers and Free Labor in Early Maryland.* Ithaca, N.Y.: Cornell University Press, 2012.

Dowd, Gregory Evans. *War Under Heaven Pontiac, the Indian Nations, and the British Empire.* Baltimore: Johns Hopkins University Press, 2002.

Downs, Gregory. *After Appomattox: Military Occupation and the Ends of War.* Cambridge, Mass.: Harvard University Press, 2015.

Drescher, Seymour. *Abolition: A History of Slavery and Antislavery.* New York: Cambridge University Press 2009.

Dunn, Walter Scott. *Choosing Sides on the Frontier in the American Revolution.* New York: Greenwood, 2007.

DuVal, Kathleen. *Independence Lost: Lives on the Edge of the American Revolution.* New York: Random House, 2016.

DuVal, Kathleen. "Indian Intermarriage and Métissage in Colonial Louisiana." *William and Mary Quarterly* 65 no. 2 (April 2008): 267–304.

Earle, Carville V. "A Staple Interpretation of Slavery and Free Labor." *Geographical Review* 68 no. 1 (January 1978): 51–65.

Edleson, S. Max. *The New Map of Empire: How Britain Imagined America Before Independence.* Cambridge, Mass.: Harvard University Press, 2017.

Edmunds, David, and Joseph Peyser. *The Fox Wars: The Mesquakie Challenge to New France.* Norman: University of Oklahoma Press, 1993.

Edwards, Laura F. "Enslaved Women and the Law: Paradoxes of Subordination in the Post-revolutionary Carolinas." In *Women and Slavery: The Modern Atlantic*, vol. 2, ed. Gwyn Campbell, Suzanne Miers, and Joseph C. Miller, 128–51. Athens: Ohio University Press, 2008.

Edwards, Laura F. *The People and Their Peace: Legal Culture and the Transformation of Inequality in the Post-Revolutionary South.* Chapel Hill: University of North Carolina Press, 2009.

Egnal, Marc. *A Mighty Empire: The Origins of the American Revolution.* Ithaca, N.Y.: Cornell University Press, 1988.

Ekberg, Carl. "Black Slavery in Illinois, 1720–1765." *Western Illinois Regional Studies* 12 no. 1 (Spring 1989): 5–19.

Ekberg, Carl J. *French Roots in the Illinois Country: The Mississippi Valley in Colonial Times.* Urbana: University of Illinois Press, 1998.

Ekberg, Carl J. *Stealing Indian Women: Native Slavery in the Illinois Country.* Urbana: University of Illinois Press, 2007.

Ekberg, Carl J., and Sharon K. Person. *St. Louis Rising: The French Regime of Louis St. Ange de Bellerive.* Urbana: University of Illinois Press, 2016.

Engerman, Stanley. *Slavery, Emancipation and Freedom: Comparative Perspectives.* Baton Rouge: Louisiana State University Press, 2007.

Evans, Linda. "Abolitionism in the Illinois Churches: 1830–1865." PhD diss., Northwestern University, 1981.

Faragher, John Mack. *Sugar Creek: Life on the Illinois Prairie.* New Haven, Conn.: Yale University Press, 1986.

Fehrenbacher, Don E. *The Slaveholding Republic: An Account of the United States Government's Relations to Slavery.* New York: Oxford University Press, 2001.

Ferrer, Ada. *Freedom's Mirror: Cuba and Haiti in the Age of Revolution.* New York: Cambridge University Press, 2015.

Fett, Sharla. *Reclaimed Africans: Surviving Slave Ships, Detention, and Dislocation in the Final Years of the Slave Trade.* Chapel Hill: University of North Carolina Press, 2017.

Fields, Barbara J. "Ideology and Race in America." In *Region, Race, and Reconstruction: Essays in Honor of C. Vann Woodward*, ed. J. Morgan Kousser and James M. McPherson, 143–77. New York: Oxford University, 1982.

Finch, Aisha K. *Rethinking Slave Rebellion in Cuba: La Escalera and the Insurgencies of 1841–1844.* Chapel Hill: University of North Carolina Press, 2015.

Finkelman, Paul. "Evading the Ordinance: The Persistence of Bondage in Indiana and Illinois." *Journal of the Early Republic* 9 no. 1 (Spring 1989): 21–51.

Finkelman, Paul. *An Imperfect Union: Slavery, Federalism, and Comity.* Clark, N.J.: Lawbook Exchange, Ltd., 2000.

Finkelman, Paul. "Slavery and the Northwest Ordinance: A Study in Ambiguity." *Journal of the Early Republic* 6 no. 4 (Winter 1986): 343–70.

Foley, William E., and C. David Rice. *The First Choteaus: River Barons of Early St. Louis.* Urbana: University of Illinois Press, 1984.

Foner, Eric. *The Fiery Trial: Abraham Lincoln and American Slavery.* New York: W. W. Norton, 2010.

Foner, Eric. *Free Soil, Free Labor, Free Men: The Ideology of the Republican Party Before the Civil War.* New York: Oxford University Press, 1970.

Forret, Jeff. *Slave Against Slave: Plantation Violence in the Old South.* Baton Rouge: Louisiana State University Press, 2015.

Ford, Lacy. *Deliver Us from Evil: The Slavery Question in the Old South.* New York: Oxford University Press, 2009.

Fowkes, Henry L., ed. *Historical Encyclopedia of Illinois.* Vol. 1. Christian County, Ill.: Munsell Publishing, 1918.

Franklin, John Hope, and Loren Schweninger. *Runaway Slaves: Rebels on the Plantation.* New York: Oxford University Press, 2000.

Freamon, Bernard K. "Straight No Chaser: Slavery, Abolition, and Modern Islamic Thought." In *Indian Ocean Slavery in the Age of Abolition*, ed. Robert Harms, Bernard K. Freamon, and David W. Blight, 61–80. New Haven, Conn.: Yale University Press, 2013.

Fuentes, Marisa J. *Dispossessed Lives: Enslaved Women, Violence, and the Archive.* Philadelphia: University of Pennsylvania Press, 2016.

Furstenberg, Francois. "The Significance of the Trans-Appalachian Frontier in Atlantic History, c. 1754–1815." *American Historical Review* 113 no. 2 (June 2008): 647–77.

Gallay, Alan. *The Indian Slave Trade: The Rise of the English Empire in the American South, 1670–1717.* New Haven, Conn.: Yale University Press, 2003.

Games, Alison. "Beyond the Atlantic: English Globetrotters and Transoceanic Connections." *William and Mary Quarterly* 63 no. 4 (October 2006): 675–92.

Gellman, David. *Emancipating New York: The Politics of Slavery and Freedom 1777–1827.* Baton Rouge: Louisiana State University Press, 2006.

Genovese, Eugene. *Roll Jordan Roll: The World the Slaves Made.* New Orleans: Polyanthos, 1968.

Gienapp, William E. *The Origins of the Republican Party, 1852–1856.* New York: Oxford University Press, 1987.

Gigantino, James, II. *The Ragged Road to Abolition: Slavery and Freedom in New Jersey, 1775–1865.* Philadelphia: University of Pennsylvania Press, 2014.

Gitlin, Jay. *The Bourgeois Frontier: French Towns, French Traders, and American Expansion.* New Haven, Conn.: Yale University Press, 2009.

Gliozzo, Charles A. "John Jones: A Study of a Black Chicagoan." *Illinois Historical Journal* 80 no. 3 (Autumn 1987): 177–88.

Goetz, Rebecca Anne. "Indian Slavery: An Atlantic and Hemispheric Problem." *History Compass* 14 no. 2 (Spring 2016): 59–70.

Gorsuch, Alison Mileo. "Race and Labour Contracts in the Upper Mississippi Valley." In *Legal Histories of the British Empire: Laws Engagements and Legacies*, ed. Shaunnagh Dorsett and John McLaren. New York: Rutledge, 2014.

Gorsuch, Alison Mileo. "To Indent Oneself: Ownership, Contracts, and Consent in Antebellum Illinois." In *The Legal Understanding of Slavery: From the Historical to the Contemporary*, ed. Jean Allain, 135–51. New York: Oxford University Press, 2012.

Gould, Eliga H. "Comparing Atlantic Histories." *Reviews in American History* 38 no. 1 (March 2010): 8–16.

Gould, Eliga H. *The Persistence of Empire: British Political Culture in the Age of the American Revolution.* Chapel Hill: University of North Carolina Press, 2000.

Gould, Eliga H. "Zones of Law, Zones of Violence: The Legal Geography of the British Atlantic, *circa* 1772." *William and Mary Quarterly* 60 no. 3 (October 2003): 471–510.

Green, Jack P., and Philip Morgan, eds. *The Atlantic World: A Critical Appraisal.* New York: Oxford University Press, 2008.

Griffin, Patrick. *American Leviathan: Empire, Nation and the Revolutionary Frontier.* New York: Hill and Wang, 2007.

Grivno, Max. *Gleanings of Freedom: Free and Slave Labor Along the Mason-Dixon Line, 1790–1860.* Urbana: University of Illinois Press, 2011.

Gronningsater, Sarah L. H. *The Arc of Abolition: The Children of Abolition and the Origins of Freedom National.* Philadelphia: University of Pennsylvania Press, Forthcoming.

Gronningsater, Sarah L. H. " 'On Behalf of His Race and the Lemmon Slaves': Louis Napoleon, Northern Black Legal Culture, and the Politics of Sectional Crisis." *Journal of the Civil War Era* 7 no. 2 (June 2017): 206–41.

Guasco, Michael. *Slaves and Englishmen: Human Bondage in the Early Modern Atlantic World.* Philadelphia: University of Pennsylvania Press, 2014.

Guasco, Suzanne Cooper. *Confronting Slavery: Edward Coles and the Rise of Antislavery Politics in Nineteenth Century America.* DeKalb: Northern Illinois University Press, 2013.

Guasco, Suzanne Cooper. "The Deadly Influence of Negro Capitalists: Southern Yeomen and the Resistance to the Expansion of Slavery in Illinois." *Civil War History* 47 (March 2001): 9–10.

Gudmestad, Robert. *Steamboats and the Rise of the Cotton Kingdom.* Baton Rouge: Louisiana State University Press, 2011.

Hahn, Steven. *A Nation Without Borders: The United States and Its World in an Age of Civil Wars, 1830–1910.* New York: Viking, 2016.

Hahn, Steven. *The Political Worlds of Slavery and Freedom.* Cambridge, Mass.: Harvard University Press, 2009.

Hall, Gwendolyn Midlo. *Africans in Colonial Louisiana: The Development of Afro-Creole Culture in the Eighteenth Century.* Baton Rouge: Louisiana State University Press, 1992.

Hall, Matthew W. *Dividing the Union: Jesse Burgess Thomas and the Making of the Missouri Compromise.* Carbondale: Southern Illinois University Press, 2015.

Hammond, John Craig. *Slavery, Freedom and Expansion in the Early American West.* Charlottesville: University of Virginia Press, 2007.

Hammond, John Craig. "Slavery, Settlement, and Empire: The Expansion and Growth of Slavery in the Interior of the North American Continent, 1770–1820." *Journal of the Early Republic* 32 no. 2 (Summer 2012): 175–206.

Hammond, John Craig. "Slavery, Sovereignty, and Empires: North American Borderlands and the American Civil War, 1660–1860." *Journal of the Civil War Era* 4 no. 2 (June 2014): 264–98.

Hammond, John Craig. " 'Uncontrollable Necessity': The Local Politics, Geopolitics, and Sectional Politics of Slavery Expansion." In *Contesting Slavery: The Politics of Bondage and Freedom in the New American Nation*, ed. John Craig Hammond and Matthew Mason, 138–60. Charlottesville: University of Virginia Press, 2012.

Hancock, David. *Citizens of the World: London Merchants and the Integration of the British Atlantic Community, 1735–1785.* New York: Cambridge University Press, 1995.

Hansen, Stephen, and Paul Nygard. "Stephen A. Douglas, the Know-Nothings, and the Democratic Party in Illinois, 1854–1858." *Illinois Historical Journal* 87 (Summer 1994): 109–30.

Harris, Leslie. *In the Shadow of Slavery: African Americans in New York City, 1626–1863.* Chicago: University of Chicago Press, 2002.

Hatfield, April Lee. *Atlantic Virginia: Intercolonial Relations in the Seventeenth Century.* Philadelphia: University of Pennsylvania Press, 2004.

Havard, Gilles, and Cecile Vidal. *Histoire de l'Amerique Francise.* Paris: Editions Flammarion, 2003.

Heerman, M. Scott. "In a State of Slavery: Black Servitude in Illinois, 1800–1830." *Early American Studies* 14 no. 1 (Winter 2016): 113–39.

Higginbotham, Evelyn Brooks. "African-American Women's History and the Metalanguage of Race." *Signs*, 17 no. 2 (Winter 1992): 252–53.

Hilliard, Kathleen M. *Masters, Slaves, and Exchange: Power's Purchase in the Old South.* Cambridge: Cambridge University Press, 2013.

Hinderaker, Eric. *Elusive Empires: Constructing Colonialism in the Ohio Valley, 1673–1800.* New York: Cambridge University Press, 1999.

Hodges, Graham Russell Gao. *David Ruggles: A Radical Black Abolitionist and the Underground Railroad in New York City.* Chapel Hill: University of North Carolina Press, 2012.

Holt, Thomas C. *Children of Fire: A History of African Americans.* New York: Hill and Wang, 2010.

Horton, James Oliver, and Lois Horton. *In Hope of Liberty: Culture, Community and Protest Among Northern Free Blacks, 1700–1860.* New York: Oxford University Press, 1997.

Horton, James Oliver, and Lois E. Horton. *Slavery and the Making of America.* New York: Oxford University Press, 2006.

Howard, Robert. *The Illinois Governors: Mostly Good and Competent Men.* Springfield: Illinois State Historic Society, 1988.

Howe, David Walker. *What Hath God Wrought: The Transformation of America, 1815–1848.* New York: Oxford University Press, 2007.

Hughes, Michael. "Within the Grasp of Company Law: Land, Legitimacy, and the Racialization of the Metis, 1815–1821." *Ethnohistory* 63 no. 3 (July 2016): 519–40.

Hulsebosch, Daniel J. "Nothing but Liberty: 'Somerest's Case' and the British Empire." *Law and History Review* 24 no. 3 (Fall 2006): 647–57.

Hunter, T. K. "Geographies of Liberty: A Brief Look at Two Cases." In *Prophets of Protest: Reconsidering the History of American Abolitionism*, ed. Timothy Patrick McCarty and John Stauffer, 41–58. New York: New Press, 2006.

Huston, James L. "The Illinois Political Realignment of 1844–1860: Revisiting the Analysis." *Journal of the Civil War Era* 1 no. 4 (December 2011): 506–35.

Hyde, Anne F. *Empires, Nations, and Families: A History of the North American West.* Lincoln: University of Nebraska Press, 2012.

Irwin, James Reid. "Exploring the Affinity of Wheat and Slavery in the Virginia Piedmont." *Explorations in Economic History* 25 no. 3 (July 1988): 295–322.

Jaenen, Cornelius. "The Frenchification and Evangelization of the Amerindians in Seventeenth Century New France." *Canadian Catholic Historical Association Study Sessions* 35 (1968): 57–71.

Johnson, Guion Griffis. *Ante-Bellum North Carolina: A Social History.* Chapel Hill: University of North Carolina Press, 1937.

Johnson, Rashauna. *Slavery's Metropolis: Unfree Labor in New Orleans During the Age of Revolutions.* New York: Cambridge University Press, 2016.

Johnson, Reinhard O. *The Liberty Party 1840–1848: Antislavery Third Party Politics in the United States.* Baton Rouge: Louisiana State University Press, 2009.

Johnson, Walter. *River of Dark Dreams: Slavery and Empire in the Cotton Kingdom.* Cambridge, Mass.: Harvard University Press, 2013.

Jones, Martha. *All Bound Up Together: The Woman Question in African American Public Culture 1830–1900.* Chapel Hill: University of North Carolina Press, 2009.

Jones, Martha. "Time, Space, and Jurisdiction in Atlantic World Slavery: The Volunbrun Household in Gradual Emancipation New York." *Law and History Review* 29 (November 2011): 1031–60.

Junger, Richard. "'God and Man Helped Those Who Helped Themselves': John and Mary Jones and Culture of African American Self-Sufficiency in Mid-Nineteenth Century Chicago." *Journal of Illinois History* 11 (Summer 2008): 111–32.

Kantrowitz, Stephen. *More Than Freedom: Fighting for Black Citizenship in a White Republic.* New York: Penguin, 2012.

Kaye, Anthony. *Joining Places: Slave Neighborhoods in the Old South.* Chapel Hill: University of North Carolina Press, 2009.

Kaye, Anthony. "The Second Slavery: Modernity in the Nineteenth-Century South and the Atlantic World." *Journal of Southern History* 75 no. 3 (August 2009): 627–50.

Keita Cha-Jua, Sundiata. *America's First Black Town: Brooklyn Illinois, 1830–1915.* Champaign: Illinois University Press, 2002.

Kennington, Kelly. *In the Shadow of* Dred Scott: *St. Louis Freedom Suits and the Legal Culture of Slavery in Antebellum America.* Athens: University of Georgia Press, 2017.

Kennington, Kelly Marie. "Law, Geography and Mobility: Suing for Freedom in Antebellum St. Louis." *Journal of Southern History* 80 no. 3 (August 2014): 575–604.

Kiser, William S. *Borderlands of Slavery: The Struggle over Captivity and Peonage in the American Southwest.* Philadelphia: University of Pennsylvania Press, 2017.

Klein, Herbert S. *A Population History of the United States.* New York: Cambridge University Press, 2012.

Klein, Martin. "The Emancipation of Slaves in the Indian Ocean." In *Abolition and Its Aftermath in the Indian Ocean Africa and Asia,* ed. Gwynn Campbell, 198–218. New York: Routledge, 2005.

Kolchin, Peter. *American Slavery, 1619–1865.* New York: Hill and Wang, 2003.

Kolchin, Peter. "Variations of Slavery in the Atlantic World." *William and Mary Quarterly* 59 no. 3 (July 2002): 551–52.

Kren, Robert. "The 'Grand Illinois Venture': The Operations of Baynton, Wharton and Morgan Company in the Illinois Country, 1765–1771." Master's thesis, Western Illinois University, 1968.

Kuhlmann, Charles Byron. *The Development of the Flour-Milling Industry in the United States, with Special Reference to the Industry in Minneapolis.* New York: Houghton Mifflin, 1929.

LaRoche, Cheryl. *Free Black Communities and the Underground Railroad: The Geography of Resistance.* DeKalb: Northern Illinois University Press, 2013.

Leavelle, Neal. *The Catholic Calumet: Colonial Conversions in French and Indian North America.* Philadelphia: University of Pennsylvania Press, 2012.

Lee, Jacob F. "Rivers of Power: Indians and Colonists in the North American Midcontinent." PhD diss., University of California, Davis, 2014.

Levine, Bruce. *The Fall of the House of Dixie: The Civil War and the Social Revolution That Transformed the South.* New York: Random House, 2013.

Lipman, Drew. *The Saltwater Frontier: Indians and the Contest for the American Coast.* New Haven, Conn.: Yale University Press, 2015.

Litwack, Leon. *North of Slavery: The Negro in the Free States, 1790–1860.* Chicago: University of Chicago Press, 1961.

Martin, Ann Smart. *Buying into the World of Goods: Early Consumers in Backcountry Virginia.* Baltimore: Johns Hopkins University Press, 2009.

Marvin, Nathan Elliot. " 'A Thousand Prejudices': French Habitants and Catholic Missionaries in the Making of the Old Northwest, 1795–1805." In *Une Amérique Française, 1760–1860: Dynamiques du Corridor Creole,* ed. Guillaume Teasdale and Tangi Villerbu, 113–40. Paris: Les Indes Savants, 2015.

Mason, Matthew. "The Maine and Missouri Compromise: Competing Priorities and Northern Slavery Politics in the Early Republic." *Journal of the Early Republic* 33 no. 4 (Winter 2013): 675–700.

McCarthy, Timothy Patrick, and John Stauffer, eds. *Prophets of Protest: Reconsidering the History of American Abolitionism.* New York: W. W. Norton, 2006.

McDaniel, W. Caleb. *The Problem of Democracy in the Age of Slavery: Garrisonian Abolitionists and Transatlantic Reform.* Baton Rouge: Louisiana State University Press, 2013.

McKinley, Michelle. *Fractional Freedoms: Slavery, Intimacy, and Legal Mobilization in Colonial Lima, 1600–1700.* New York: Cambridge University Press, 2016.

McMurtie, Douglas C. "Negotiations for the Illinois Salt Springs 1802–1803." *Bulletin of the Chicago Historical Society* 2 no. 3 (March 1937): 86–91.

Melish, Joanne Pope. *Disowning Slavery: Gradual Emancipation and "Race" in New England 1780–1860.* Ithaca, N.Y.: Cornell University Press, 1998.

Menard, Russell R. *Sweet Negotiations: Sugar, Slavery, and Plantation Agriculture in Early Barbados.* Charlottesville: University of Virginia Press, 2006.

Metzger, John. "The Gallatin County Saline and Slavery in Illinois." Master's thesis, Southern Illinois University, 1971.

Meyer, Douglas K. *Making the Heartland Quilt: A Geographical History of Settlement and Migration in Early-Nineteenth-Century Illinois.* Carbondale: Southern Illinois University Press, 2000.

Middleton, Stephen. *The Black Laws: Race and the Legal Process in Ohio, 1787–1860.* Athens: Ohio University Press, 2005.

Miller, Joseph C. *The Problem of Slavery as History: A Global Approach.* New Haven, Conn.: Yale University Press, 2014.

Miller, Richard Lawrence. *Lincoln and His World: The Rise to National Prominence, 1843–1853.* New York: McFarland, 2010.

Milne, Edward. "Bondsmen, Servants, and Slaves: Social Hierarchies in the Heart of Seventeenth-Century North America." *Ethnohistory* 64 no. 1 (January 2017): 115–39.

Morgan, M. J. *Land of Big Rivers: French and Indian Illinois, 1699–1778.* Carbondale: Southern Illinois University Press, 2010.

Morgan, Philip. *Slave Counterpoint: Black Culture in Eighteenth-Century Chesapeake and Lowcountry.* Chapel Hill: University of North Carolina Press, 1998.

Morrissey, Robert Michael. *Empire by Collaboration: Indians, Colonists, and Governments in Colonial Illinois Country.* Philadelphia: University of Pennsylvania Press, 2015.

Morrissey, Robert Michael. "Kaskaskia Social Network: Kinship and Assimilation in the French-Illinois Borderlands, 1695–1735." *William and Mary Quarterly* 70 no. 1 (January 2013): 103–46.

Morrissey, Robert Michael. "The Power of the Ecotone: Bison, Slavery, and the Rise and Fall of the Grand Village of the Kaskaskia." *Journal of American History* 102 no. 3 (December 2015): 667–92.

Murrin, John M. "1776: The Countercyclical Revolution." In *Revolutionary Currents: Nation Building in the Transatlantic World,* ed. Michael A. Morrison and Melinda Zook. New York: Rowman & Littlefield, 2004.

Myers, Amrita Chakrabarti. *Forging Freedom: Black Women and the Pursuit of Liberty in Antebellum Charleston.* Chapel Hill: University of North Carolina Press, 2012.

Miles, Tiya. *The Dawn of Detroit: A Chronicle of Slavery and Freedom in the City of the Straights.* New York: New Press, 2017.

Miles, Tiya. *Ties That Bind: The Story of an Afro-Cherokee Family in Slavery and Freedom.* Oakland: University of California Press, 2006.

Nash, Gary, and Jean Soderlund. *Freedom by Degrees: Emancipation in Pennsylvania and Its Aftermath.* New York: Oxford University Press, 1991.

Newell, Margaret Ellen. *Brethren by Nature: New England Indians, Colonists, and the Origins of American Slavery.* Ithaca, N.Y.: Cornell University Press, 2015.

Newman, Richard S. *Freedom's Prophet: Bishop Richard Allen, the AME Church, and the Black Founding Fathers.* New York: New York University Press, 2009.

Newman, Richard S. *The Transformation of American Abolitionism: Fighting Slavery in the Early Republic.* Chapel Hill: University of North Carolina Press, 2002.

Newman, Simon. *A New World of Labor: The Development of Plantation Slavery in the British Atlantic.* Philadelphia: University of Pennsylvania Press, 2014.

Oakes, James. "Conflict vs. Racial Consensus in the History of Antislavery Politics." In *Contesting Slavery: The Politics of Bondage and Freedom in the New American Nation*, ed. John Craig Hammond and Matthew Mason, 291–304. Charlottesville: University of Virginia Press, 2011.

Oakes, James. *Freedom National: The Destruction of Slavery in the United States, 1861–1865.* New York: W. W. Norton, 2014.

Oakes, James. *The Scorpion Sting: Antislavery and the Coming of the Civil War.* New York: W. W. Norton, 2014.

Onuf, Peter S. *Jefferson's Empire: The Language of American Nationhood.* Charlottesville: University of Virginia Press, 2000.

Onuf, Peter S. *Statehood and Union: A History of the Northwest Ordinance.* Bloomington: Indiana University Press, 1985.

O'Shaughnessey, Andrew Jackson. *An Empire Divided: The American Revolution and the British Caribbean.* Philadelphia: University of Pennsylvania Press, 2000.

Paley, Ruth. "Imperial Politics and English Law: The Many Contexts of 'Somerset.'" *Law and History Review* 24 no. 3 (Fall 2006): 659–64.

Palm, Mary Borgias. "The First Illinois Wheat." *Mid-Atlantic: An Historical Review* 13 no. 3 (July 1930): 72–73.

Parkman, Francis. *France and England in North America.* New York: Library Company of America, 1983.

Patterson, Orlando. *Slavery and Social Death: A Comparative Study.* Cambridge, Mass.: Harvard University Press, 1982.

Patton, Diana. "Witchcraft, Poison, Law and Atlantic Slavery." *William and Mary Quarterly* 69 no. 2 (April 2012): 235–64.

Peart, Daniel. "Political Organization in the United States During the Early 1820s." PhD diss., University College of London, 2011.

Peterson, Jacqueline. "The People in Between: Indian-White Marriage and the Genesis of a Métis Society and Culture in the Great Lakes Region, 1680–1830." PhD diss., University of Illinois, Chicago, 1980.

Pirtle, Carol. *Escape Betwixt Two Suns: A True Tale of the Underground Railroad in Illinois.* Carbondale: Southern Illinois University Press, 2000.

Price, Richard. *Maroon Societies: Rebel Communities in the Americas.* Baltimore: Johns Hopkins University Press, 1996.

Rael, Patrick. *Eighty-Eight Years: The Long Death of Slavery in the United States, 1777–1865.* Athens: University of Georgia Press, 2015.

Reda, John. "From Subjects to Citizens: Two Pierres and the French Influence on the Transformation of the Illinois Country." In *French and Indians in the Heart of North America, 1630–1815*, ed. Robert Englebert and Guillaume Teasdale, 159–82. East Lansing: Michigan State University Press, 2013.

Resendez, Andres. *The Other Slavery: The Uncovered Story of Indian Enslavement in America.* New York: Houghton Mifflin Harcourt, 2016.

Reynolds, Terry S. *Stronger Than a Hundred Men: A History of the Vertical Water Wheel.* Baltimore: Johns Hopkins University Press, 1983.

Robertson, Stacey M. *Hearts Beating for Liberty: Women Abolitionists in the Old Northwest.* Chapel Hill: University of North Carolina Press, 2010.

Rood, Daniel B. *The Reinvention of Atlantic Slavery: Technology, Labor, Race, and Capitalism in the Greater Caribbean.* New York: Oxford University Press, 2017.

Rothman, Adam. *Slave Country: American Expansion and the Origins of the Deep South.* Cambridge, Mass.: Harvard University Press, 2007.

Royot, Daniel. *Divided Loyalties in a Doomed Empire: The French in the West from New France to the Lewis and Clark Expedition.* Newark: University of Delaware Press, 2007.

Ruby, Robert, and John Brown. *Indian Slavery in the Pacific Northwest.* Norman: University of Oklahoma Press, 1993.

Rushforth, Brett. *Bonds of Alliance: Indigenous and Atlantic Slaveries in New France.* Chapel Hill: University of North Carolina Press, 2012.

Rushforth, Brett. "'A Little Flesh We Offer You': The Origins of Indian Slavery in New France." *William and Mary Quarterly* 60 no. 4 (October 2003): 777–808.

Rushforth, Brett. "Slavery, Fox Wars, and the Limits of Alliance." *William and Mary Quarterly* 63 no. 1 (January 2006): 53–80.

Salafia, Matthew. *Slavery's Borderland: Freedom and Bondage Along the Ohio River.* Philadelphia: University of Pennsylvania Press, 2013.

Saunt, Claudo. *West of Revolution: An Uncommon History of 1776.* New York: W. W. Norton, 2014.

Schroeder, Christopher D. "Dreams of a Prairie Republic: Morris Birbeck and Settlement on the Indiana-Illinois Frontier, 1764–1860." PhD diss., University of Delaware, 2000.

Scott, Rebecca J. "Slavery and the Law in Atlantic Perspective: Jurisdiction, Jurisprudence, and Justice." *Law and History Review* 29 no. 4 (November 2011): 915–24.

Scott, Rebecca J. "Social Facts, Legal Fictions, and the Attribution of Slave Status." *Law and History Review* 35 no. 1 (February 2017): 9–30.

Sewell, Richard. *Ballots for Freedom: Antislavery Politics in the United States, 1837–1860.* New York: W. W. Norton, 1980.

Shepherd, Verene, ed. *Slavery Without Sugar: Diversity in Caribbean Economy and Society Since the 17th Century.* Gainesville: University of Florida Press, 2002.

Silver, Peter. *Our Savage Neighbors: How Indian War Transformed Early America.* New York: W. W. Norton, 2008.

Sinha, Manisha. "Coming of Age: The Historiography of Black Abolitionism." In *Prophets of Protest: Reconsidering the History of American Abolitionism*, ed. Timothy Patrick McCarthy and John Stauffer. New York: W. W. Norton, 2006.

Sinha, Manisha. *The Slave's Cause: A History of Abolition.* New Haven, Conn.: Yale University Press, 2016.

Simeone, James. *Democracy and Slavery in Frontier Illinois: The Bottomland Republic.* DeKalb: Northern Illinois University Press, 2000.

Slaughter, Tomas P. *Bloody Dawn: The Christiana Riot and Racial Violence in the Antebellum North.* New York: Oxford University Press, 1994.

Smith, Susan Sleeper. *Indian Women and French Men: Rethinking Cultural Encounter in the Western Great Lakes.* Amherst: University of Massachusetts Press, 2001.

Smith, Washington. *A History of Southern Illinois: A Narrative Account of Its Historical Progress, Its People, and Its Principle Interests.* Chicago: Lewis Publishing, 1912.

Snyder, Christina. *Slavery in Indian Country: The Changing Face of Captivity in Early America.* Cambridge, Mass.: Harvard University Press, 2010.

Spear, Jennifer. "Colonial Intimacies: Legislating Sex in French Louisiana." *William and Mary Quarterly* 60 no. 1 (January 2003): 75–98.

Spear, Jennifer. *Race, Sex, and Social Order in Early New Orleans.* Baltimore: Johns Hopkins University Press, 2009.

Stauffer, John. *Black Hearts of Men: Radical Abolitionists and the Transformation of Race.* Cambridge, Mass.: Harvard University Press, 2002.

Steiner, Mark E. *An Honest Calling: The Law Practice of Abraham Lincoln.* DeKalb: Northern Illinois University Press, 2006.

Steinfield, Robert. *The Invention of Free Labor: The Employment Relation in English and American Law and Culture, 1350–1870.* Chapel Hill: University of North Carolina Press, 1991.

Steinke, Christopher. "The *Code Noir* in the Illinois Country: Slavery and the Law in a French-Indigenous Borderland." January 2011. Unpublished manuscript.

Taylor, Alan. *The Divided Ground: Indians, Settlers, and the Northern Borderland of the American Revolution.* New York: Knopf, 2005.

Taylor, Nikki M. *Frontiers of Freedom: Cincinnati's Black Community 1802–1868.* Athens: Ohio University Press, 2005.

Tomich, Dale. *Through the Prism of Slavery: Labor, Capital, and World Economy.* New York: Rowman and Littlefield, 2003.

Tomlins, Christopher. *Freedom Bound: Law, Labor, and Civic Identity in Colonizing English America, 1580–1865.* New York: Cambridge University Press, 2010.

Tomlins, Christopher L., and Bruce H. Mann, eds. *The Many Legalities of Early America.* Chapel Hill: University of North Carolina Press, 2001.

Twitty, Anne. *Before* Dred Scott*: Slavery and Legal Culture in the American Confluence, 1787–1857.* New York: Cambridge University Press, 2016.

Usner, Daniel. *Settlers, Indians, and Slaves in a Frontier Exchange Economy: The Lower Mississippi Valley Before 1783.* Chapel Hill: University of North Carolina Press, 1992.

Van Cleve, George William. "Mansfield's Decision: Toward Human Freedom." *Law and History Review* 24 no. 3 (Fall 2006): 665–71.

Van Cleve, George William. *A Slaveholders' Union: Slavery, Politics, and the Constitution in the Early American Republic.* Chicago: University of Chicago Press, 2010.

Van Cleve, George William. "'Somerset's Case' and Its Antecedents in Imperial Perspective." *Law and History Review* 24 no. 3 (Fall 2006): 601–45.

Van Kirk, Sylvia. *Many Tender Ties: Women in Fur Trade Society 1670–1870.* Norman: University of Oklahoma Press, 1986.

VanderVeld, Lea. *Redemption Songs: Suing for Freedom Before* Dred Scott. New York: Oxford University Press, 2014.

Varon, Elizabeth. *Appomattox: Victory, Defeat, and Freedom at the End of the Civil War.* New York: Oxford University Press, 2013.

Vidal, Cecil. "Africains et Europeens au Pays des Illinois Durant la Periode Francaise (1699–17656)." *French Colonial History* 3 (2003): 31–68.

Vidal, Cecile. "Antoine Bienvienu, Illinois Planter and Mississippi Trader: The Structure of Exchange Between Lower and Upper Louisiana." In *French Colonial Louisiana and the*

Atlantic World, ed. Bradley Bond, 111–33. Baton Rouge: Louisiana State University Press, 2005.

Warren, Wendy. *New England Bound: Slavery and Colonization in Early America.* New York: W. W. Norton, 2016.

Weaver, Jace. *The Red Atlantic: American Indigenes and the Making of the Modern World, 1000–1927.* Chapel Hill: University of North Carolina Press, 2014.

Weiner, Dana Elizabeth. *Race and Rights: Fighting Slavery and Prejudice in the Old Northwest, 1830–1870.* DeKalb: Northern Illinois University Press, 2013.

Weiner, Dana Elizabeth. "Racial Radicals: Antislavery Activism in the Old Northwest 1830–1861." PhD diss., Northwestern University, 2009.

Welch, Kimberly. *Calling to Account: Black Litigants in the Antebellum American South.* Chapel Hill: University of North Carolina Press, 2018.

White, Richard. *The Middle Ground: Indians, Empires, and Republics in the Great Lakes Region, 1650–1815.* New York: Cambridge University Press, 1991.

White, Shane. *Somewhat More Independent: The End of Slavery in New York 1790–1810.* Athens: University of Georgia Press, 1995.

White, Sophie. *Wild Frenchmen and Frenchified Indians: Material Culture and Race in Colonial Louisiana.* Philadelphia: University of Pennsylvania Press, 2013.

Whitman, Stephen T. *The Price of Freedom: Slavery and Manumission in Baltimore and Early National Maryland.* Lexington: University of Kentucky Press, 1997.

Wigmore, Gregory. "Before the Railroad: From Slavery to Freedom in the Canadian-American Borderland." *Journal of American History* 98 no. 2 (September 2011): 437–54.

Wilentz, Sean. *The Rise of American Democracy: Jefferson to Lincoln.* New York: W. W. Norton, 2006.

Williams, Heather Andrea. *Self Taught: African American Education in Slavery and Freedom.* Chapel Hill: University of North Carolina Press, 2005.

Wood, Gordon S. *Empire of Liberty: A History of the Early Republic.* New York: Oxford University Press, 2010.

Wright, Gavin. "Slavery and American Agricultural History." *Agricultural History* 77 no. 4 (April 2003): 527–52.

Zilversmit, Arthur. *The First Emancipation: The Abolition of Slavery in the North.* Chicago: University of Chicago Press, 1967.

INDEX

Accault, Michel, 22
Act Concerning the Introduction of Negroes and Mulattoes into this Territory, 79–80, 82–83, 88, 104–6, 130
Adams, Charles, 116, 132
Adams, Maria, 116, 132
Aelsey, 120, 122
African Methodist Episcopal Church, 109, 127
Alexander County, Ill. *See* Cairo, Ill.
Allen, Joe, 102
Alton, 140, 163
American Antislavery Society, 140
Amy, 104
Anderson, Nathaniel, 89
Andre, 50
Antoine, 95
Aspasia, 138
Atlantic world, 7–9, 19–20, 44–45

Bailey, David, 135
Baltimore, John, 109
Baltimore, Priscilla, 109
baptism, 4, 23, 25–27, 28, 49–50, 70, 91–92, 113, 141
Baptiste, Jean, 147
Baynton, John 44
Baynton, Wharton, and Morgan, 38–39, 44, 46, 49, 52, 56, 72–78
Beauvais, Elenne, 48
Beauvais, Jean Baptiste, 49
Beauvais, Michel, 91, 95
Bedford County, Tenn., 126
Ben, 74
Bennet, 114
Bennington Boon v. Juliet, a woman of color, 145
Betsy, 73
Bienvenu, Antoine, 32–33, 39, 78
Bienville, Jean Baptiste Le Moyne, 30–31
Birney, James, 142
Black Codes, 14, 100–101, 111–13, 123, 143, 153–54, 162–65
black convention movement, 154–55, 160, 163
black freedom villages, 11, 14, 109–10, 112, 127–30
black laws. *See* Black Codes
Blay, Anthony, 122
Bob, 90
Boisbriand, Pierre Durgé, 22, 28–29
Bond, Shadrach, 78, 99
Boulduc, Louis, 73
Bowles, William, 97
Boyce, Jean, 74
Brazile, 93
British Empire, 40–41, 53–54
Brooklyn, Ill., 109, 126–28
Buchet, Antoine, 33

Cahokia, 23, 42, 62, 93, 114. *See also* St. Clair County, Ill.
Cairo, Ill., 4–5, 150–51
Calvert, George, 149
Camp, Ichabod, 68
Canada, 21
Cape Girardeau, Mo., 5, 131
Carbondale, Ill., 152
Caribbean, 32, 34, 38–40, 46
Carlinville, Ill., 149
Carr, William, 114, 117
Catherine, 93
Catholic Church, 1–2, 22, 25, 28, 48–50, 91
census data, 32, 83, 86, 118, 123, 142
Charleston, S.C., 82
Charleville, Francois, 73
Charleville, Pierre, 39, 74
Chicago, Ill., 118, 127, 142–45, 149–50, 152–54, 162, 164

Chickasaw Indians, 30
Chouteau, Therese, 58
Churchill, George, 124
Clark, George Rogers, 62–63, 66
Clark, N.D., 131
Codding, Ichabod, 143–44
Code Noir, 11, 23, 41–42, 53, 148. *See also* law of slavery
Coles, Edward, 101–3
Congo, 96
Cons, Jean, 73
convention movement (1824), 101–2
Cornelius, Joseph, 93
Cosby, John, 132
Costly, Nance Cromwell, 105–6, 135, 157, 167
Costly, William, 167
Cox, Jane, 105
Cox, Thomas, 91, 105
Crenshaw, John, 132
Croghan, George, 44, 45
Cromwell, Nathan, 105, 135
Cynthia, 122
Cynthia Ann, 91–92

Davenport, Venus, 120
David Bailey vs. William Cromwell (1841), 136, 145
Davis, Eva, 129
Dearborn, Henry, 75
demography. *See* census data
Derousse, Pierre, 92
Dice, 105
Douglas, Stephen A., 136, 138, 155–58
Douglass, Frederick, 127
Dred Scott v. Sanford (1857), 157
Duclos, Antoine, 48
D'Ulloa, Don Antonio, 47
Dumoulin, John, 76
Dunky, 82

Eastman, Zebina, 142–43
Eddy, Henry, 116–18, 120
Edgar, John, 73, 76, 101, 122
Edwards, Benjamin, 132
Edwards, Ninian, 93, 95, 99–101, 103–4, 116, 125
Edwards, Ninian Wirt, 132
Edwardsville, Ill., 125, 149
Elizabeth, 116
Emancipation Proclamation, 158, 160, 164
enslaved men, 24, 121–24
enslaved women, 25–27, 120–22, 149

Farmer, Benjamin, 102
File, 68
Finney, James, 132
Fisher, John, 93, 125
Fort Chartres, 42, 46
Fort Duquense, 35
Fort Massac, 72
fox wars, 29–30
Francois, 93
Frank, 96
Franky, 102
freedom suits, 82, 90, 104, 116–18, 121, 128–29
free labor ideology, 102, 155–58
Freeport, Ill., 156
Freeport Doctrine, 156
French, Augustus, 5, 151
French Negroes: and black towns, 109; children born as, 90; court proceedings, 5–6, 146–47; creation of legal category, 60, 64, 103–4; diverse sources of, 7, 92; eighteenth-century origins of, 3; emancipation process, 110, 122, 136–37, 141; emerged in U.S. period, 80–81; exempted from northwest territory, 69–70, 83–84; eve of the U.S. Civil War, 8; Illinois State Constitution, 99; kidnapping of, 4–5, 150–51; selling to traders, 49
Fugitive Slave Act (1850), 151–54, 163

Gage, Thomas, 44, 47, 52–55
Gallatin County, Ill., 97, 102, 116–18, 120, 123, 125, 132
Garrison, William Lloyd, 140, 142
Gaston, William, 130
gender. *See* enslaved men; enslaved women; slavery
Genius of Liberty, 141
Girualt, Jean (Lieutenant), 67
godparents, 49. *See also* Catholic Church
Golconda, Ill., 126, 127, 131. *See also* Pope County, Ill.
Graff, Nancy, 150
Granger, Frank, 117
de Guyenne, Father Alexandre Xavier, 1–2

Hale, Albert (Reverend), 140
Hale, John, 145

Harrison, William Henry, 76, 87
Hay, Andrew, 82
Hayes Creek, 126
Heathcock, Edwin, 154
Henry, John, 93
Henry, Patrick, 62
Hicks, Ephraim, 127
Hicks, William, 127
Hillsborough, 1st Earl of (Will Hills), 44, 47, 54
Holy Family (Parish), 70, 91

Illinois: Atlantic world, 19–20, 45; British Empire, 43–46; convention movement, 101; defining boundaries, 13; economy after statehood, 94–95; French Empire, 22; migration into, 13, 22–23, 46–48, 59, 67–68, 77, 86, 98, 110, 111, 118, 129; salt production, 96; Somerset principle, 146; statehood, 98; trans-Appalachian West, 58; Upper South, 85–86
Illinois antislavery politics, 102, 111, 133, 137–38, 149. *See also* Republican Party
Illinois Anti-Slavery Society, 140, 142–43
Illinois Emigrant, 116
Illinois Indians, 20, 30
Illinois Republican, 131–32
Illinois State Constitution (1818), 84, 98–99, 101, 107
Illinois Supreme Court, 3–5, 84, 100–101, 104–6, 121, 130, 135, 145, 164
Immaculate Conception (Parish), 1–2, 25, 70, 91
indentured servants: earning freedom, 116, 130–31, 135, 148; laws regarding created, 79–80; legality of system, 103–7; process of indenturing, 86–90, 97, 98; slaves becoming, 3–4, 82–84; white migrants as indentures, 119. *See also* Act Concerning the Introduction of Negroes and Mulattoes into this Territory
Indian slavery, 1–2, 9–10, 18, 20, 25–26, 49–50, 71, 84, 92. *See also* Rushforth, Brett

Jack, 94
Jackson County, Ill., 117
Jacksonville, Ill., 140, 149–50
Janette, 65
Jarrot, 95
Jesuits, 1–2, 21–22, 27
John, 124
Johnson, Moses, 153
Johnson, William, 44
Johnson County, 93, 125
Jones, Elizabeth, 116
Jones, John, 123 160–63, 164–65
Jones, Mary, 160
Jonesboro, Ill., 156
Joseph Jarrot, alias Pete, a colored man v. Julia Jarrot, 5–6, 150–51
Judith, 3–4, 7
Juliet, 130

Kane, Elias Kent, 101
Kaskaskia, Ill., 1–2, 22–23, 38, 42, 62, 82, 121. *See also* Immaculate Conception (Parish); Randolph County, Ill.
Kaskaskia Indians, 23, 36
Kentucky, 68, 75, 80, 83–84, 90, 93–94, 97–99, 123
kidnapping, 4–5, 113, 137, 149, 150, 153
King, Austin, 5, 151
Kuykendall, Simon, 132

LaChapelle, Baptiste, 91
LaChapelle, Elizabeth 91
LaChance, Antoine, 73
Langlois, Etienne, 74
Langlois, Pierre, 67
La Salle County, Ill., 145
Lasonde, Pierre, 93
Lasource, Jacques, 48
law of slavery, 11, 41–42, 53–54, 58–59, 63–64, 68, 70; slaves knowledge of, 66, 110, 127–22. See also *Code Noir*; Northwest Territory Ordinance (1787)
Lea, Lucinda, 149
Leavitt, Joshua, 144
Lewis, Moses, 129
Liberator, 140, 167
Liberty Party, 144–45
Lincoln, Abraham, 135, 138, 147, 155–58
Lindah, 3–4, 7
Lisette, 17
Louis, 2, 7
Louvien, Antoine (dit Amour), 73
Lovejoy, Elijah, 140
Lovejoy, Owen, 145
Lucinda, 116

Lydia, 90, 122
Lyon, Matthew, 98

Manuel, 64–67
Maria, 116
Marie, 92
Marie Jeanne, 17–19
marriage patterns, 18, 22, 28, 36, 48–50
Martin, 65
Mary (Beauvais family), 91
Mary (Menard family), 121
Massac County, Ill., 152
Mathilda, 152
Matis, Jerome, 17–19
Maurepas, Jean Frédérick Phélypeaux, 29
McCoy, J. W., 131
McCoy, Thomas, 131
McIntyre, John, 93
McWorter, Frank, 127
Menard, Francois, 93, 96
Menard, Pierre, 58, 74, 93, 95, 99, 138, 141
Merry, John, 113
migration, 13; African Americans into Illinois, 110, 129; northern migration into Illinois, 111, 118; slaves into Illinois, 22–23, 46–48; slaveholders into Illinois 59, 67–68, 77; from Upper South, 86, 98
Miller, Harrison, 126–27
Miller Grove, 126–28
Milly, 97
Mississippi River: and Atlantic commerce, 19–20; as border, 59, 62; British settlement in, 44; convoys on, 17, 29, 33, 36; slaves on, 94; smuggling across, 46–47, 56; warfare in, 29–30, 63; wheat economies, 24
Missouri statehood, 100
Mitchel, Jincy, 90, 122
Mitchell, Bill, 125
Montgomery County, Tenn., 123
Morain, Antoine, 52
Moreau, 64–67
Morgan, George, 39–40, 44, 49, 51, 54–55, 72
Morris, David, 131
Morris, Elijah, 131
Morris, James, 131
Morris, Katherine, 131
Morris, Martha, 131
Morrison, John, 116
Morrison, William, 58, 70, 76, 82, 91, 95

Nance, a woman of color v. John Howard (1828), 104–6, 135
Nancy, 122
Ned (ferry worker), 96
Ned (indentured servant), 89
Nelly, 120
Nelson, 163
Nelson, James, 89
New Orleans, La.: commercial connections to Illinois, 6, 95; convoys from Illinois, 17, 29, 33, 36, 72, 74; Illinois slaves kidnapped to, 114, 120; Superior Council of, 18; trade with St. Louis, 41
New Philadelphia, Ill., 126–27
Nicolles (family), 65
northern abolition, 87, 108, 133, 139, 140
Northwest Territory Ordinance (1787): exceptions to, 69, 91, 103; Illinois State Constitution, 99; after Illinois statehood, 105–7, 148, 164; passage of, 68; petitions to repeal, 58, 75–78; slaveholders evading, 3–4, 83

O'Reilly, Alejandro, 48
Ottawa, Ill., 150, 155
Ously, Jonathan, 74

Padfield, Abraham, 128
Patterson, Orlando, 8, 8 n.19, 9 n.20, 13 n.37
Pelagie, 120
Pensoneau, Ettienne, 104
Pensoneau, Louis, 92, 113
Peoria, Ill., 125
Peoria Indians, 23, 36
Peter, 150
Pet Pet, 95
Philips, Joseph, 105
Phillis, 97
Phoebe, a woman of color v. William Jay (1828), 104, 106–7
Pompe, 67
Pontiac's Rebellion, 45
Pope, Nathaniel, 91–92
Pope County, Ill., 93, 110, 119, 121, 123, 127, 129. *See also* Golconda, Ill.
popular sovereignty, 155–58
Posey, John, 97
print culture. *See* Illinois antislavery politics
process of emancipation, 114–15, 120, 139–40

Proclamation Act (1763), 52
Pulaski County, Ill., 152

Quinn, William Paul (Reverend), 109, 127

Randolph County, Ill., 88, 93–95, 119, 121, 136. *See also* Kaskaskia, Ill.
Raum, John, 119–20, 131, 133
registered servants, 88, 130–31. *See also* indentured servants
Reid, Thomas, 46, 53
Republican Advocate, 104
Republican Party, 6, 137–38, 154, 157
Reynolds, John, 86, 101–2
Robinson, William, 125
Rocky Fork, Ill., 126
Rouensa, Maria, 22
Rumsey, James, 38–39
runaway slaves, 113–15, 124–25, 127
Rushforth, Brett, 9, 18 n.12, 37 n.107

salt mines and marshes, 60, 75, 84, 96–97, 125
Sam, 93
Sangamon County, Ill., 102, 119. *See also* Springfield, Ill.
Sarah, 122
Sasa, 65
Saucier, Jean Baptist, 93
Saucier, Jeanne Marie, 48
second slavery, 10
Shawnee Indians, 36
Shawnee National Forest, 130
Shelby County, Tenn., 123
Shelbyville County, Tenn., 126
Shreeve, Israel, 72
Sides, Henry, 129
Sides, Robert, 127
slavery: adaptations to, 3, 8–11, 28, 60, 70, 84, 87, 109–10, 114, 118–19, 123, 136–37, 148, 166; in Atlantic world, 7; definition of, 12; failed abolition, 91; institutional analysis, 6; law of, 11, 41–42, 53–54, 58–59, 63–64, 68, 70; men's experiences, 121–24; race, 18; women's experiences, 25–27, 120–22, 149
Sloan, William, 131
Smith, Theophis, 105
smuggling. *See* Mississippi River
Snider, Ephraim, 152
Somerset principle, 146
Spanish Empire, 44, 73
Springfield, Ill., 105, 118, 135. *See also* Sangamon County, Ill.
St. Clair, Arthur, 69
St. Clair, William, 76
St. Clair County, Ill., 93–95, 109, 114, 119, 121–22, 128, 136, 146
Stephenson, John G., 114
Sterling, Thomas, 46–47
St. Genevieve, Mo., 1, 48–49, 73
St. Louis, Mo.: founding, 40–41; Illinois slaves in, 82, 93; Illinois slaves kidnapped in, 113; kidnappers in, 149; Elijah Lovejoy in, 140; trade with Illinois, 73, 96; trade with New Orleans, 41; U.S. settlers in, 77
Sukey, 117
Superior Council of New Orleans, 18, 47

Tackey's Rebellion, 39
Tallmadge, James, 99
Tardiveau, Barthelemi, 74
Tempe, 138
Therese (free woman), 116
Therese (of the Jesuits), 2
Thomas, 129
Thomas, Jesse, 99–101
Tipton County, Tenn., 117
Todd, John, 63, 67, 71
Tom, 102
trans-Appalachian West, 58, 62
Treaty of Fort Wayne, 75
Trottier, August, 114
Trumbull, Lyman, 5, 138, 146
Turpin, Louis, 26

Underground Railroad, 152, 160
Upper South, 13, 83, 87, 99, 110, 123–24, 129
U.S. Civil War, 18, 158
U.S. Congress, 11, 58, 77, 81, 98–99, 145
U.S. Continental Congress, 67–68
Vallard, Paul, 125

Vallé, Francois, 74
Vaudreuil, Pierre de Rigaurd, 31
Vincent, 97
Virginia Act of Cession (1784), 67, 76, 103

Wade, 4, 7, 151
Walker, David, 127
Wardman, Joseph, 147

Western Citizen, 142–45, 163
Wharton, Samuel, 44, 56
wheat cultivation, 24, 51–52
Wickliffe, Nathaniel, 150
Wilkins, John, 46
William, 89
Wilson, William, 3–4, 88
Winney, 97
Winnie, 122
Winny, 129
Winston, Richard, 67
Wynn, Lewis, 147

Yates, Richard, 150, 167

ACKNOWLEDGMENTS

It is strange to bid farewell to this book project, which has been in my life in one way or another for over a decade. To paraphrase Henry Higgins, I've grown accustomed to its face; it almost makes the day begin! Yet reflecting on the manuscript reminds me that turning the draggletailed guttersnipe of a draft into a book with at least some modest refinement was not done alone. Countless people helped at every step of the way, ensuring that the final draft is not an incarnate insult to the English language.

At the University of Maryland, Ira Berlin provided me endless support. He encouraged me as I launched this project, and he helped push the manuscript to its final version. He constantly reminded me that history was a full-contact sport and that arguments are what drive our work. Clare Lyons helped me conceive of the project so that it could appeal to broad audiences. She has my gratitude for the hours and hours of conversations that over the years moved my intellectual work toward bolder terrain. Glenn McNair and Robert Bennett lit a spark in me to pursue this project while I was in the ACM Program at the Newberry Library. Alice and Randall Shrock served as intellectual parents for me, encouraging me to keep plugging away on this quirky paper I had written on slavery in Illinois. At the University of Maryland, Leslie Rowland, David Sartorious, Mike Ross, and Julie Greene each read parts of the project, and their commentary helped in ways big and small.

From 2013 to 2015, I had the good fortune to be the Patrick Henry Scholar at the History Department at Johns Hopkins University. The faculty welcomed me warmly, and Phil Morgan and Toby Ditz deserve special thanks for reading the manuscript and offering careful, constructive criticisms, which improved this work in many ways. They were excellent mentors, and I cannot thank them enough. I had the opportunity to present at "The Seminar," where my colleagues' probing questions led me to rethink major issues in the closing two chapters of the book. I also presented much of the material of the book, in some form or another, at the Atlantic Seminar, and the sharp questions from its participants did the book a world of good.

At the University of Miami, I have a welcoming intellectual home. Several of my colleagues helped me with revisions, in particular Michael Bernath, Kate Ramsey, Dominique Riell, and Ashli White. Mary Lindemann's support as department chair stands out, making sure I had the time and resources to get my work done.

Since I first talked with Bob Lockhart about this project, he has been everything I could have hoped for in an editor and more. His detailed reading greatly improved the manuscript, and his edits always were spot on. He helped turn a semi-revised project into a fully revised manuscript, and we shared some nice dinners along the way. As part of the team at the University of Pennsylvania Press, Steven Hahn's insights enabled me to connect the story of Illinois to larger global developments, ensuring that this would not be a regional study. He was a constant companion as this project ended, and his mentorship means the world to me. Mary Jo Binker and Martha Shulman both provided expert editing of the manuscript, elevating the writing and cleaning up after my sloppiness.

Beyond the various departments that I have worked in, several colleagues read chapters and offered important suggestions for revision: Matthew Fox-Amato, Rick Bell, Caleb Daniels, John Demos, Eric Hinderaker, Jacob Lee, Matt Mason, Bob Morrissey, and Bethel Saler. Others went above and beyond, both reading the work and engaging me in extended conversations, at times over several years, always pushing me and the project to go further. Nathan Connolly's incisive commentary allowed me to conceive of black agency in whole new ways. Woody Holton read most of the project and had much more to say about it. He pushed me to think about the creation of the American nation and its importance for my work, to imagine black intellectual history in new ways, and to search for a better title, even if I never took all his suggestions. It must be said that he'd do anything, yes, anything, for me. Brett Rushforth offered his sharp eye on material in the opening chapters, and he challenged me to make the argument focused and the interventions clear. Sophie White has also been an important colleague, reading the work with a careful eye, offering countless suggestions for more archival research, and from time to time sharing a cup of Pimms to make the work all the more enjoyable.

A few people deserve special thanks because I have leaned on them especially hard. Sarah Gronningsater read the entire manuscript when it was nearly complete, and her detailed, extensive comments helped me tie various parts together. She read the introduction and some final revisions more than once, despite being in the throes of a new job. She was throughout the perfect lunch companion and travel buddy to conferences. Paul Polgar has known me since 2005 and has been hearing of this project ever since. Never one to shy away from a fight, he grappled with the bigger arguments of the project at every turn. Always in good cheer, he has been a wonderful friend to me as I worked through all forms of revisions. Christina Snyder has been this project's biggest cheerleader when it needed it the most. Her enthusiasm for the book always gave me an extra jolt of energy to keep working away at it. Reading it in full more than once, she always saw the potential of the project, even when I didn't. She never doubted I could make this project work in all of its complexity, and her voice helped me with publishers, fellowships, article revisions, and so much more. I owe her a couple rounds of Sazeracs. Last, Kim Welch is the Mary Poppins of colleagues—practically perfect in every way. From our summers in Oxford, springtime in Nashville, and everywhere in between, she has been a critic, enthusiast, therapist, mentor, and friend. She read the final draft of the manuscript, catching factual errors, flagging tangents, probing inconsistencies, demanding that I flesh out the argument in key spots, and reminding me of our mentor's mantra: "there is no such thing as good writing, only good rewriting." It is my great fortune to have her as a colleague, and my thanks here cannot repay all she has done for me.

Several grants and fellowships came at key times in the project's development, making the work of first writing and then revising a book possible. In 2011, the Council of Library and Information Resources provided a year of generous support, and the University of Maryland followed it up with the Anne Wylie grant in 2012. The William Clements Library awarded me a Jacob M. Price fellowship, and the Illinois Historic Preservation Agency awarded me a King V. Hostick grant to support my research at the Abraham Lincoln Presidential Library and Museum. The Newberry Library hosted me as a short-term fellow, and working there was a pure delight. Other organizations helped as I turned the manuscript into a monograph. The Filson Historical Society provided me with a travel grant, as well as a good measure of bourbon, to help expand the research. The J. Franklin

Jameson fellowship from the American Historical Association allowed me to spend an extremely productive summer at the Kluge Center at the Library of Congress, where I completed essential research in the manuscript reading room. The wonderful staff at the Kluge Center made the work that much more enjoyable. The Office of the Provost at the University of Miami provided me with summer research funds to travel to the British Archives. Saving the best for last, Huntington Library awarded me the Barbara Thom Fellowship, which allowed me to complete final research and revisions of the manuscript. The intellectual community, depth of the collections, support of the staff, and beauty of the grounds at the Huntington have no peer.

More than any other group of people, the librarians, archivists, and county and circuit clerks who organized, guarded, and preserved the documentary basis of this work deserve my greatest thanks. I do not have the space to thank each one personally, but as they see their collections in my notes, they should know that each citation is a small thank you. However, several people went above and beyond what I could have reasonably hoped for, and they deserve special thanks. Karl Moore at the Illinois State Archives introduced me to the core documents that sustained most of the project and helped me navigate the state's public records, answering a flurry of questions both quickly and without complaint. Emily Lyons and Sister Mary Kennon Wolf helped me unlock the French colonial sources in Illinois and understand their importance to a wide array of histories. John Hoffman and Ryan Ross at the Illinois History and Lincoln Collection opened up the extensive collection they manage and were affable discussants about myriad aspects of Illinois history. Additionally, the entire staff at the Chicago History Museum helped me tap into the wealth of data housed in their collection.

My final thanks go to my family. They instilled a love of history in me from a young age, which is fitting in light of the fact that both my parents were history teachers. My parents helped me pursue my passions and always generously helped me travel to an archive or buy a new book. My father saw this project begin but did not live to see it to completion. In an odd way, that is fitting—because he never had any doubt I would complete this book, even if I doubted it along the way. He didn't need to see it completed to know that it would all come to pass. Christopher Richmond deserves my most heartfelt gratitude. He has put up with my rigorous travel schedule, and has always helped me see a bigger picture while I was mired in the details. He willingly read the entire manuscript more than once and spent countless dinner hours listening to me work out my ideas. A better storyteller than I will ever be, Christopher made this project more readable and engaging at every turn. For these reasons and for many more, this work is dedicated to him.